CW00689869

DEMOCRACY
THE CURSE OF CROMWELL

BY THE SAME AUTHOR

Clippers: The Ships that Shaped the World

Power to the People: And to Hell with Cromwellian Totalitarianism

The Book Of Tephi by J A Goodchild (Editor)

DEMOCRACY
THE CURSE OF CROMWELL

DANIEL J NOLAN

MALBAY PUBLISHING
IRELAND

First published in Ireland in 2015 by
Malbay Publishing
Bray, County Wicklow

The moral right of Daniel Nolan to be
identified as the author of this work has been
asserted in accordance with the Copyright,
Designs and Patents Act, 1988.

All rights reserved. No part of this publication
may be reproduced or transmitted in any form
or by any means, electronic or mechanical,
including photocopy, recording, or any
information storage and retrieval system,
without permission in writing from the publisher.

A CIP catalogue record for this book is available
from the British Library

ISBN 978-1-908726-03-2

Printed and bound in Ireland by Central Press, Bray Ltd

For the victims of Cromwellian Totalitarianism worldwide

The invention of the Ogham is attributed in bardic history to Ogma, son of Elatan, a prince of the Tuatha de Dananns, that people whom all our national traditions represent as a more cultured race than any of the other colonies that took possession of this island in primitive times.

John Healy

CONTENTS

PROLOGUE

All republicanism is based on Oliver Cromwell.

Paul A Rahe[1]

While the English had been fighting the two civil wars, a separate but related conflict had been going on in Ireland. The upshot was that the fledgling English Republic was forced to send over an army to pacify those areas of Ireland still unsubdued to forces friendly to it.

Diane Purkiss[2]

The wicked unsheathe their swords;
>   They string their bows
To fell the poor and oppressed,
>   To slaughter those whose way is upright.

Psalm 37: 14[3]

Indeed, Fleetwood could not have wondered at the reason for the lack of enthusiasm of the citizens of Wexford as he surveyed the ruined, powder-blackened walls of the old town; the breaches where Oliver Cromwell's artillery had pounded its ancient foundations, allowing his infantry to pour in. The Parliamentary soldiers had surged through the narrow streets pushing the people towards the market place, Market Cross, in the north of the town. There the soldiers slaughtered nearly 1,500 of the inhabitants, including 250 women, as many children, five Franciscan Priests and two Franciscan Friars. The charred ruins of the Franciscan Friary in John Street bore mute witness to the massacre. The memory was too sharp for the survivors of Wexford to make pretence of welcoming Cromwell's son-in-law.

Peter Beresford Ellis[4]

If you have men who will exclude any of God's creatures from the shelter of compassion and pity, you will have men who will deal likewise with their fellow men.

St Francis of Assisi[5]

If you are neutral in situations of injustice, you have chosen the side of the oppressor.

Desmond Tutu[6]

A nation cannot be made virtuous by diktat or by government inspectors. The experience of the major-generals [Cromwell's], and their troops and horse behind them, also helped to augment the national hatred of standing armies.

Peter Ackroyd[7]

War is the continuation of politics by other means.

Carl von Clausewitz[8]

The repression of the Vendee [Peasants] revolt, which is thought to have taken 300,000 to 600,000 lives . . . suggests that the French Revolution contained the ideological germs of the kind of limitless brutality more usually associated with totalitarian regimes of the 20th century . . . In the village of Savenay on Dec. 23, 1793, General Westermann routed the tenacious Vendee rebel army, boasting that he had "trampled children under horse feet" and massacred "women who will no longer give birth to brigands." When he returned to Paris he reported: 'I have no prisoner to worry about, I have exterminated everything.'

James A Markham[9]

For two centuries, people have been made to be ashamed to be from the Vendee, but the truth is that all the great terrorists of the 20th century have taken Robespierre as their model.

Philippe de Villiers[10]

As Hampden and Sidney waned other more potent symbols of power and order waxed and two of those were of the Old World – Napoleon Bonaparte and Oliver Cromwell. These two men of Iron had not been greatly admired by the generations that loved Hampden and Sidney. After all, Washington had rejected Cromwell's mantle at Newburgh. Forty years after the incident John Lovett's poetic celebration of Washington's birthday has the father of his country tell his Newburgh troops (Freedom's Sons): "O, damn it not to raise a Cromwell's fame." Others warned of Cromwell's usurpation "or some such ferocious animal" if a large standing army were to be created or if the Union was to be imperilled.

Peter Karsten[11]

Washington, March 10.

Wood, Manila:—
I congratulate you and the officers and men of your command upon the brilliant feat of arms wherein you and they so well upheld the honor of the American flag.

(Signed) Theodore Roosevelt

His whole utterance is merely a convention. Not a word of what he said came out of his heart. He knew perfectly well that to pen six hundred helpless and weaponless savages in a hole like rats in a trap and massacre them in detail during a stretch of a day and a half from a safe position on the heights above, was no brilliant feat of arms—and would not have been a brilliant feat of arms even if Christian America, represented by its salaried soldiers, had shot them down with Bibles and the golden rule instead of bullets. He knew perfectly well that our uniformed assassins had *not* upheld the honor of the American flag, but had done as they had been doing continuously for eight years in the Philippines—that is to say, they had dishonoured it . . . We see the terrified faces. We see the tears. We see the small hands clinging in supplication to the mother; but we do not see those children that we are speaking about. We see in their places the little creatures whom we know and love. The next heading blazes with American and Christian glory like to the sun at its zenith: *"Death List is now 900."*

I have never been so enthusiastically proud of the flag till now!

Mark Twain[12]

While Leonardo had met the Signoria's request, his fresco also exposed in the crudest terms the horror of war, which Leonardo described unhesitatingly as *"una pazzia bestialissima"* (a most bestial folly). Indeed, Vasari's description of the painting opens with the words: 'Fury, hate, and rage are as visible in the men as in the horses.' Apart from Pouissin's *Massacre of the Innocents*, Goya's *Tres de Mayo*, and Picasso's *Guernica* there is probably no picture in the history of art as violent, brutal, and terrible as the battle of *Anghiari*. As Leonardo saw it, the painter had to reach the onlookers heart, move him, force him to think, and edify him. He hated war and in his fresco sought to communicate to others the horror it inspired in him.

Serge Bramly[13]

What difference does it make to the dead, the orphans or the homeless, whether the mad destruction is wrought under the name of totalitarianism or the holy name of liberty or democracy?

Mahatma Gandi[14]

Spain owned the Phillipines from 1521 to 1898, and America from 1898 to 1946. Pundits summarize this history as "four hundred years in a convent, and fifty years in a whorehouse".

P J O'Rourke[15]

The backwoodsmen had pushed the Spaniards from the Mississippi, had set up a slave-holding republic of Texas and had conquered the Californian gold-fields in the sheer masterful exercise of might . . . In our long settled communities there have always been people who opposed every war which marked the advance of American civilization at the cost of savagery. The opposition was fundamentally the same, whether these wars were campaigns in the old West against the Shawnees and the Miamis, in the new West against the Sioux and the Apaches or in Luzan against the Tagals. In each case, in the end, the believers in the historic American policy of expansion have triumphed.

Theodore Roosevelt[16]

For over a century and a half after his death the memory of the greatest Englishman of the seventeenth century was looked upon with horror by the leaders of English thought, political and literary; the very men who were carrying to fruition Cromwell's policies being utterly ignorant that they were following in his footsteps. At last the scales began to drop from the most far-seeing eyes. Carlyle, with his eminently sane and wholesome spirit, held Cromwell and the social forces for which he stood – Puritanic and otherwise – at their real worth, and his judgment about them was, in all essentials, accurate . . . In England there was practically peace during the first forty years of the century, but it was an ignoble and therefore an evil peace . . . Those who doubt this would do well to study the condition of England during the reign of James I., and during the first part of the reign of Charles I. England had then no standing army and no foreign policy worthy of the name. The chief of her colonies was growing up almost against her wishes, and wholly without any help or care from her.

Theodore Roosevelt[17]

Nationalism is an infantile disease, the measles of mankind.

Albert Einstein[18]

Among the FBI's principal targets was Nobel Prize winner Dr Martin Luther King, Jr., who labelled the U.S. government "the greatest purveyor of violence in the world today".

Oliver Stone & Peter Kuznik[19]

He delivered an inaugural address with more references to poverty, hunger and suffering than FDR, Eisenhower, Truman, or any other president to follow. After declaring 'man holds in his mortal hands the power to abolish all forms of human poverty and all forms of human life . . .' Dirksen had insisted on going into the Rose Garden when they first spoke about it (threat to ratification of test ban treaty) during the winter of 1961, they probably went outside, where there was less risk of having their conversation overheard or intercepted by whatever bugs the CIA, FBI, or other government agencies might have installed in the White House without Kennedy's knowledge . . . The author and peace activist Norman Cousins, who had been serving as a clandestine intermediary between Kennedy and Khrushchev, spoke of "a new spirit of hopefulness" abroad in the world that summer, writing, 'Nothing is more powerful than an individual acting out of his conscience, thus helping to bring the collective to life' . . . (Adlai) Stevenson liked the idea (of an accommodation with Castro) but said, 'Unfortunately the CIA are still in charge in Cuba' . . . [JFK] 'These brass hats have one great advantage in their favour. If we listen to them, and do what they want us to do, none of us will be alive later to tell them that they are wrong . . . men tend to like the idea of war until they have tasted it.'

Thurston Clarke[20]

When my Dad was fighting in Europe in the war, he made a bargain with God. He promised God if he got home alive, he'd never own another gun.

Barbara Bush[21]

All governments suffer a recurring problem: Power attracts pathological personalities.

Frank Herbert[22]

Giant Trusts and Cartels everywhere, at the present time, as they coalesce, approach the economic pattern of the soviet state.

Wyndham Lewis[23]

My faith in the people governing is, on the whole, infinitesimal; my faith in the People governed is, on the whole, illimitable.

Charles Dickens[24]

Both Montesquieu and Voltaire were liberal pioneers and consistent and courageous advocates of human freedom. However both men exhibited a clearly antidemocratic temperament; they had no interest in the illiterate masses as political subjects and thus were incapable of imagining mass collective identification with a kingdom or political homeland.

Shlomo Sand[25]

Where are the kings and queens and warriors now? Gone with all their glory! The present day and present men? Paltry, mean, tight, and tedious. Bah.

Sean O'Casey[26]

CHAPTER 1

DEMOCRACY: THE GREAT CON

An imbalance between rich and poor is the oldest and most fatal ailment of republics.

Plutarch[27]

Democracy, the euphemism for Parliamentarianism, is a Con, the greatest confidence trick ever played on the Human Race. For the vast majority of people in the world democracy means being punitively taxed, corporately exploited, machine-controlled, brainwashed, lawyer-ridden, and war weary. Parliaments' principal role is to legalise Grand Larceny. Multiparty government is anarchy, while more established parliaments are frequently bipolar:

> They asked a peasant woman if she had food. She told them it had been stolen. "Russians or Germans?" Frank asked. "Thieves" the woman replied impassively.
>
> Giles MacDonough.[28]

Benjamin Disraeli's definition of British Democracy is truer today than when he wrote:

> . . . all thoughts and things have assumed an aspect and title contrary to their real quality and style: Oligarchy has been called Liberty; an exclusive Priesthood has been christened a National Church; Sovereignty has been the title of something that has had no dominion, while absolute power has been wielded by those who profess themselves the servants of the People. In the selfish strife of factions, two great existences have been blotted out of the history of England, the Monarch and the Multitude; as the power of the Crown had diminished, the Privileges of the People have disappeared; till at length the sceptre has become a pageant, and its subject has generated again into a serf.
>
> Benjamin Disraeli[29]

HISTORY

History is mostly a pack of lies. The Greek Herodotus (484–425 BC), the "Father of History", was also known for recording fanciful stories which earned him the less complimentary title "Father of Lies."[30] John Willis Griffiths (1809–1882) of New York, probably the greatest shipwright and naval architect since Archimedes and the shipbuilders of Tyre, was scathing about historians:

> In scanning the musty folios of the past, it would seem that a second deluge had swept every page of the history of mechanical science from the face of the earth. Our reductive energies are shackled by historians, who have delighted to luxuriate on the rise, progress and ruin of their race, while the most prolific minds of Science and Art have been left unexplored; the most valuable discoveries to the commercial world have been consigned to the incendiary's torch, or doomed to the tomb of the Capulets; the exuberance of the language has been exhausted to laud the hero, and foster a spirit of military glory; the bloody riots of butchers of their race, and the desolating march of tyrants, have been narrated with redundant effusion. The irretrievable loss of information respecting the prominent mechanics of earlier ages, may be attributed to the unsophisticated dogmas of such men as Plato, who poured out ebullitions of wrath against his followers for debasing the excellence of geometry, by applying it to sensible things . . . The light of science, mental, moral, and physical have dispelled the gloom of barbarism, and given a powerful impetus to man's career, down to the latest future in the vista of time; alas, for the scruples of Plato and his coadjutors.
>
> John W Griffiths[31]

Read no history – nothing but biography, for that is life without theory [lies]. . . If the history of England be ever written by one who has the knowledge and the courage, and both qualities are a equally requisite for the undertaking, the world would be more astonished than when reading the Roman annals of Niebuhr. Generally speaking, all the great events have been distorted, most of the important causes concealed, some of the principle characters never appear, and all who figure are so misunderstood and misrepresented, that the result is a complete mystification, and the perusal of the narrative about as profitable to an Englishman as reading the Republic of Plato or the Utopia of Moore, the pages of Gaudentio di Lucca or the adventures of Peter Wilkins.

Benjamin Disraeli[29]

OLIVER CROMWELL

Having unsuccessfully summoned the garrison [of Drogheda] to surrender, he breached the ramparts with his cannon, and at the third assault, which he led himself, stormed the town. There followed a massacre so all-effacing as to startle even the opinion of those fierce times. All were put to the sword. None escaped; every priest and friar was butchered. The corpses were carefully ransacked for their valuables. The ferreting out and slaughter of those in hiding lasted till the third day. The war continued in squalid murderous fashion for two years after Cromwell left Ireland. Cromwell in Ireland, disposing of overwhelming strength and using it with merciless wickedness, debased the standards of human conduct and sensibly darkened the journey of mankind. The consequences of Cromwell's rule in Ireland have distressed and at times distracted English politics down even to the present day. Upon all of us there still lies "The Curse of Cromwell".

Winston Churchill[32]

To solve the problems of society he looked not to the arguments of rational men, but to the dynamic, charismatic powers of "the leader – the true Leader," the Führer. Such a leader drew no authority from the existing laws; those were the "shams" which it was his function to destroy. The only visible tests of this power are sincerity and success. Cromwell was sincere, a man of his word: he did what he said he would do to the Irish, as Hitler to the Jews, and he succeeded. Success justified all his methods, as it justified, in Frederick the Great, aggression, fraud, breach of faith. The end justifies the means. Might is right. Might is right . . . the phrase runs like a refrain through Carlyle's works.

Hugh Trevor-Roper[33]

ROYAL MARTYR KING CHARLES I

The Venetian physician Marco de Cola in Iain Pears's *An Instance of the Fingerpost*:

Public life was steeped in blood, and murder of a king aroused no more repugnance on the breasts of many than did the slaughter of a domestic beast. We had become inured to the most horrendous of sins, and thought of them as instruments of policy . . . England had only recently been in the grip of fanatical sectarians, and I knew their influence was far from dissipated – my colleagues in the coach to Oxford overnight had informed me with glee of the new persecutory laws against us [Catholics] that the Parliament had forced the king to adopt . . . Then I walked to Westminster and saw the Palace and gazed in awe at the very window from which King Charles stepped to his bloody martyrdom, covered now in black crêpe to commemorate that evil deed, and reflected awhile on the punishments the nation had endured because of that sinful act.

Iain Pears[34]

Rightly was King Charles surnamed the Martyr; for he was the holocaust of direct taxation. Never yet did man lay down his heroic life for so great a cause: the cause of the Church and the cause of the Poor.

Benjamin Disraeli[29]

In 2009 the exhibition at the British Library was titled: 'Taking Liberties: The Struggle for Britain's Freedom and Rights' which celebrated: 'The First Year of Freedom 1649.'[35] Sixteen forty-nine was the year of Regicide and the year of Genocide. King Charles I was beheaded on Oliver Cromwell's orders on 30th of January. Immediately afterwards the executioner, who was masked and disguised for fear of being recognised, held the King's head high in front of a large crowd, held back by the Cromwell's soldiers. According to observer Philip Henry:

> A moan as I never before and desire I may never hear again rose
> from the assembled crowd of People.
> en.wikipedia.org/Charles_I_of_England[36]

Among the soldiers were those who would later take part in the massacres in Droghda and Wexford, the beginning of a campaign of Ethnic Cleansing of the Native Irish population that would reduce their numbers by nearly a third. And who controls the British Library? The library is a non-departmental public body sponsored by the Department of Culture, Media and Sport[37] of the Cromwellian Institute, as Westminster Parliament should be called; the sooner it becomes a museum the better!!

Churchill was equally forceful in condemning Cromwell's Parliamentary rule:

> To the mass of the nation however the rule of Cromwell mani-
> fested itself in the form of numberless and miserable petty
> tyrannies, and thus became hated as no Government has ever
> been hated in England before or since. For the first time the
> English people felt themselves governed from a centre in the
> control of which they had no say. Anger and hatred welled the
> stronger because their expression was difficult. The old kings
> might have harried the nobles and taxed the rich; but here were
> personages who had climbed up by lawless, bloody violations,
> and presumed to order the life and habits of every village and
> to shift custom from the channels which it had cut in the flow
> of centuries. What wonder that under the oak-leaves, broad and
> far throughout the countryside, men dreamed fondly of what

they called the good old times and yearned for the day when "the King shall enjoy his won again".

Winston Churchill[32]

I asked him a bit more sharply than was strictly necessary who exactly, was John Thurloe? 'Never heard of him?' he (Wood) said with an air of amazement. 'Many in Venice have. And almost everywhere else in Europe. For near ten years that man murdered, stole, bribed, and tortured his way across this land and others' . . . Certainly they were active; scarcely a month went by without one scheme or another — arising here, an assassination there. If these had come to fruition, Cromwell would have been dead a dozen times before he died in his bed . . . 'Thurloe is a traitor and should have been hanged years ago' . . . the glorious news that Cromwell was dead.

Iain Pears[34]

John Thurloe was Oliver Cromwell's brutal chief of security. Thousands are reputed to have disappeared during his Reign of Terror. Little wonder that Sir Isaiah Berlin, the well known Oxford philosopher, is quoted as saying that history ended with Cromwell!

Sir William Petty MD FRCP FRS a founding Fellow of the Royal Society, would afterwards describe Cromwell as a usurper and Parliament as usurping government.[38] In 1651 Petty arrived in Ireland as Physician to Cromwell's army, and not long afterwards he took on the task of mapping Ireland for the Cromwellian Settlement. Self made, he was one of the great polymaths of the time. He was probably born a Catholic and may have been a closet Catholic throughout his life. He left school at the age of twelve and took a job as a cabin boy. Shortly afterwards he sustained a broken leg and left his ship in Caen, where he enrolled in the local Jesuit school. There he taught English in return for tuition in arithmetic, mathematics and Latin. Petty returned to England but shortly afterwards went back to Continental Europe because of the English Civil War, and studied Medicine in Amsterdam, Leiden, Utrecht and Paris before returning to England. He registered at Oxford University for an MD degree, and had to wait three years before he could graduate. He spent much of the time trading in London to maintain himself. He subsequently became Reader in Anatomy at Oxford University and Vice-Principle of Brasenose College. Petty became famous for resuscitating the body of Anne Green who was hanged in Oxford.[39]

No parliament has ever been anything other than a DOT (Den of Thieves), and if Westminster is the Mother of Parliaments, then Oliver Cromwell was the father of the Mother of all Parliaments![40] And the thieving started in earnest with the English Long Parliament of 1642–1649. In February of 1642 a group of London merchants approached the House of Commons with a scheme by which the Irish Rebellion would be put down by troops financed by them at the end of which "they may have such satisfaction out of the rebel's estates." The members of the House of Commons were not slow to contribute to this promising scheme. Oliver Cromwell paid just over £2,000. On 30 July the treasurers of the fund were asked to hand over £100,000 by the Commons which was never repaid.[41] Britain is a *de facto* Republic and has been so since the time of Cromwell, except for a short period under the reign of the Magnificent Monarch, King Charles II.

By 1649 the Irish Rebellion was long over and the only purpose of Cromwell's invasion of Ireland was ethnic cleansing of the Native Irish population and the acquisition of their land. Between 1841 and 1651 the population of Ireland was reduced by over 30 percent from 1,466,000 in 1641 from war, famine and bubonic plague; about 50,000 men, women and children were sent into slavery in the West Indies, nearly all to Barbados: "To Hell or Barbados;"[42] about 40,000 soldiers, who had surrendered, were allowed to leave and join the armies of France and Spain. To consolidate Cromwell's policy most of the remaining Catholics, whether owners or tenants, were hunted out of their homes and land and ordered to go: "To Hell or to Connaught".[4] About 2.5 million acres of their best land was confiscated and divided among Cromwell's soldiers in lieu of pay, and to City of London Adventurers who had funded his campaigns. Lecky in the eighteenth century described Cromwell's policy as "the chief cause of the political and social evils of Ireland".[43]

One who was aware of his ancestors' expulsion from County Carlow by Cromwell's soldiers was Lieutenant-Colonel John Philip Nolan RA (Royal Artillery), who as Captain Nolan became a Nationalist MP (Member of Parliament) for Galway in 1874. Two years earlier he had contested the seat and polled 2,823 votes compared to his opponent, Conservative William le

Letter is from The Churchill Documents *Volume 5*
At The Admiralty 1911–1914 (2007, page 1666–1667)

Lord Stamfordham to WSC

(Royal Archives)

4 November 1912

Admiralty

My dear Churchill,

Your letter to me of the 1st instant has been laid before the King. I cannot conceal from you His Majesty's regret that you suggest that he should reconsider his objection to the name of *Oliver Cromwell* for one of the new Warships.

The arguments you adduce do not alter the King's views on the subject. You express your conviction that the name would be extremely well received; but may I remind you that when the Government of the day in 1895 proposed to erect out of public funds a Statue of Oliver Cromwell they were rigorously opposed by the Irish and the Opposition and defeated by a majority of 137.

In debate Mr Justin McCarthy stated that what the Duke of Alva was in the memories of the people of the Netherlands so was Oliver Cromwell in the minds of the Irish, and 'he could not understand how a Liberal Government and above all a Home Rule Government could propose what was an insult to the Irish People'.

Mr Redmond described Cromwell as 'a murderer and a canting hypocritical murderer' and said the Irish would be false to the tradition of their country and its history, false to their forefathers, their religion and nationality if they did not protest.

Colonel Nolan condemned Cromwell as a 'treacherous brute'.

Colonel Saunderson on the other hand said no proposal would be more dear to the hearts of the Nonconformist but that Government had decided to give away their Nonconformist supporters in obedience to the orders of their masters in Ireland .

Mr. Balfour as Leader of the Opposition disputed the point Cromwell was the founder of the Naval Power of England; for the Navy was already before Cromwell's advent to power the greatest in the world. 'As to Parliament Government he absolutely succeeded in uprooting its whole system.'

Sr W. Harcourt as Leader of the House of Commons admitted Cromwell's character was one upon which many people held different opinions: even he himself might not regard him as a hero; nor could the House of Commons admire some parts of his career!

If the idea of a Statue aroused so much animosity it is reasonable to expect not less opposition to the association of Cromwell with a Warship costing millions of public money.

Whatever His Majesty's own personal feelings may be with regard to Cromwell he is satisfied that your proposal would revive similar feelings of antagonism and religious bitterness to those of 17 years ago, and especially now at a time when there are alas, and especially in Ireland, signs that 'the bitterness of the rebellions of the past' have by no means 'ceased to stir men's minds.'

Stamfordham

Poer Trench's 658.[44] But Trench contested the result and the Cromwellian Institute's local legal functionary Judge William Keogh, found in favour of Trench. The Catholic bishops and priests had spoken out on behalf of Nolan because Le Poer's family was active in proselytizing. In his judgement, Keogh said that the bishops and priests had intimidated the voters by urging them to vote for Nolan. Keogh's decision was deeply divisive. Nolan would be instrumental in preventing the British taxpayer from paying for the statue of Oliver Cromwell that now stands in front of the Cromwellian Institute, and also in preventing the Admiralty from naming a warship "Oliver Cromwell" (Figure 1). Cromwell's statue with the bible in one hand and the sword in the other is most appropriate for a man who was a religious fundamentalist, brutal military dictator, regicide, genocidal psychopath and Ireland's nemesis.[40]

> Power is not a means, it is an end. One does not establish a dictatorship in order to safeguard a revolution; one makes a revolution in order to establish a dictatorship.
>
> George Orwell[45]

Before the Gaddafi regime was overthrown Jeremy Bowen, who was in Libya for the BBC (British Broadcasting Company), said: 'This is a Police State.' Libya was not a police state; it was a brutal military dictatorship. Muammar Gaddafi's crimes pale into insignificance compared to those of Oliver Cromwell!!!

CHAPTER 2

HEBERNIA: THE LOST CIVILIZATION

It is a misfortune that the Celtic mind prefers literature to history. Celtic writers of the present day may be greatly attracted by the later Arthurian legends, and their mythological connections, and write on them at great length; but they will not give any of this attention to the historical discussions of the real facts, on which the immense pile of romance has been raised. The fiction occupies twenty times the space of the historical material in the Encyclopaedia. It is this constitutional frame of mind in both Welsh and Irish which, from ancient to modern times, has prejudiced the solid information which rests in their hands.

W M Flinders Petrie.[46]

. . . an alternative view has been put forward by two Kells residents who claim that the funeral games were those of Queen Teia Tephi who had journeyed from the near East in company with Jeremiah and the Ark of the Covenant. "The Queen has also brought with her the Israeli system of law as outlined in Deuteronomy which then became the law in Ireland — a felicitous turn of events, since the theory also holds that Irish people are all descendents of the Tribe of Dan. Teia had a palace at Teltown and died August 1st 534 BC. The Ark of the Covenant is believed to rest in Tara."

Paul Murphy[47]

The further you look back the further you can look forward, according to Churchill.[48] Ireland before the Viking invasions was one of the most civilized and advanced societies of its time. Monarchy had existed for about two-and-a-half thousand years. One of the first known kings of Ireland was Sreng of the Firbolgs who may have been a contemporary of Abraham.[49]

It was Calcol son of Zerah, one of the twin sons of Judah, son of Jacob (Israel), and great-great-grandson of Abraham, who created the Ulster and subsequently the O'Neill (Uí Néill) dynasty, as well as other European royal dynasties.[50,51] The name Ulster (Uladh) is reputed to come from Eladah a great grandson or grandson of Ephraim, son of Joseph son of Jacob.[52] Calcol's brother Darda founded Troy. Jacob's family had moved to Egypt about 1700 BC, from where they subsequently migrated. Ulster's symbol, the Red Hand of Zerah, is often displayed on a white background of the six-pointed (hexagram) Star of David. The Red Hand originates from the birth of the twins Perez and Zerah to Tamar, as described in the *Book of Genesis:*

> When the time for delivery came there were twins in her womb. While she was giving birth, one put out his hand; and the midwife took and tied a crimson thread on his hand . . . but as he withdrew his hand his brother came out . . . so he was called Perez . . . Afterward his brother, who had the crimson thread on his hand, came out; he was called Zerah (A Hebrew word for the red light of dawn, alluding apparently to the crimson thread).
>
> Genesis[53]

THE PHOENICIANS

The Phoenicians at an early age, perhaps as early as the foundation of Carthage (the middle of the ninth century BC), had planted colonies on the shores of Spain. The colonists, filled with the adventurous spirit of their ancestors, had passed beyond the Pillars of Hercules, reached Britain, and discovered the tin mines at its southern extremity. To supply from these newly discovered mines the ports of the Mediterranean with tin, they found to be a lucrative employment, especially as long as they enjoyed a monopoly of the trade. To preserve that monopoly they kept the position of Britain a secret, and all that the other nations knew either of Britain or Ireland was that in some far distant part of the Western sea were the Cassiterides or Tin Islands, so distant and difficult of access that only Phoenician energy and skill in navigation could reach them. At a later date, Herodotus had heard of the Cassiterides or Tin Islands, but of their position he had no knowledge. Both Britain and Ireland were shrouded in impenetrable gloom and on the map of the world as known to him they found no place. The Carthaginians were as daring, as skilful in navigation, and as keenly anxious to acquire wealth by commerce as their Phoenician kinsfolk, and in an expedition under Hamilco they discovered those famous Tin Islands which they had long sought in vain.

E A D'Alton[54]

The first Phoenicians appear to have been Canaanites and their base was Tyre, reputedly established around 1500 BC. They were a Semitic people who spoke a similar language to Hebrew. Great traders by land and particularly by sea, their ships were responsible for bringing Cornish tin to Israel for use in the building of the Temple of Solomon. They also built Solomon's fleet of ships and his "Temple Square". There are evidences that the Phoenicians also ranged as far as the Western Hemisphere as early 1447 BC.[55] They were unrivalled masters of the sea, and were famed "traders in purple" because of their monopoly on the precious purple dye of the murex snail[56,57] Their leading city was Tyre, which established about 300 colonies and trading posts on the coasts of the Mediterranean and beyond.

The Phoenicians were also experts in woodcraft:

> The workers in wood seemed to have more prestige. The Phoenicians in Asia, who sold Lebanese pine and cedar to Egypt and Palestine, had already made a reputation for themselves as carpenters, and Solomon called upon one of them when he was building his temple . . . In the first century AD wooden beams were still to be seen in Melqart's (Apollo's) temple in Uticia, built in 1101 BC. The most important work of the woodworkers was the building and repairing of ships, at which they were past-masters as the Greeks willingly acknowledged.[58]

By the twelfth century BC Danite Israelites had gone to sea with, and were part of the Phoenicians as recorded in *The Book of Judges*: 'Why did Dan spend his time in ships?[59] Capt says the Dan was in ships as early as 1296 BC.[60,61] The Tribe of Dan would subsequently come to dominate the Phoenicians: "Danite

Phoenicians." The Phoenicians went into decline after the fall of Carthage to the Romans in 146 BC.

'Canaan found her pathways to the hiding of men's desires.' This quotation from the *Book of Tephi* [62,63] tells us how the Phoenicians kept their sea and ocean trade routes outside the Seagate, later "The Pillars of Hercules" and now the Strait of Gibraltar, in great secrecy as they did when they discovered tin deposits in Cornwall.

Articles made in Tyre were on sale in Ireland in the sixth century BC:

> Of the bards there came fourscore
> In green; then a chosen band of Elatha's men from the shore
> Came next in their varied raiment, the purples of them that sold
> The Tyrian wares, and scarlet and azure, whilst ruddy gold
> Gleamed in their belts and brooches, flashed from their helms of brass
> Like a marsh-flower mead.
> John A Goodchild & Daniel J Nolan [62,63]

The Phoenicians' syllabic writing system, phonetic rather than pictorial in its characters, had its origins in Classical Hebrew. [64] The alphabet, shaped by the Hebrews, originally contained twenty-one characters; vowels were added later. Through their maritime trade, the Phoenicians spread the use of the alphabet to North Africa and Europe where it was adapted by the Greeks and Romans. Hebrew was the first written language of Britain and Ireland, [64] and is often used to aid translations of Phoenician inscriptions:

> She liked the Hebrew and the English tongue
> And said there was analogy between 'em
> She proved it somehow out of sacred song,
> But I must leave the proofs to those who've seen 'em
> But this I heard her say, and can't be wrong
> And all may think which way their judgements lean 'em,
> Tis strange the Hebrew noun which means "I am,"
> The English always use to govern d—n.

> 'He was what Erin calls, in her sublime
> Old erse or Irish, or it may be Punic;

> The antiquarians whom settle time,
>   Which settles all things, Roman, Greek, or Runic,
> Swear that Pat's language sprung from the same clime
>   With Hannibal, and wears the Tyrian tunic
> Of Dido's—alphabets and this is rational
>   As any other notion, and not rational.
>
> Lord Byron[65]

There is a river DoN in Yorkshire; part of it named DuN.[66] The River Tamar separating Devon and Cornwall is named after Tamar Tephi, as Teia Tephi was known by some[67,68] Tamar is the name of the RNLI's (Royal National Lifeboat Institution) latest class of all-weather lifeboat.[69] England's capital city is LonDoN, and Albion is the oldest known name of England:[70]

> Bring in these men out of Albion, and bid the ollamhs unroll
> The message they bring with the token from him that hath writ us a scroll.
>
> John A Goodchild & Daniel J Nolan[62,63]

Marazion is where the Prophet Jeremiah, and the chief of Cornwall Elatha wept over the fall of Jerusalem to the Babylonians; Mara Zion apparently means "bitter for Zion".

> Now Elatha communed much with the Prophet, and wept and grieved
>   Upon Zion greatly. . .
>
> John A Goodchild & Daniel J Nolan[62,63]

DoNald, MacDoNald and MacDoNnell are Irish and Scottish surnames names: a river in Aberdeenshire is the DoN;[71] and the Rosemarkie 'Daniel Stone'[72] in Rosss-shire depicts Daniel's head in the lion's mouth. Lochlann appears to be the oldest known name of Scotland, and the floating rocks may have been whales:

> And amber from wizard lands at whose dread the Lochlann mocks
> When he sails his hidebound boat through the sea of the floating rocks.
>
> John A Goodchild & Daniel J Nolan[62,63]

Place names with D~N abound in Ireland: Donegal, Dún Loaghaire, Dunboyne *et al.* The encrypted code engraved on many of the ancient monuments and known as Ogham, exclusive to Ireland and based on the alphabet, was created by Ogma in the sixth century BC:[73]

> In warfare or peace, save Ethan, was no man broader that he,
> > And these twain I set together for truth and service to me,
> With En, and with Sri, and with Ogma, my husband's champion and
> > friend,
> > My almost brother, for these were faithful unto the end,
> And helpful in my beginning . . .
> > > John A Goodchild & Daniel J Nolan[62,63]

And places in Europe where the Tribe of Dan inhabited before moving on: Rivers DaNube, DoN and DNieper, as well as DeNmark (DaNmark). DoNetsk in the Ukraine was recently engulfed in conflict.[74]

> The antiquities of this island bear uncommon and indelible marks of very remote times. Phoenician monuments are scattered over the surface of it, and what is more extraordinary Phoenician names of things and places, are retained even to this day.
> > > Charles Vallancey:[75]

> The Tuatha Dé Danann have long since retreated into the chambers and vaults and mounds and raths, waiting there to be aroused for a great battle to restore Ireland's glory.
> > > Anthony Murphy[76]

On page 16, Murphy illustrates a "Neolithic carving".[76] This is presumably an example of Phoenician art referred to by General Vallancey. It would have been carved by the Danites, known as the Tuatha Dé Danann in Ireland. Tuatha Dé translates "The Chosen People", Tuatha Dé Dána translates "The Chosen People of Dan"[77] kinsfolk of the Danite Phoenicians.

... However, it was Bezalel, son of Uri, son of Hur, of the tribe of Judah who made all that the LORD commanded Moses. And he was assisted by Ololiab, son of Ahisamach, of the tribe of Dan, who was an engraver, an embroiderer and a weaver of variegated cloth of violet, purple and scarlet yarn and of fine linen.

Exodus[78]

Another Irish authority, Kenrick, believes that the towers have a Phoenician origin, which is the same as saying the Tuatha Dé Danann were the builders. Childress indicates a Phoenician origin as well when he likens the round towers to similar towers in the Mediterranean.[79]

Whence Northward and West they sailed till the Island of Towers was won.

John A Goodchild & Daniel J Nolan[62,63]

CARTHAGE 814–146 BC

Lovely Æneas, these are *Carthage* walles,
And here Queene *Dido* weares th'imperiall Crowne,
Who for *Troyes* sake hath entertained us all,
And clad us in these wealthie robes we weare.

Christopher Marlow[80]

Carthage was the great Phoenician city-state in North Africa, in what is now Tunisia. It was founded as Kar-Hadasht by Queen Elissa, afterwards named Dido by the Greeks. Elissa fled Tyre following the murder of her husband in an attempt by her younger brother, the King of Tyre, to bolster his own power. At its peak Carthage was called the "shining city", ruling 300 other cities around the western Mediterranean and leading the Phoenician world.[81]

The most famous Carthaginian was the Danite general Hannibal.

Apart from the famous story of his (Hannibal) hatred of Rome, no anecdotes have come down to us from his childhood such as enliven the biographies of the famous Greeks and Romans that the Greek biographer and philosopher Plutarch compiled under the title *Parallel Lives* . . . being a regular correspondent, Hannibal wrote several books in Greek. One was an address to the people of Rhodes, demonstrating the ruthlessness of the Romans.

Robert Garland[82]

For much of its history, Carthage was on hostile terms with Greeks in Sicily and the Roman Republic.[82] At the height of its power Carthage's massive merchant fleet traversed the trade routes mapped out by Tyre. Carthage produced the extremely valuable dye Tyrian purple following Tyre's capture by the Babylonians in 573 BC after a thirteen-year siege. The Phoenicians removed almost everything of value by sea during the siege, which took place while Tephi was on her way to Ireland and during her first ten years in the Seagirt Isle:

And the spoils of all outer peoples have builded the fanes of Tyre
Which shall fall, even now are falling . . .

John A Goodchild & Daniel J Nolan[62,63]

Carthage produced finely embroidered silks, dyed textiles of cotton, linen and wool; artistic and functional pottery. Its artisans worked expertly with ivory, glassware and wood, as well as with alabaster, bronze, brass, lead, gold, silver, and precious stones to create a wide array of goods including mirrors, furniture, cabinetry, beds, bedding and pillows, jewellery, arms, implements and household items. They excelled at wood-carving, ceramics and glass blowing.[83] Carthage was also the home of a famous worker in Bronze, Boetus, son of Apollodorus, whose signature has been deciphered on the pedestal of a statue at Ephesus.[84]

Carthage traded in Atlantic salted fish and fish sauce and brokered manufactured, agricultural and natural products of almost every Mediterranean people. In addition Carthage practiced highly advanced irrigation farming, producing a wide variety of fruit and agricultural products. After the second Punic War Hannibal promoted agriculture to help restore Carthage's economy and pay the war indemnity to Rome, and was largely successful. Its olive oil was processed and exported all over the Mediterranean. Carthage sent caravans into the interior of Africa and Persia. Fine horses were raised by the Carthaginians, the ancestors of today's Barb (Berber) horses. Aristotle considered Carthage to have had the best governing institutions along with the Greek states of Sparta and Crete.[85]

At the end of the third Punic War (149–146 BC) Carthage, with a population of over 500,000 people, was destroyed. The Roman soldiers under Scipio Aemilianus went from house to house slaughtering and enslaving people. The victorious Roman general Scipio reserved all gold, silver and sacred objects for Rome, before turning the city over to his troops.[86] When appetites had been satiated and everything of value removed, the city was set ablaze and the ruins of Carthage were levelled to the ground. Sketches of ruined Carthage show devastation similar to that of Hiroshima and Nagasaki after their destruction by the atomic bombs.

No one survived the massacre with the result that there are no surviving witness records. The cities which had stood by Carthage were also destroyed while those which had sided with Rome were rewarded. Land was given to the Numidians who had deserted to the Romans while the remainder, some 5,000 square miles, became a new Roman province.[87]

> So total was the destruction wrought on Carthage that, though the Phoenician race was not completely exterminated in North Africa, it lost its identity through gradual assimilation and left no readily discernible religious, political, or social heritage. An eastern civilisation had been planted in the western Mediterranean but, after a period of luxuriant growth, it had been violently uprooted and destroyed.
>
> Nigel Bagnall[86]

> The destruction of Carthage and Corinth in 146 BC stood as a bloody memorial to the cost of resistance to Rome, and a suitably apocalyptic fanfare for Rome's coming of age as a world power.
>
> B H Wormington[87]

In 157 he (Marcus Porcius Cato) was one of the deputies sent to Carthage to arbitrate between the Carthaginians and King Massinissa of Numidia. The mission was unsuccessful and the commissioners returned home.

But Cato was so struck by the evidences of Carthaginian prosperity that he was convinced that the security of Rome depended on the annihilation of Carthage. From then on he concluded all his speeches with *Carthago delenda est*. He was known for saying this at the conclusion of his speeches, regardless of the topic.[88]

> CATO, in pronouncing the dread fiat, could scarcely have contemplated in anticipation a more complete fulfilment of the words *"delende est Carthago"* than that which actually took place. The Roman battle-axe was laid to the fair and flourishing tree and the mingled fires of Roman envy and material flame combined to wipe out Carthage from the face of the earth.
>
> Richard Miles[89]

> And when Polybius, who was with him [Cornelius Scipio Aemilianus], asked him what he meant, he turned and took him by the arm saying: 'This is a glorious moment, Polybius; and yet I am seized with fear and foreboding that someday the same fate will befall my own country.'
>
> Nigel Bagnell[86]

The destruction of Carthage by the Roman Savages transferred power from the more civilized, peaceful and talented Semitic peoples to an Aryan tyranny, with far-reaching consequences. Its culture and records were destroyed by the Romans leaving very few primary sources. And it explains why the Irish and Hebridean Scottish Christians refused to accept the authority of Rome until forced to do so by the Normans. Hannibal's failure to crush Rome in 211 BC remains one of the greatest, if not the greatest, military disaster of all time. Rome's newly found status was expressed not only in the power to obliterate, but also in the power to justify the unjustifiable.[89]

With the fall of Carthage the Phoenicians lost their most important city state and with it their role as the world's leading trader. Less than a hundred years later Julius Caesar invaded Britain (55–54 BC) to obtain access to the tin mines of Cornwall. And in the reign of Claudius the Romans controlled the world's supply of tin.[90]

The inscription on the tophet of Cirta mentions scribes, a doctor, a smelter, a sculptor, carpenters, and a bow-maker and they all have Punic names. Thus at the end of the fourth century AD in the district round Hippo a patois was still spoken which was doubtless very much crossed with Libyan, but contained enough Punic words for St Augustine's flock to recognize it as a near relation to Biblical Hebrew, and to declare themselves as Canaanites.

Gilbert Charles Picard, & Colette Picard[91]

Most of the ruins of Carthage and adjacent towns lie inaccessible under Roman, Byzantine, Arab and present day Tunisian settlements. Archaeologists discovered the remains of Kerkouane, the name bestowed by them.[92] It was one of the manufacturing sites of the famous Phoenician purple dye.

However, what really surprised the archaeologists who excavated Kerkouane was the sheer number of bathrooms, and their technical ingenuity. Unlike in Carthage, where the hip baths were free-standing, many of those in Kerkouane were built into the room, with the most elaborate having a stepped seat, arm rests and basin all of which were covered in water-resistant render. Some bathrooms were split between changing and washing facilities. Whereas in many Greek houses the bathroom was connected to the kitchen area, in Kerkouane many were situated off the entrance vestibule or passageway leading from the street into the house.

Mabel Moore[92]

CHAPTER 3

TEIA TEPHI: QUEEN OF IRELAND 583–534 BC

The Harp dates back to 719 BC when it was brought to the country by the Irish King David. Today the harp is usually represented with a carved body depicting Tea Tephi, an early Irish Queen, whose wings denote her guardianships of the island.

Nigel Groom[93]

Teia Tephi became queen of Ireland on 21st June 583 BC and was later wrongfully Deified as a mythical goddess called Bo/Bovinda, which is why over the passage of time she became lost in the realms of myth and fantasy ceasing to be remembered as real flesh and blood queen who came to Ireland from Jerusalem, that she really was . . .

jahtruth.net/liafail[94]

Teltown, located about ten kilometres from Kells in the direction of Navan, originally called Tailte Teia (Teia's land – Tailtiu) was built in the sixth century BC by Queen Teia Tephi, after whom it is named. Teia Tephi was Queen of Tara and ruled Ireland from there while living in her palace (Rath Dubh) at Teltown until her death on the August 1, 534 BC at Teltown. Teia (*known affectionately as the [Dubh] "Black-haired Heifer," later wrongfully Deified as Bo/Bovinda*)[95] gave birth to four children: three boys and a girl. They were called Aedh (flame) who died whilst still a teenager and was buried at the eastern entrance of the Mound of Hostages at Tara; Ainge (her daughter); Aengus (Mac Oc "the younger son") who ruled as Ard Ri and built Newgrange for his tomb (*as confirmed by the fact that his name is carved in Ogham Script on Stone C4 inside Newgrange*) and Armad, as she explained in her book "Book of Tephi Queen of Tara and Gibraltar". Before her death Queen Teia Tephi asked the Irish people to hold a fair and games, every year; which were to be non-competitive; to commemorate her reign and death.[95] (The games were subsequently known as the Tailteann Games and only ceased following the arrival of the Normans)

Teia Tephi became Queen of Eriu after arriving there, following the fall of Jerusalem to the Babylonian King Nebuchadnezzar in 587 BC.[62,63] Tephi, of the Tribe of Judah, was a direct descendant of King David. Her father Zedekiah and her brothers were captured and killed after the fall of Jerusalem. Tephi escaped to Egypt with her sisters Maacha and Bathba, the Prophet Jeremiah and Jeremiah's scribe Baruch ben Neriah. From there they made their way to Ireland in seven stages by sea: by way of the Nile Delta, Carthage, the mouth of a then unknown river now known to be the Tiber, Gibraltar, Galicia in north-west Iberia, Cornwall, Holy Island (Anglesey) arriving at Howth, then known as Pen Edair, on 18 June 583 BC. Baruch, Jeremiah's scribe, died in Gibraltar and was buried there. Tephi's journey and her early time in Ireland are well described by John A Goodchild in his epic narrative poem *The Book of Tephi*, her apparent autobiography.[62] Goodchild, an English physician, antiqarian and poet, practised Medicine in Italy. *Tephi* is based on translations of ancient manuscripts by Standish O'Grady, Whitley Stokes and others.

Shortly after arriving in Ireland Tephi married the High King Eochaidh, and was crowned Queen on the Stone of Destiny (Liá Fáil) brought to Ireland by Jeremiah. The Kings of Israel were previously crowned on the Stone (Jacob's Pillar). According to the Old Testament it was the Stone on which Jacob laid his head when he stopped on the way from Beer-Sheba to Haran and dreamt of a stairway reaching from the ground to the heavens.[96] It was on this hallowed Stone that the High kings of Ireland were crowned until it was borrowed by the Scots for the crowning of their king in 501 AD and not returned. In 1296 it was taken to London by King Edward I and placed in Westminster Abbey, where it remains to this day as the Coronation Stone.

Tephi faced a challenge from a number of warlords, notably Balor the leader of the Firbolgs, but with the support of the Tuatha Dé Danann was victorious at the battle of Moytura (Magh Turedh). Tephi introduced laws based on the Torah, afterwards known as Brehon Laws. They were administered by Brehons who prescribed restitution rather than punishment and banishment for serious offences. Many years of relative peace followed, reinforced by the arrival of St Patrick. Between the arrival of Tephi and the first Viking raids at the end of the eighth century AD, a period extending over nearly 1,400 years, Ireland was a centre of craft, culture, learning and enlightenment. Brehon Laws began to be replaced by Norman Law in the reign of

King Henry II and ceased to exist by the end of the Tudor era. Henry II also brought the Irish Christian Church under Roman domination nearly 800 years after the Emperor Constantine made Christianity the official religion of the Roman Empire.

> Christianity had begun as a humble movement of Jewish sectaries, but when it was adopted as the official religion of the Roman Empire, it soon made peace with war.
>
> Nigel Cliff[97]

The High Kingship was destabilised when Brian Boru usurped the throne and made himself Ard Rí, as the High Kingship of Ireland was known. Boru unseated Máel Sechnaill MacDomnaill, known as Malachy II, the last Tuatha Dé Danann King of Ireland, in 1002. Malachy had defeated a Viking army at the Battle of Tara.[98] The Battle of Tara is regarded as a far more decisive defeat of the Norse of Dublin than Brian Boru's more famous victory at Clontarf in 1014. Malachy regained the High Kingship after Boru's death at Clontarf and retained it until his death in 1022. But Boru's usurpation destabilised the Irish monarchy, and from then on squabbling between claimants resulted in divisions and alliances with subsequent invaders particularly the Normans, resulting in the eventual demise of the High kingship of Ireland.

Donald III (Domnall mac Donnchada in medieval Gaelic)[99] was probably the last Danann King of Scotland. He reigned from 1093 to 1097 with an interruption in 1094. Domnall is *Gaelic* for Daniel, a fact that seems to be completely unknown to historians and language experts alike in both Ireland and Scotland! The so-called medieval spelling, Domnall, was how the author's forename was spelt at school!! There was a minor difference, a dot called a "boulte" was over the m; Mac Domnall translates: "Son of Daniel".

The "Daniel Stone"[72] is one of the fourteen Rosmarkie sculpture fragments, Pictish slabs and stone fragments discovered in Rosemarkie, on the Black Isle of Easter Ross in Scotland. They are currently displayed in Groam House Museum at Rosemarkie.

> The latter [Daniel Stone] is so named because of the tendency among scholars and enthusiasts to give every Pictish stone a Christian interpretation. In this case, the depiction of a man's

head at the jaws of a wolf-like beast depicts the Old Testament story of Daniel in the Lion's Den . . .

Rosemarkie Sculpture Fragments [72]

Ireland was called Hibernia, and there were the Hebrides Islands and numerous places in Gaul and other Celtic areas whose name contained the root "eber" meaning Hebrew.

britam.org/namesakes [100]

What is the truth about the Celtic lands? I am only a sailor, amateur historian and novelist. I make no claim to have an answer to my own question. All I know for certain is that there is a need to seek an answer and that I intend to take part in the continuing search. That's all.

Larsson, Björn [101]

The most likely answer to Björn Larsson's question: Danite-Phoenician!!!

CHAPTER 4

FROM ABRAHAM TO *DANNY BOY*: DAN – DANIEL – TRIBE OF DAN – DANAAN – DANITES – TUATHA DÉ DANANN

Jacob-Israel had twelve sons, who fathered the twelve tribes of Israel, the fifth of whom was called Dan[102] and he fathered the Tuatha de Danann (*the Tribe of Dan*). Dan was the fifth son of Jacob, and the first of Bilah, who was Jacob's concubine and the maid of Rachel, who was Jacob's wife.[103] Dan travelled with Jacob and family from Padan Aram to Canaan, and later to Egypt. When Jacob blessed his sons he stated that Dan would achieve justice for his people.[104]

The Tribe of Dan is reprimanded in the Old Testament's *Song of Deborah* for not participating in the war against the Canaanites.[59] The tribe of Dan failed to conquer the portion of the land of Israel that was given to them as their original inheritance. The failure forced them to move north, where they took over the land called Laish, renaming it Dan.[105] That became the northern limit of Israel.

The Scales of Justice emblem of the Tribe of Dan[106] is displayed with emblems of the other eleven tribes of Israel at HaPoel HaMizrachi Central Synagogue in Bnei Brak, Israel (See figure 2 oppos).[107] Bnei Brak is located in the Dan metropolitan region near Tel Aviv which recently merged with the ancient port of Jaffa to become Tel Aviv-Jaffa.

The second year after the Israelites came out of the land of Egypt a census was taken of all men aged between 20 and 60 years-of-age who were fit for military service. There were four brigades, each brigade made up of three tribes positioned around the Tabernacle Encampment.[108] The brigade leaders were Ruben, whose standard was a MAN; Judah, whose standard was a LION; Joseph/Ephraim whose standard was a CALF/UNICORN; Dan's standard was an EAGLE.[109]

> The Tribe of Dan, by its enterprise and vigour, has made itself one of the most conspicuous branches of Jacob's family.
>
> John Cox Gawler [110]

The invention of the Ogham is attributed in bardic history to Ogma, son of Elatan, a prince of the Tuatha de Dananns, that people whom all our national traditions represent as a more cultured race than any of the other colonies that took possession of this island in primitive times.

John Healy[111]

Irishman John Wilson's book, *Lectures on Our Israelitish Origin* (1840, four editions subsequently, and an American edition in 1851), established his reputation as the "True Father of the Rediscovery of Israel". He substantiated the traceable migratory path of the Tribe of Dan, carrying its eagle standard (See figure 3 overleaf) from the Near East by way of the Caucasus Mountains into Western Europe.

Neil Baldwin[112]

DAN

The Irish people are mostly descended from Dan and came to Ireland at various times, under various names, as they migrated by different routes and arrived at various times, having picked up new names on the way. One of those names makes their identity more obvious than the others and that name is the Tuatha de Danann – the Tribe of Dan; who was the fifth of Jacob/Israel's twelve sons. Jacob/Israel's twelve sons fathered the twelve tribes of Israel. Prior to the De Dananns were the Nemidians (Sons of Heaven) who came from Carthage which was a Phoenician Danite settlement or Sanctuary (Nemidth), in what is now Tunisia. The Phoenician sailors of ancient history were mostly Israelis from the tribe of Dan; Gad and Simeon.

jahtruth.net/bkofke[109]

Then Elatha the kinsman of Ith gave counsel to rest awhile
Till swift boats be sent to Eriu to question the men of that isle

44

Where the princes of Dan abode, and chiefly o Jochad, the son
Of Duach, him that their landsmen had chosen as Heremon,
    Whose fathers came out of Japho wherein they were held too
                          straight
By the kings of Gath and of Eckron, and spreading their sails to fate
    Drew their swords unto kingship in Chittim, Rhodan, and Lud,
And ruled Ar Kadesh, and mingled the stream of the chosen blood
    In many a mountain torrent, on many a peopled coast
Ere they lighted on green Eriu a little, a noble host,
    Which fought the cause of the landsmen. This fame, and their
                        names therein
    The prophet foreknew of the Dannites, the furthest of Jacob's kin.
With these he would leave in the sun's path the twig of the lofty tree
    The small green bough of the olive, in the midst of the deep to be
Even yet in Abraham's bosom, the home of his sons afar
    Who replenish their strength in the isles, ere they gather to seek the
                        star
Of Isaac and Jacob their fathers, when Israel filleth the earth
    With joy in the sound of his coming, and music and songs of
                        mirth.
Five weeks we abode at Pensauel till the men of the land returned
    With tidings whereat the Prophet rejoiced, and my spirit burned.
At Pen Edair they heard of peace, how Eriu yearned for the choice
    Of a guard against evil rulers, and the aire cried with one voice
Upon Jochad, the son of Duach, a prince of the tribe of Dan,
    A champion wise and mighty, and sprung of that chosen clan
Which had captained miledhs in Javan, and their hosts throughout
                        Eberled.
            John A Goodchild & Daniel J Nolan[62,63]

. . . and indicates that the tin used in Dan of the Galilee came
from Britain. Later one of the names given to Cornwall and
Devon was Daunonia and Dannonia. The Phoenician mines in
Cornwall according to local tradition are all connected to the
JEWS meaning in their terms, HEBREWS from ISRAEL.
           ensignmessage.com/archives/tracingdan[113]

. . . Archaeologists have also unearthed an 8th century BC Hebrew seal with the emblem of a ship. It is an obvious inference that the ancient Irish Tuatha de Danann, who trace their origin to the East, are related to both the Danaan of early Greece and the Biblical tribe of Dan. It is a known fact that the old word, 'tuatha,' means tribe; 'Tuatha de Danaan' therefore means 'tribe of Dan.' Well-respected modern archaeologist, Cyrus Gordon, (who was called the leading American archaeologist of the 20th century by *Archaeology Magazine* in 1966), also tied the tribe of Dan to the Tuatha de Danann of early Ireland.

israelite.ca/research/source/[114]

Irish tradition holds that the [round] towers were built by the Tuatha de Danann. The towers were "specifically constructed for the twofold purpose of worshipping the Sun and Moon, as the authors of generation and vegetable heat . . ."

Henry O'Brien[115]

Early Irish annalists referred to the Ó Nualláins (the O'Nolans) as the "ancient ones of Leinster." Oral tradition further holds that they were descendants of the Tuatha De Danann, the mythical Tribe of Dan, who, in their early wanderings, gave their name to the "Danube" river and the country of "Denmark," . . . According to historical writings and recent archaeological discoveries, the homeland of the Tuatha De Danann was Scythia, a vast region extending northwards from the Black Sea and covering most of the Ukraine. Modern-day archaeology further states that the Scythians had a thriving agricultural economy supplying wheat to the Greek empire in exchange for wine and other goods. . . . The Scythians were also renowned for their metallurgical skills, creating exquisite pieces of gold jewellery, tableware and even gold ornaments for their horses.

nolanfamilies.org/index[116]

The Native Irish excelled in metallurgical skills and created magnificent pieces such as the Tara Broach[117] and the Ardagh Chalice.[118] In addition they illustrated manuscripts, creating such exquisite art as the Book of Kells.[119] And during the centuries before the Christian Era their culture was of a very high standard, in some respects the highest in the world.[120] Yair Davidy quotes Peter Beresford Ellis who said that Physicians in ancient Ireland were skilled in performing Caesarean operations, amputations and even brain surgery; and records a hospital being established in Ulster around 377 BC.[52,120] Hospitals were regulated by the "Brehon Law" requiring them to be staffed by qualified personnel, free from debt, be freely available to the sick, feeble, elderly and orphans, and have four doors and fresh water. Diancecht was the sixth century BC Danann physician who tended Jodhad, husband of Teia Tephi: 'Six months my watchings endured, and my sorrow and toil was great, ere Diancecht, the mighty healer, cured him, yet not to the state wherein he had strength before.'[62,63] Women also practiced leechcraft, as the art of healing was then known.[62]

CHAPTER 5

VIKINGS TO CROMWELL:
DEMISE OF A CIVILIZATION

> Despite attempts to rehabilitate them in recent times, the
> Vikings, with their thirst for blood and glory and their gruesome
> human sacrifices, were not surprisingly regarded with horror
> by the settled Anglo-Saxons, who witnessed their monasteries
> being torched, their gold and silver treasures being looted, their
> precious illuminated manuscripts being destroyed, their young
> men and women being led away as slaves, and anyone who stood
> in the way being mercilessly put to the sword.
>
> Marc Morris[121]

The Viking with their raids starting in 795 on Rathlin Island off the north
Antrim coast, and later with their settlements in Dublin, Wexford, Water-
ford, Cork and Limerick, brought an end to the great Hebernian (Native Irish
Hebrew) Civilization.

> But they [Vikings] are the forerunners of most of the European
> societies which we know today: including our own in the United
> Kingdom and Ireland.
>
> Vikings-Neil-Oliver [122]

In 1169 the Normans arrived in Ireland. The Normans were a few generations
down from the Vikings, and could best be described as "Vikings in sheep's
clothing". They played a leading role in the discredited Crusades; Native Irish
Christians took no part. The first Crusade was from 1095 to 1099. The three
leading Norman families who acquired much of their Irish land by conquest
were the de Burgs (Burkes), Butlers and Fitzgeralds. When the Tudor Terror
was visited on the people, many of the descendents of the Norman Conquerors
conveniently converted to the Protestant religion. And, more recently, they
have been influential in rewriting Irish history. Almost every Irish schoolchild

is told how "The Normans became more Irish than the Irish themselves". These nine words hide successful campaigns of violence and plunder in the pursuit of land and wealth at the expense of the Native Irish.

The century that followed Henry II's visit to Ireland marked the height of Norman expansion. More than half the country was by now directly subjected to the knightly invaders. Among them was Gerald of Windsor, ancestor of the Fitzgerald family, and branches of which as the Earls of Kildare and lords of much else, were for long to control large tracts of southern and central Ireland. There was William de Burgh, brother of the English Justicer and ancestor of the Earls of Ulster; and Theobold Walter, King John's butler and founder of the powerful Butler family of Ormond, which took their name from his official calling. But there was no organised colonisation and settlement. English [Norman] authority was accepted in the Norse towns on the southern and eastern coasts, and the king's writ ran over varying areas of country surrounding Dublin. The hinterland of the capital was significantly known as the "Pale", which might be defined as defended Closure. Immediately outside lay the big feudal lordships and beyond these were the "wild" unconquered Irish of the West. Two races dwelt in uneasy balance, and the division between them was sharpened when a Parliament of Ireland evolved towards the end of the thirteenth century. From this body the Native Irish were excluded; it was a parliament in Ireland of the English only.

Winston Churchill[123]

The Norman de Bourg/Bourke dynasty was founded by William de Burgh (1160–1206), who was closely associated with King John.[124] Henry II appointed him Governor of Limerick and granted him large estates in Leinster and Munster. He was Royal Governor of Munster 1201–1203. He married an O'Brien of the Thomond Dynasty and in 1199 to 1202 carried out a military campaign in Desmond with O'Brien, conquering and plundering Connaught as well as churches. The Arms of the de Burgh, Red Cross of St George on a gold shield, has its origins in the first Crusade.[125,126]

Many descendants of the leading Norman families have, over the centuries, retained their power and influence by conforming to the prevailing religious and political mores of the day. Many of the Fitzgeralds, descendants of Gerald of Windsor, have retained their power and influence by doing so. The former C-in-C (Commissar-in-Chief) Garrett Fitzgerald, a man not renowned for his intellect and with a paucity of social skills, had a State Funeral in Dublin with the coffin wrapped in the Fenian Tricolour. Interesting, when one realizes that it was the powerful Fitzgerald family, Earls of Kildare and afterwards Dukes of Leinster, who first used St Patrick's saltire as their emblem before it became the flag of pre-Nineteenth century Ireland!

The Duke of Ormond (1610–1668) became Viceroy shortly after the Restoration of 1660. Unlike King Charles II, who intended to convert to the Catholic faith, Ormond harboured a hatred of Catholicism:

> . . . and when the Irish Parliament hastened to welcome him, and to express a hope that Popery would be further discouraged, the Catholics knew that the resources of bigotry were not yet exhausted, and that further repressive legislation was to come. In the session of 1704, such legislation did come, when the 'Bill to prevent the further growth of Popery' became law.
>
> E A D'Alton[127]

The 2nd Duke of Ormonde was one of the principal Williamite supporters in Ireland. Most of the Dukes' Butler relatives remained Catholic. A path around the headland Bray Head in County Wicklow is named *Slí de Búitléar*; in English: De Búitléar's Way!! It is likely to have been named after a local Butler, an Irish Army officer of that name, who in the middle of the twentieth century required his family to speak *An Gaelge* at home. He was presumably one of the Ormond Butlers who, having taken much of the lands of the Princes of Foharta (Forth), the O'Nolans (Ó Nualláins), demoted them. The principal families of County Carlow following the Normans Conquest were:

Barons: Butler
Lords: O'Cavanagh, O'Moore, O'Nolan and O'Ryan
Chieftains: MacGorman, O'Cahill and O'Doran
No title designated: Clevers, Coke, Eustace, Fitzgerald, Grace,

Lombard, MacMurragh, MacTigue, O'Bolger, O'Doyle, O'Doyne, O'Kinsella, Sarsfield, Strongbow, Tallon and Wall.

Oliver Cromwell and his army came ashore at Dublin on August 15, 1649.

> Mr McCourt, don't you care about the babies burned with napalm in Vietnam? I do, and I care about the babies in Korea and China, in Auschwitz and Armenia, and the babies impaled on the swords of Cromwell's soldiers in Ireland.
>
> Frank McCourt[128]

The Norman Conquerors were not the only invaders whose descendants behave as though they are more Irish than the Natives!!

> . . . a slave-based fortune paid for the splendid buildings by Hawksmoor at All Souls College, Oxford; . . .
>
> Hugh Brogan[129]

The present owner of Tullynally Castle, Castlepollard, County Westmeath is Tom Pakenham, 8th Earl of Longford.[130] His sister is Lady Antonia Fraser. In her biography of Oliver Cromwell, Fraser states:

> Great estates were built up, as many officers were also under another hat Adventurers. Captain Henry Pakenham, for example, of Abbott's dragoons, built up his Westmeath estate by three methods: land owing to him as an adventurer, military debentures, and outright acquisition by purchase.
>
> Antonia Fraser [41]

Colonel Daniel Abbott's Regiment of Dragoons was specifically raised by Oliver Cromwell for his Irish campaign.[131] Captain Henry Pakenham was obviously an officer in the Parliamentary Army of Oliver Cromwell when it arrived in Dublin on the August 15, 1649, and introduced Cromwellian Totalitarianism: autocracy, bureaucracy, democracy, plutocracy, hypocrisy, militarism, republicanism, capitalism, and communism to Ireland.

Oliver Cromwell was the hero of the rabid psychopath Vladimir Lenin[132] whose bloody Red Russian Revolution resulted not only in the brutal killing of the Imperial Royal family[133] but also as the initiator of Soviet State Terror that resulted in the deaths of millions. Ivan Bunin, who was afterwards awarded the Dynamite Prize for Literature as an exile, was accidentally connected to a conversation within the Kremlin in March 1918:

> 'I have fifteen officers and Lieutenant Kaledin. What should I do to them?' The voice at the other end of the line did not hesitate: 'Shoot them right away.' Later Bunin received an order requiring the registration of "all bourgeois" . . . His suspicions that their registration was the prelude to execution proved entirely correct. Fortunately Bunin managed to flee Russia into exile and save his life. In his private diary he wrote: 'the "Great Russian Revolution" is a thousand times more bestial, filthy and stupid than the vile original which it claims to copy because it exceeds – step by step, item for item, and in a horribly shameless and explicit way – the bloody melodrama that had played itself out in France.'
>
> Tim Tzouliadis[134]

On 11 August 1918, Lenin wrote to the party leaders in Penza giving instructions on how to deal with the peasants:

> Comrades! The revolt by the five kulak voloists [smallest rural administrative subdivisions in Imperial Russia][135] must be suppressed without mercy . . . You need to hang (hang without fail, so that the public sees) at least 100 notorious kulaks, the rich and the bloodsuckers . . . execute the hostages – in accordance with yesterday's telegram. This need to be accomplished in such a way that people for hundreds of miles around will see, tremble, know and scream out: let's choke and strangle those blood-sucking kulaks. Telegraph us acknowledging receipt and execution of this. Yours Lenin. PS Use your toughest people for this.
>
> Tim Tzouliadis; Diane P Koenker & Ronald D Bachman[134,136]

Here also was Lenin's order for the 'execution by firing squad' of the priests of Shuia, his instruction to Nikolai Krestinsky: It is necessary and secretly – and urgently – to prepare the terror', and his admission in 1920: 'We do not hesitate to shoot thousands of people.' Was it surprising, therefore, that Lenin, who began the process, gave way to Stalin, who accelerated the disappearance of millions? Stalin methodically and ruthlessly applied the same methods on a larger scale, but with the rhetorical 'When we are reproached with cruelty, we wonder how people can forget the most elementary Marxism' was Lenin's own. The consequences of Stalinism were therefore neither accident nor a 'socialist aberration', as Khrushchev sought to portray. The Terror was a historical continuity within a political system which glorified 'Bolshevik ruthlessness' and denigrated the value of human life ... The Soviet nuclear scientist turned dissident Andrei Sakharov estimated that between fifteen and twenty million perished as victims of the Stalin era ... seven million shot.

Tim Tzouliadis[134]

On September 10, 1649 Cromwell and his troops stormed Drogheda. In a letter dated 17 September to the John Bradshaw, President of the Council of State, Cromwell stated:

It hath pleased God to bless our endeavours at Drogheda. The enemy was about 3,000 strong in the town ... Before we entered we refused them quarter; having the day before summoned the town. I do not think Thirty of the whole number escaped with their lives. Those that did are in safe custody for Barbadoes.

Sean O'Callaghan[42]

And who was this man John Bradshaw? Bradshaw was President of the High court of Justice for the trial of King Charles I when many more prominent lawyers had refused the position. During the trial he was flanked by an impressive personal guard and carried a sword at his side. He wore scarlet robes and broad-brimmed, bullet proof beaver hat, which he had covered over with velvet and lined it with steel. He also wore armour underneath his robes.[137]

In the years following Cromwell's invasion, many thousands more Irish men, women and Children were shipped into slavery in Barbados and other colonies.[42] Of the 50,000 people Irish people sent into slavery in the West Indies most were sent to Barbados, where they had to work in appalling conditions on the sugar plantations. Two of the sugar plantations in Barbados were owned by the Codrington family where many of the Irish, sent by Cromwell's men, would have ended their days. They did not live long, as they were less tolerant of the great heat of the Sun than the African slaves.

> 'Those sold to the heretics in America are treated by them more
> cruelly than the slaves under the Turks; nor is any attention paid
> to youth or the decrepitude of old age, to sex or rank, sacerdotal
> orders to religious life', according to Cardinal Giovanni Battista
> Rinuccini, papal nuncio to the Confederation of Kilkenny 1645–
> 1648.
>
> Sean O'Callaghan[42]

The Codrington Library is the library of All Souls College, Oxford. It was endowed by Christopher Codrington (1668–1710) a fellow of the College who amassed a fortune through his plantation slavery in the West Indies. He bequeathed books worth £6,000 and £10,000 to provide a building to house the books.[138] The magnificent library was designed by Nicholas Hawksmoor and completed in 1751. A cold shiver runs down my spine each time I walk past All Souls!!!

Many Irish soldiers crossed over to England and fought on the side of King Charles I against Cromwell in the English Civil War.

> On the 24th of the same month, October, 1644, the Parliament
> promulgated its Rhadamanthine Ordinance, to 'hang any Irish
> Papist taken in arms in this country . . .'
>
> Thomas Carlyle[139]

When the Parliamentarians captured Shrewsbury in February 1645, they took fifty Irish prisoners. Colonel Mytton, the parliamentary commander, selected twelve by lot and hanged them in the town square. In retaliation Price Rupert ordered the hanging of thirteen Roundheads taken at Oswestry. Parliament protested vigorously against the 'outrage' and ordered the Earl of Essex to explain to Rupert that 'there was a very great difference between Englishmen and Irishmen'. . . . Sir William Brereton hanged every Irish prisoner he took. In the same year, 1645, Captain Swanley, a parliamentary naval officer, captured a ship out of Dublin bound for Bristol with seventy soldiers and two women on board. He threw them overboard, tied back to back. One of the London newspapers, the *Perfect Diurnal,* wrote approvingly of Captain Swanley's action and stated that he 'made water rats of the papish vermin'. Parliament acclaimed his action and presented Captain Swanly with a gold chain worth £200.

Sean O'Callaghan[42]

PENAL LAWS

Following the Cromwellian Invasion of 1649 control of the Irish Parliament passed into the hands of the Cromwellian Planters, who passed the Penal Laws specifically targeting the Catholic Native Irish who became disenfranchised to such an extent that our ancestors became non-people in their own country.

This then was the lot of the Catholic tenant: A mud cabin fit for a pig, and which they shared with that animal, a patch of ground at a Rack-Rent, precarious and ill-paid labour, chronic starvation, and ever impending famine, rags for his wife and children, extortionate tithes for an alien church, a coarse and brutal landlord with an insult often, and sometimes a blow, and, worst of all, a persistent attempt by government and law to shut him out from the Kingdom of Heaven. Another aftermath of the Cromwellian Invasion and the Planters Parliament was the large number of people who were homeless: In 1742 there were more than 30,000 beggars in Ireland.

E A Dalton[127]

The eulogistic description of the lives of her Cromwellian Planter ancestors by Eliza Pakenham in her *Soldier, Sailor: An Intimate Portrait of an Irish Family*[140] is downright offensive:

> I have something else that will help to set the scene. It is a careful pencil sketch made in the journal of George Edward Pakenham, the great-uncle of the Napoleonic generation of Pakenhams. He came to stay with his elder brother in Ireland in the autumn of 1737. It shows the place where they were all brought up as it was at the time of their grandfather, Thomas Pakenham. The foreground is all fields and hills, a pack of hounds and huntsmen chasing a fox, just visible leaping away in the corner. Beyond, on the opposite slope, is an elaborate formal garden of avenues, canals and basins, laid out like a miniature Versailles. Far away in the distance is the house, a plain square box, as small as a postage stamp, Pakenham Hall, Westmeath.
>
> The scene looks bucolic. In his journal George Edward can't help a touch of envy creeping into his description. His brother's house was a bustling, prosperous place with 'a steward, a butler, gardener and several helpers... ten men in livery, 8 or 10 hunters, a fine pack of hounds and a set of horses' – in short, all that a fox-hunting squire could desire. But even a hard-up younger brother could see there were drawbacks to owning an Irish estate. He found his brother's fellow squires boorish and drunken; and the peasantry were miserably poor and (to his English Protestant eyes) kept in a state of ignorance and servitude by their local priests. And his brother's few surviving letters reveal a still dangerous and unsettled country with bands of outlaws (probably dispossessed Catholics) hidden in the wild oak woods that edged the nearby lake of Derravaragh.
>
> Eliza Pakenham[140]

The authorities also resorted to Cromwell's policy of transportation. During the 1660s large numbers of Tories [disposed Catholics who had become outlaws] were 'Barbadoed', or sent to Jamaica. We know this because the viceroy of Ireland, Berkley, gave permission to Archbishop Plunkett to negotiate with them, offering thirty-seven of their leaders free pardon and transport out of Ireland to Flanders. In September 1670, fifteen accepted the offer, including Patrick Fleming, their leader, but instead of sending them to the continental countries, the government broke its word and sent them as slaves to Barbados.

Sean O'Callaghan[42]

CHAPTER 6

CAPITALISM: TRIUMPH OF MACHEVILLISM

In a country well governed poverty is something to be ashamed of; in a country badly governed, wealth is something to be ashamed of.

Confucius[141]

I found this type of book [Nicolò Machiavelli's *The Prince*] to be written by an enemy of the human race. It explains every means whereby religion, justice and any inclination towards virtue could be destroyed.

Cardinal Reginald Pole[142]

Out of his surname [Machiavelli's] they have coined an epithet for a knave, and out of his Christian name a synonym for the Devil.

Thomas Babbington Macauley[143]

Power is a poison well known for thousands of years. If only no one were ever to acquire material power over others! Power is not an attraction – it is an intoxication . . . Do you think you can build a just society on a foundation of self-serving and envious people?

Aleksandr Solzhenitsyn[144]

World peace, however noble, was no more the capitalists' primary concern than was achieving wealth and power through the marketplace. Through a dizzying array of formal and informal business agreements, a network of multinational corporations based in the United States, England, and Germany colluded to capture markets and control prices.

Wyndham Lewis[23]

'The whole country's in a state o' chassis' wrote Sean O'Casey.[145] And much more so now than when he wrote *Juno and the Paycock*! The Recovery was a hoax, Growth is a mirage, economics is a form of Voodoo, politics is lying through one's teeth, Business is exploitation, Privatisation is Grand Larceny, and Public Private Partnerships are partnerships in crime. Advertising, marketing, sponsorship and spin are propaganda, and as George Orwell said: 'All propaganda is lies'.[146] If competition rather than cooperation had been the way forward from the beginning of time we would still be hunter gatherers living in caves!!

Privatisation is an extension of the Enclosure Acts of Parliament which enclosed open fields and common land in the country, creating legal property rights to land that was previously considered common:

> Between 1604 and 1914, over 5,200 individual closure acts were put into place, enclosing 6.8 million acres of land (about 11,000 square miles). Enclosure acts for small areas had been passed sporadically since the 12th century, but with the rise of the Industrial Revolution they became more commonplace. In search of better financial returns, the landowners looked for more efficient farming techniques. Enclosures were also created so that landowners could charge higher rent to people working the land. This was at least partially responsible for peasants leaving the land to work in the city in industrial factories.
>
> en.wikipedia.org/wiki/Inclosure_Acts[147]

> Peasants have been under siege since time immemorial by those intent on prying from them agricultural surpluses or the means of agricultural production. Sometimes the weapons used against them were tithes and taxes, sometimes agrarian reforms, sometimes enclosures or privatization.
>
> Gail Kligman & Katherine Verdery[148]

Agrarian laws enabling large landowners to wrestle land from farmers and peasants go back to Rome:

By the 2nd century BC, wealthy landowners had begun to dominate the agrarian areas of the empire by "renting" large tracts of public land and treating it as though it were private. This began to force out smaller private farmers with competition; the farmers were forced to move to the cities for this and a number of other factors including battles, making living in rural areas dangerous. Roman cities were not good places to get jobs; they were also dangerous, overcrowded and messy.

en.wikipedia.org/wiki/Agrarian_law[149]

Two needs clashed when red met white; and so did two great principles; the principle of private property and the principle of common ownership.

Hugh Brogan[129]

'I am told' continued Egremont, 'that an impassable gulf divided the Rich from the Poor; I was told that the Privileged and the People formed Two Nations, governed by different laws, influenced by different manners, with no thoughts or sympathies in common; with an innate inability of mutual comprehension . . .'

Benjamin Disraeli[29]

The brutal property laws of the English penal code came over side by side with Trial by Jury and the Writ of Habeas Corpus.

Wyndham Lewis[23]

'Yes the Russians come here too. I think they're frightened. Capitalism is causing more problems than Communism did. Everything is failing. You see our temple too, it's crumbling. I could not see this; only the dark hills touched it with desolation.'

Colin Thubron[150]

Russia's flirtation with crony capitalism proved equally insane.

Oliver Stone & Peter Kuznik[19]

MACHEVIL AND THE PSYCHOPATH:
TUDOR TERROR UNLEASHED

The very poor were very numerous in Tudor and Stuart England.

Hugh Brogan[129]

[Enter] Machevil.
Albeit the world thinke *Machevil* is dead,
Yet was his soule but flowne beyond the *Alps* . . .

Christopher Marlowe[151]

And who was one of the first to put into practice the exhorting of the Anti-Christ Niccolò Machiavelli? None other than the banker, lawyer, land-grabber and altar-stripper Sir Thomas Cromwell![152] Cromwell is reputed to have obtained a pre-publication copy of Machiavelli's *The Prince*[153] during his time as a banker in Florence, and to have shown it to King Henry VIII.[154] Henry was persuaded by Cromwell to embark on the confiscation of the monasteries and their land, and plunder their wealth.

> No comparable transfer of wealth (the confiscation of the monasteries and the selling of monastic lands) had occurred since the Norman Conquest. The consequences did more than anything to prepare the English nation for the modern age.
>
> Simon Jenkins[155]

To call it a Reformation is an affront to Abrahamic Christianity.[156] Cardinal Reginald Pole (1550–1558) whose maternal grandparents were George Plantagenet, 1st Duke of Clarence and Isabella Neville, Duchess of Clarence, and a grand-nephew of Kings Edward IV and Richard III, incurred the wrath of Henry VIII and Thomas Cromwell.[142] Pole was known for his strong condemnation of Machiavelli's *The Prince* which he had read in Italy. He is said to have labelled Thomas Cromwell an "Emissary of Satin". He escaped the wrath of Henry by going to Paris. His mother Margaret Pole, 8th Countess of Salisbury, who was in no way guilty of disloyalty to Henry, spent two-and-a-half years in the Tower of London under appalling conditions before being executed in a barbarous manner. Margaret Pole was one of the last surviving members of the House of Plantagenet and under some circumstances that descent could have made Reginald a contender for the throne if he had not entered the clergy. After the death of Henry VIII, Reginald Pole became the last Catholic Archbishop of Canterbury.

Winston Churchill[32] describes how Cromwell handled what was called the dissolution of the monasteries with cold-blooded efficiency. It appealed to the well-to-do. The high nobility and country gentry acquired on most favourable terms large tracts of land and estates. Sometimes a neighbouring merchant or a syndicate leased or bought the confiscated land. In some cases a local squire who had been steward of monastic lands, which he had managed for generations, bought them.

Anyone who stood in Henry's way was put to the sword. Queens, chief ministers, abbots, monks, priests and ordinary people who dared resist the royal will were put to death. Roman Catholics and Calvinists alike were burnt for heresy and religious treason. At the beginning of 1537 a revolt broke out in the North of England and Lincolnshire because the people objected to the taxes and the suppression of the monasteries. The revolt collapsed and Henry dealt ruthlessly with the ringleaders. Seventy were hanged as traitors at Carlisle assizes alone and when Norfolk the victorious general was inclined to clemency Henry sent word that he desired a large number of executions. Altogether about 250 insurgents were put to death.[32]

The Tudor Terror continued under Queens Mary and Elizabeth. The confiscation of the monastic lands resulted in impoverished peasants flocking into urban centres, particularly London. Previously the monks had cared for the poor but there was no one to look after their huge numbers in the aftermath of Henry VIII's and Thomas Cromwell's great land grab. The Tudor system of indentured servitude which paved the way for African enslavement evolved out of Tudor methods of dealing with the unemployed and beggars. Their harshness resembled the colonial slave codes. This is especially true of the statute of 1547, which provided for the branding and enslaving of vagrants, whom their masters might beat, chain, half-starve and put to labour "how vile so ever it be". But this statute was so harsh as to be unenforceable, and was repealed within three years.[157] According to Holinshed, who wrote after Henry VIII's death, 71,400 thieves and vagabonds were hanged during his reign. The generally accepted statement that during the reign of Henry VIII there were seventy-two thousand thieves and vagabonds hanged, appears to have been founded upon the loose estimate that about two thousand were hanged in each year of that reign.[158]

TUDOR TERROR IN IRELAND

The Native Irish were subject to the Tudor Terror, as were Christians in England who refused to convert to the Protestant religion. Persecution continued in Ireland during the reigns of Mary and Elizabeth, where there was widespread confiscation of land, especially in the North in preparation for the "Plantation of Ulster". In 1537 the last strongholds of the O'Nolans (Ó Nualláins) fell to the Tudor invader:

> From Offaly Grey [Henry VIII's Lord Deputy of Ireland] proceeded to MacMurrogh country, took two castles of the O'Nolans and compelled the Kavanaghs to give new pledges of good behaviour.
>
> E A D'Alton[159]

To consolidate Tudor Protestant rule in Ireland, Trinity College was established by Queen Elizabeth in 1592, in the confiscated Augustinian Priory of All Hallows. Trinity was planned to be the first of a number of constituent colleges of the University of Dublin. From the beginning the main purpose of Trinity College was to suppress the Native Irish and all knowledge of their Hebernian roots.

> Once a country is habituated to liars it takes generations to bring the truth back.
>
> Gore Vidal[160]

> Peter Lombard who was titular Archbishop of Armagh in the reign of Queen Elizabeth states 'English governors endeavoured to destroy or carry away every monument of antiquity belonging to the Irish which they could gain possession; and that a great number were shut up in the Tower of London, and consigned to

forgetfulness, which, if translated, would throw new and interesting light on religion and letters. The Dane and the Briton were alike hostile to the proofs of former glory; and what the pagan spared the Christian sought to demolish.' . . . we cannot, with Doctor Lynch and others, but lament the fatal policy of the English, who, until the reign of James the first, took all possible means to destroy our old writings, as they did those of Scotland, in the reign of Edward the first.

Henry O'Brien[161]

Catholics would not be allowed to become students until the nineteenth century. Among the first casualties was the poet, historian and Catholic priest Geoffrey Keating (1569–1644)[162] He circulated his comprehensive "History of Ireland" in manuscript form, as he was not allowed to have it printed because it was deemed pro-Catholic!

Neither France nor Spain was willing to tolerate any religion but Catholicism, and, in consequence, history has to condemn the horrors of the Inquisition and the banishment of the Huguenots. Nor would England allow her subjects to be anything but Protestants. Even the non-conforming Protestants laboured under disabilities; but the Catholics, above all, were trampled on and oppressed. Their attachment to Rome was held to be inconsistent with loyal subjects; and for such disloyalty no punishment was too severe.

E A D'Alton[163]

CHAPTER 7

UNHOLY ALLIANCE: "ORANGE" BALFOUR, *SINN FÉIN*-IRA AND ZIONISM

> Belfast had become the Mecca of Unionism. Thither went Mr.
> Balfour in April [1893] and Lord Salisbury in May, both to rouse
> the militant bigotry of Ulster Orangeism.
>
> E A D'Alton[163]

As the twenty-first century dawned it has become fashionable for the Irish ruling elite to be anti-Catholic. Norman Grandee Mary Robinson, one of the Burkes of Ballina and former President of Ireland:

> I gave up arguing with her [mother], but deep inside me I
> queried her sense that because the Bourke's had a crest, because
> the local Protestant church contained memorial tablets to
> Victorian generals – one, my father's great uncle Paget, had been
> captain of the Queen's bodyguard at Buckingham Palace – that
> somehow he was special . . . I took comfort from the fact that on
> my Grandmother Macaulay's side, her uncle Thomas Macauly
> had been jailed as a Fenian, for belonging to the Irish Republican
> Brotherhood . . .
>
> The Irish Constitution and laws reflected the ethos of the
> Catholic Church whose prominent position in society was
> guaranteed in article 44. The effect was to marginalise those of
> the Protestant tradition, the small Jewish community and those
> who were not religious.
>
> Mary Robinson[164]

Robinson appears to have been badly advised. The Irish Free State Constitution of 1937 in no way marginalised the Jewish community.

> I regarded Zionism as a magnificent inspiration, but I was not
> personally concerned — as you have observed, I was somewhat

preoccupied with my activities as an Irishman. Then, too, I was fortunate in living in a country where Jews were subject to no persecution and very little prejudice, far less even than in the United States of America. The terrible pressures which forced European Jews into compact, self-defensive communities were totally absent in Ireland . . . People have sometimes wondered how I reconciled my loyalties to Ireland and to my race. That was not a problem. The only time they could possibly have clashed was on the question of Ireland's neutrality — whether from the point of view of a Jew it would have been better for Ireland to enter the war. As you have seen I had no difficulty in resolving the question — I am an Irishman who happens to be of the Jewish faith. However, there are far more bonds between Ireland and Israel than differences.

Robert Briscoe[165]

The 1937 Constitution was the brainchild of the duplicitous American-born Spaniard Eamon de Valera and placed the Irish Language *An Gaelge*, considered by the majority of people a dead language and which few spoke or wished to speak, as the first official language. The English Language was recognised as second official language. Throughout his political career one of De Valera's most staunch supporters was the Jewish Robert Briscoe.[166] Although Briscoe declared little concern for Zionism in its earlier years he subsequently became as fanatical about Zionism as he was about Fenian Republicanism. Briscoe swore the oath to the "Irish Republic" on becoming a member of Fianna Eireann. Subsequently as an IRA (Irish Republican Army) gunrunner he arranged multiple shipments of arms from Germany for the guerrilla leader and Ireland's "Robespierre", Michael Collins.

Robert Briscoe accompanied De Valera on his money raising tour of the United States during the IRA Insurgency of 1919–1921. He was a member of the DOT, *Dáil Eireann* for 38 years followed by his son Ben's 37 years. Both served as Lord Mayors of Dublin. In the 1972 election Ben narrowly held on to his seat following a challenge from Mary Robinson.[164]

In the early hours of October 14, 1958 a bomb exploded in the stairwell of the Anshe Emet Synagogue in Peoria, Illinois, USA. The following is a letter from

James Staver, published in the Chicago Sunday Tribune five days later. Under the heading "Briscoe at Peoria":[167]

> Chicago Oct. 15 – There can be few people in Illinois who would disagree with President Eisenhower's characterization of the bombing of the Peoria edifice as 'Shocking and deplorable'. Surely Gov. Stratton speaks for the whole state when he says "We abhor violence" – "We're not going to allow this sort of thing in Illinois". And Rabbi Joseph Ginsburg of the temple subjected to this outrage is correct in saying that the real damage is not material but that "the moral and spiritual damage to our American way of life can be more expensive and far-reaching than any physical damage to the edifice".
>
> The problem of moral and spiritual damage is universal and should be treated as such. Before the damage becomes extensive as Rabbi Ginsburg fears, it is necessary for all of us to examine our consciences and our positions. There should be no exceptions. The feted guest of Rabbi Ginsburg's temple on Oct. 14, the day following the outrage, was the former Lord Mayor of Dublin, Robert Briscoe, internationally known as an ex-gun smuggler and leader of the terrorist and bomb-throwing Irish Republican army, against not only the British but his own fellow countrymen. Later Briscoe taught similar tactics to the militant terrorists of the Zionist movement. There is no question of this. He openly writes this in his autobiography *For the Life of Me*, reviewed in the Chicago Tribune Oct. 12. Inviting this man of violence into their midst and honouring him at an Israel bond rally gave open sanction to such tactics.
>
> James Staver [167]

The anti-British Briscoe had Irgun's first leader, Ze'ev Jabotinsky, trained in guerrilla tactics in Ireland for use against the British in Palestine:

> Jabotinsky came to Ireland to learn all he could of the methods we had used in training our young men and boys for the revolution

against England in order to form a physical force movement in Palestine on exactly the same lines as Fianna Eireann and the IRA . . . I taught Jabotinsky how we had secretly trained our Fianna Eireann boys in the time of peace; and the methods we had found most effective in the guerrilla war. I explained British military weakness and where their strength lay and how to profit by the first and combat—or evade—the second. In fact, I appointed myself to a full professorship of the Chair of Subversive Activity against England . . . Fianna was, in fact, the organization which trained the boys of Ireland to fight when they became men. Instead of learning to tie knots, the Fianna boys were taught to shoot to kill; how to use hand grenades and land mines. Instead of woodcraft they were taught the techniques of ambush and sabotage. Long before they were old enough to fight they were the secret messenger boys of the Irish Republican Army.

Robert Briscoe[165]

What Briscoe did not realise was that he was living in the Promised Land!!

And thus in this far off strand [Howth]
My heart might be cheered within me with sight of the Promised
  Land.

John A Goodchild & Daniel J Nolan[62,63]

Irgun were a particular ruthless organization. They carried out random attacks on Arab policemen, Arab civilians and targeted attacks on British Intelligence officers, British soldiers and British policemen[168] There was a lull in Irgun activity between 1939 and 1944. Following Menachem Began's accession to the leadership of Irgun in 1943 some of the worst atrocities were carried out. Ninety-one people died in the King David Hotel bombing on July 22, 1946 and between 107 and 120 Arabs were massacred in the village of Deir Yassin near Jerusalem during April 9–11, 1947. Two British Intelligence officers were hanged and their bodies booby-trapped on July 29, 1947. Begin harboured a particular hatred for Britain. His Irgun units launched sabotage operations against British military instillations in Germany, planted a substantial bomb at the Colonial Office in London, which did not explode, threatened to assassinate Bevin and Atlee, sent letter-bombs to Cabinet ministers and blew up the British embassy in Rome.[169] The other Zionist guerrilla groups in Palestine were the Stern Gang and Haganh. Yitzhak Shamir was a member of Irgun until it split in 1940 to become another militant faction Lehi, better known as the "Stern Gang". Shamir used the *nom de guerre* 'Michael' after Michael Collins.[170] The violent Zionism of Begin and Shamir, created by Briscoe and Jabotinsky, is euphemistically known as 'Revisionist Zionism'!!

Menachem Began's party was branded terrorist, Nazi and Fascist by Albert Einstein and twenty-seven other prominent Jewish intellectuals in a letter to the *New York Times* published on December 4, 1948:[171]

> Among the most disturbing political phenomena of our time is the emergence in the newly created state of Israel of the 'Freedom Party' a political party closely akin in its organization, methods, political philosophy and social appeal to the Nazi and Fascist parties . . . Terrorist bands attacked this peaceful village, which was not a military objective in the fighting, killing most of its inhabitants – 240 men, women and children – and kept a few of them alive to parade as captives through the streets of Jerusalem . . . But the terrorists, far from being ashamed for their act, were proud of their massacre, publicized it widely and invited all the correspondents present in the country to view the heaped corpses and the general havoc at Deir Yassim . . . During the last years of the sporadic anti-British violence the IZL and the Stern groups inaugurated a reign of Terror in the Jewish community. Teachers were beaten up for speaking against them; adults were shot for not letting their children join them. By gangster methods, beatings, window-smashing and wide-spread robberies the terrorists intimidated the population and extracted a heavy tribute.
>
> Albert Einstein *et al* [171]

The behaviour of Menachem Began and his Revisionist Zionists was little different to that of Michael Collins and his IRA's war on the RIC and the Irish People. Begin's pathological hatred of Britain led him to supply weapons of war to Argentina during the Falklands War.[172] In 1978 Menachem Began was awarded the Dynamite Peace Prize.[173] [The author refuses to call it by its given name as Alfred Nobel was an armament manufacturer and the inventor of dynamite.][174,175] When Begin went to Oslo to receive the Prize, there were such violent demonstrations against him that the award ceremony had to be moved to Akershus fortress.[173]

The anti-Catholic and anti-Semitic Arthur Balfour and *Sinn Féin*-IRA, between them, created a Zionist Republic and planted it in Palestine with disastrous consequences. In addition, the Zionists resurrected and modernised a dead language, as *Sinn Féin*–IRA had done in Ireland, to the detriment of Biblical Hebrew – The Classical Language!!

> There appears to be a conundrum about Arthur Balfour. On the one hand, his name is inseparable from the declaration he signed as Foreign Secretary on 2 November 1917, which read in part: 'His Majesty's Government views with favour the establishment in Palestine of a nation home for the Jewish people, and will use their best endeavours to facilitate the achievement of this object …' On the other hand as Prime Minister he brought in emigration controls aimed specifically against Jews from Eastern Europe.
>
> Brian Klug[176]

There was considerable opposition throughout the Jewish community to Balfour's Declaration, notably from Edwin Samuel Montague[177] a Liberal politician who became a member of the Cabinet and in the same year issued a memorandum entitled, 'Montagu Memo[178] on the Anti-Semitism of the British Government' (August 23, 1917):

> . . . Zionism has always seemed to me to be a mischievous political creed, untenable by any patriotic citizen of the United Kingdom. If a Jewish Englishman sets his eyes on the Mount of Olives and longs for the day when he will shake British soil from his shoes and go back to agricultural pursuits in Palestine, he has always seemed to me to have acknowledged aims inconsistent with British citizenship and to have admitted that he is unfit for a share in public life in Great Britain, or to be treated as an

Englishman. I have always understood that those who indulged in this creed were largely animated by the restriction upon and refusal of liberty to Jews in Russia. But at this very time when these Jews have been acknowledged as Jewish Russians and given all liberties, it seems to be inconceivable that Zionism should be officially recognised by the British Government, and that Mr Balfour should be authorised to say that Palestine was to be reconstituted as the "national home of the Jewish people". I do not know what this involves, but I do assume that it means that Mahommedans and Christians are to make way for the Jews and that the Jews should be put in all positions of preference and should be peculiarly associated with Palestine in the same way that England is for the English or France with the French, that Turks and other Mahommedans in Palestine will be regarded as foreigners, just in the same way as Jews will hereafter be treated as foreigners in every country but Palestine. Perhaps also citizenship must be granted only as a result of a religious test . . . I feel that the government were asked to be the instrument for carrying out the wishes of a Zionist organisation largely run, as my information goes, at any rate in the past, by men of enemy descent or birth, and by this means have dealt a severe blow to the liberties, position and opportunities of service of their Jewish fellow-countrymen. I would say to Lord Rothchild that the Government will be prepared to do everything in their power to obtain for Jews in Palestine complete liberty of settlement and life on an equality with the inhabitants of that country who profess other religious beliefs. I would ask that the government should go no further.

jewishvirtuallibrary.org/source/history/montagumemo [178]

Keith Jeffrey in *MI6: The History of the Secret Intelligence Service 1909–1949*:

Aaron Aaronsohn a fervent Zionist. In October 1917 Cummings [Head of MI6] contact with Aaronsohn also provided the British government with back-channel communication to Jewish groups in Palestine. In November 1917 Aaron Aaronsohn's

brother (who was then in London) was given an advance copy of
the Balfour Declaration (in which the British government stated
that they viewed 'with favour the establishment in Palestine of
a national home for the Jewish people') for him to smuggle into
Palestine in order to encourage Jews with their work in support
of the Allied war effort. Cummings, too, liaised with the Zionist
leader Chaim Weizmann, meeting him several times to discuss
Jewish affairs.

Keith Jeffrey[169]

The Zionist Republic in Palestine should be called ZR (Zionist Republic)!!!

Jahtruth:

> The British Coat-of-Arms is the Coat-of-arms of the twelve
> tribed Kingdom of Israel and Christ their Rightful KING. The
> true Israel people have on their "Coat of Arms", a Lion and a
> Unicorn which is shown as a white horse "rampant" with one
> horn. The amber Lion "rampart" on the left side of the emblem
> is the two-tribed "House of Judah" and the Unicorn or white
> Wild-Ox "rampant" on the right side is the emblem of the
> ten-tribed "House of Israel", collectively making the 12-tribed
> "Kingdom of Israel". The word British is Hebrew. It means
> "the People of the Covenant" or in other words "the People of
> Israel" whose written constitution; under which there are no
> poor people, is then foolishly rejected by almost everyone, in
> favour of inferior and unjust laws and economics which cause
> poverty and therefore also crime brought about by deprivation
> and desperation.

jahtruth[179]

George Orwell said that no revolutionary was ever an Internationalist.[180]
Revolutionary leaders are nearly always dysfunctional misfits, losers, gang-
sters or psychopaths. Begin's behaviour was similar to Collins's *Sinn Féin*-IRB,
subsequently *Sinn Féin*-IRA, war against the RIC (Royal Irish Constabulary)

labelled "Crown Forces" by him, and anyone else who got in his way. Ultimate control of the RIC lay with the Cromwellian Institute's Lloyd George, who treated them appallingly when he signed The Treaty with Collins *et al.* The highly respected RCMP (Royal Canadian Mounted Police) is modelled on the RIC.[181]

Imperial Stormtroopers: If Neil Jordan's movie *Michael Collins*[182] is a good indication, then the popular memory of the Black and Tans and Auxiliaries has changed very little since Beaslai's[183] time. The British police make a few brief but memorable appearances on Jordan's biopic. First ominous music accompanies actual newsreel footage. A NEW FORCE OF HIS MAJESTY'S FINEST ARRIVES IN IRELAND, say the title cards, TO RID THE TROUBLED LAND OF ITS BLIGHT OF TERROR. Cut to the yard of Dublin Castle, where an Auxiliary troupe swaggers past the camera. They wear Naziesque leather coats, and cigarettes dangle from their lips. Festooned with ammunition belts and bandoliers, they tote a variety of weapons, British Lee-Enfield rifles and Lewis light machine guns, an American Browning automatic rifle, even a double-barrelled shotgun. Soldiers drill in the background, underlining the lack of discipline and uniformity in the foreground. His majesty's finest indeed.

David Leeson[184]

During the Irish War of Independence, under the malignant influence of Conservative and Unionist ministers who had themselves encouraged both rebellion and mutiny to forestall Home Rule before the Great War, the British government conducted a large-scale version of the Stanford Prison experiment, in Ireland. Between the passage of the Restoration of Order in Ireland Act in August 1920, and the signing of the Truce in July 1921, police and insurgents fought over the social roles of guard and prisoner, punisher and offender, killer and victim, in a looking glass world of crime without criminals, police without laws, trials without judges or juries, and sentences without appeal. For a year during its war of Independence, The Island of Saints became Devil's Island.

David Leeson[184]

According to Roy Hattersley in his biography of David Lloyd George:[185]

Lloyd George did not possess any clear or strong view on either the justice or the necessity of Home Rule . . . and he had never hidden his view that the future of Ireland was less important than the electoral success of the Liberal Party . . . The King [George V] had sensibly suggested to Lloyd George that the probable result arising from MacSweeny's [the *Sinn Féin*–IRA Lord Mayor of Cork who was on hunger strike] death would be far more serious and far more far-reaching than if he were taken out of prison where his wife could look after him . . . Lloyd George was inundated with messages begging for MacSweeny's release. Some argued the case on humanitarian grounds. Others echoed the King's warning about the damage that his death in custody would do . . . General Sir Nevil Macready was made Commander-in-Chief in Ireland with instructions not to compromise with terror. It was assumed that he was appointed to act towards Republicans with increased ferocity. His communiqués, sent to Lloyd George via Frances Stevenson, suggest otherwise: 'Ever since my days in Ulster in 1913-1914 I have always looked on the (Orange) movement as rebels. . . In the ranks of Sinn Fein are men of substance and deep religious feeling'. . . . The advice of the policeman who had been sent to intimidate Ireland was far too conciliatory to appeal to either the general public or the Unionist Party. In consequence the Prime Minister [Lloyd George] rejected it. Later, after an offer of talks by *Sinn Féin*: The first draft of the King's Belfast speech — prepared by George V's advisors — simply represented the government's outdated determination to crush terror. Lloyd George rejected it. General Smuts— an authority in the conversion of rebels into patriots supervised the composition of a new version. It was agreed by the King and accepted in both northern and southern Ireland with astonished delight.

Roy Hattersley[185]

Hattersley's excellent account of the events surrounding the death of Republican martyr Terence MacSweeny sets the record straight by nailing the lie that the Police were controlled by the Crown!! The criminals who control the Cromwellian Institute have for centuries been sheltering under the Crown!!!

Before the outbreak of violence in Ireland King George V was more concerned about the treasonous behaviour and incitement to violence policies of the Ulster Unionist leaders Edward Carson and Andrew Bonar Law, neither of whom was from Ulster. In 1912 Law had merged the Conservative and Unionist parties to become the 'Conservative Unionist Party', and is believed to have subsequently paid for the Ulster Volunteers' guns.

Robert Blake's biography of Andrew Bonar Law:[186]

> As Mr Churchill and Colonel Seely, the War Minister, left their seats they were assailed with cries of "Rats", and Mr Churchill turned round to wave his handkerchief in ironical acknowledgement of these remarks. Enraged by this gesture Ronald McNeil, an Ulster M.P., seized the Speaker's copy of the standing orders and hurled it with great accuracy at Churchill's head. Thus ended one of the worst scenes of Parliamentary disorder in modern times.
>
> Apologies were made the following day, and calm more or less restored. Eventually a formula was discovered whereby the traditional procedure of the house was not violated. It was, however, significant of the passions raised that Bonar Law in no way repudiated or condemned the conduct of his followers. On November 14th at the Albert Hall he said: 'I did not suggest a disturbance, but I have this responsibility; I did not in any way try to interfere with what my colleagues desired to do . . . I did not try it, and under similar circumstances I never shall try it.'
>
> There was also the question of the Royal Veto. Bonar Law was

no courtier and was ready to speak his mind with vigour as the following conversation shows. It took place after a dinner given by the King on May 4th, 1912. Our authority is Austin Chamberlain who jotted down Bonar Law's account of the conversation that evening. The King observed, 'I have just being saying to Sir Edward Carson that I hope there will no violent scenes this session' Chamberlain's account goes on:

'May I talk freely to Your Majesty?' asked Boner Law.

'Please do. I wish you to,' replied the King.

'Then I think, Sir, that the situation is a grave one not only for the House but also for the throne. Our desire has been to keep the Crown out of our struggles, but the Government has brought it in. Your only chance is that they should resign within two years. If they don't you must either accept the Home Rule Bill or dismiss your ministers and choose others who will support you in vetoing it – and in either case half your subjects will think you have acted against them.'

The King turned red and Law asked, 'Have you never considered that, Sir?'

'No,' answered the King, 'It is the first time it has been suggested to me.'

Law added: 'They may say that your assent is a purely formal act and that the prerogative is dead. That was true as long as there was a buffer between you and the House of Commons, but they have destroyed that buffer and it is true no longer.'

Describing this conversation to Austin Chamberlain, Bonar Law said: 'I think I have given the King the worst five minutes that he has had for a long time.'

It was certainly strong language to use, and the king, who had not yet seen enough of Bonar Law to become accustomed to his bluntness of speech, may well have resented it. Sir Harold Nicolson tells us, speaking of the situation a year later: 'Moreover he [the King] had no personal desire at all to see Mr. Bonar Law succeed Mr. Asquith, for whom he had acquired (and for ever retained) feelings of warm affection.' It is reasonable to surmise that the king's very different feelings for Bonar law originated from the episode just described, and the frosty interview, which Bonar Law was to have with the King when the latter invited him to form a Government in December 1916, suggests that even four years later this feeling had not wholly vanished. But it need scarcely be said that, whatever his personal sentiments, the King invariably treated Bonar Law with complete correctness and gave him all proper support when he finally became prime minister.

What was the attitude of Asquith during these three months? Naturally he was not going to let the inflammatory discourses of the Unionists pass without comment. Bonar Law's Blenheim speech aroused his special wrath. 'The reckless rodomontade at Blenheim in the early summer', he declared, '. . . furnishes for the future a complete grammar of anarchy.'

Asquith's biographers have revealed that he seriously contemplated legal action on grounds of sedition against the extremists of the Unionist Party, particularly against Carson and F. E. Smith, and Craig, the leaders of Ulster. There is no doubt that a strong case existed under the law. But there was no doubt also that, whatever the law might be, an Ulster jury would never convict. Moreover it would have been difficult to avoid similar action against Bonar Law whose language was at least as violent as that of Carson: and, for a government in the twentieth century to initiate a criminal prosecution against the Leader of the Opposition, was an action at which the boldest Prime Minister might pause.

Robert Blake[186]

I have loved this country and these people all my life and I would do anything or sacrifice anything for them. They are so infernally emotional. If they could only be got to realize the true character of such leaders as de Valera.

Sir John French[187]

Once Sinn Féin's resurgence drifted away from political disaffection towards violence in 1919, the savagery of terrorism and counter-terrorism became inevitable. At Kilmichael Tom Barry's guerrillas did what guerrillas do.

John A Murphy[188]

The following is a letter from Pierce Martin, published in the Irish *Sunday Independent* under the heading 'Michael Collins is not my hero', on Sunday October 3, 2010:[189]

Sir – To encourage anyone to venerate Michael Collins as a national hero ('A man who can make us believe', Brendan O'Connor Sunday Independent, September 26, 2010), is to request of them that they abjure their obligation to historical objective truth, intellectual honesty, and respect regarding the just war theory as laid out by Thomas Aquinas. Had Collins been fighting a great evil, then the encomium heaped upon him by O'Connor and Michael McDowell would be justified. However, Collins patently wasn't. An intelligence officer of the IRA in mid-summer of 1919 – with the terror and murder campaign against the Royal Irish Constabulary in full swing - - Collins formed the Squad in order to escalate republican generated anarchy, by assassinating detectives and specified government officials. The rationale was to provoke Crown forces into a blunderbuss reaction in which innocent Catholics would be killed by government security forces, thus driving moderate nationalists into the arms of the IRA.

One must surmise that O'Connor and McDowell consider this tactical innovation as indicative of Collins genius. Obviously for O'Connor and McDowell, an incapacity to imagine a man forced to kneel in his nightclothes, inside his own home, and cold-bloodly shot dead in front of his screaming pleading wife and hysterical children, with his blood spattered upon their faces has its advantages when one belongs to the Collins cult of ritual slaughter. By the end of the republican terror 4,000 people were dead or wounded, the majority of these killings and woundings, according to the late Peter Hart, were committed by the IRA and the proto-Nazi Squad.

We don't need a young killer like Collins born in the era of Queen Victoria to make us believe. And in what? That power lies through sadism and murder? That is what the Continuity IRA believes. Obviously O'Connor and McDowell believe superfluous wars are just dandy, especially the home-grown variety. The truth is, Collins was a psychopath.

Pierce Martin [189]

To the surprise of RIC officers who were discreetly monitoring the occasion [3,000 spectators at a Gaelic League match at Croke Park on April 6, 1919], de Valera made no attempt to address the crowd. At the Ard Fheis held two days later, de Valera declared emphatically that he was against any form of violence towards the RIC, a statement which (according to a Police spy who was in the hall) 'was well received by moderate members, resented by extremists.' Darrell Figgis, on the other hand, formed the opinion that the meeting was packed by IRB and IRA men (a term now coming into widespread use for the first time) who had been instructed by Collins to vote against those members of the Executive who sought a constitutional solution. Figgis was, in fact, soundly defeated for the post of Secretary by Harry Boland and felt ruefully that the militants had gained the upper hand. Michael [Collins] himself, only four weeks later, was complaining that the political activists were squeezing out the supporters of physical force in the party.

James MacKay [190]

The policy of waging war on the RIC appears to have been Collins's, and his alone. A certifiable psychopath was Charles William St John Burgess, alias Cathal Brugha. Burgess, who served on various committees preparing for the *Sinn Féin* convention on 25-26 October 1917, was largely responsible for article 2 of the new constitution which stated that "*Sinn Féin* aims at securing the International recognition of Ireland as an Independent Irish Republic".[191] Burgess was elected to the executive when de Valera was elected president. Burgess brought the army under the control of the Dáil on 20 August 1919, by ensuring that the volunteers take an oath of allegiance to *Dáil Éireann*, an important step in making the volunteers the Irish Republican Army.[191] His main contribution to the fight seems to have been to undermine the Director of Intelligence [Michael Collins] at every turn, and to continue proposing hare-brained schemes which were quite impracticable. From exterminating the entire government front bench in the House of Commons with machine-guns, he moved to the more flexible ploy of mowing down the densely packed queue outside a London cinema.[190] When Burgess persisted with this crazy scheme Richard Mulcahy, Chief of Staff, countermanded the orders which only intensified Burgess's hatred of Collins. The surname Burgess comes from the French word bourgeois!!

Confusion concerning *Sinn Féin* and violence results from the split personality the party developed when *Sinn Féin* came under the control of the ultra-nationalist IRB in 1917. In 1915 when the IRB had taken control of the Gaelic League, its President and founder Douglas Hyde resigned. The IRB was a secret society whose members took their oath of allegiance to an "Irish Republic" in great secrecy. The IRB, as a secret society was strongly opposed by the Catholic Church with its members liable to excommunication if their names became known. So, on 25th of October 1917, when de Valera was elected President of *Sinn Féin* thereby ousting Arthur Griffith, and two days later Michael Collins, a long standing member of *Sinn Féin*, was elected as Director of the Organisation of the Volunteers and around the same time of the IRB, the general public were totally unaware that *Sinn Féin* had come under the complete control of die-hard Republicans bent on human sacrifice, violence and intimidation, particularly as Griffith remained on in *Sinn Féin*–IRB to avoid a split. In doing so Griffith did a great disservice to the People of Ireland; not long afterwards *Sinn Féin*-IRB became *Sinn Féin*-IRA as it remains to this day.

Griffith, a fickle journalist, created *Sinn Féin* in 1905 as a monarchist party. He considered the Act of Union of 1800 illegal and sought a return of the dual monarchy which existed between 1782 and 1800.

> . . . and he was going about with some of them Sinn Fein lately or whatever they call themselves talking his usual trash and nonsense he says that little man he showed me without the neck is very intelligent the coming man Griffith is he well he doesn't look it thats all I can say.
>
> James Joyce[192]

In 1918 Collins played a leading role in formulating the list of *Sinn Féin* candidates for the general election, enabling many hard-line Republicans to be elected under the *Sinn Féin* banner unknown to the electorate.[190]

> I saw they'd got to the agrarian laws of Caius Gracchus, and I wondered if they knew anything about the agrarian troubles in Ireland. All they know about Ireland is that Dublin is on the Liffey.
>
> W S Maugham[193]

Arthur Balfour of the Declaration was the most oppressive Chief Secretary of Ireland, "Bloody" Balfour, who earned the sobriquet because of his attitude during the Land League's campaign to improve the lot of smallholders who were being obliged to pay rack-rents to their absentee landlords, and who were evicted in large numbers when they were unable to do so. Balfour is said to have written the new Northern Ireland government advising them to form a Special Auxiliary Police Force of Protestants, who became known as the "B Specials", because he branded former RIC officers who were Catholic and joined the newly formed RUC (Royal Ulster Constabulary) as untrustworthy.

From 1919 to 1936 the chief Rabbi of Ireland was Yitzhak HaLevi Herzog.[194] Herzog, was a supporter of Irish Ultra-Nationalism and a friend of de Valera, as well as being fluent in *An Gaelge*. Known as the "*Sinn Féin* Rabbi", he went to Palestine in 1936 where he was Ashkenazi Chief Rabbi of the British Mandate and subsequently of Israel. On February 28, 1944 Herzog as Chief Rabbi of Jerusalem sent Pope Pius XII a personal message:

> The people of Israel will never forget what His Holiness and his illustrious delegates inspired by the eternal principles of religion which is the very foundations of true civilization, are doing for us unfortunate brothers and sisters in the most tragic hour of our history, which is living proof of Divine Providence in this world.
>
> michaeljournal.org/piusXII [195]

Rabbi Herzog's son Chaim became involved with the Federation of Zionist Youth while in school at Wesely College, Dublin. In 1935 Chaim Herzog[196] went to Palestine and joined the Haganah guerrillas. He served in the British Army during World War II, having gained a law degree at London University, and was a tank commander before joining the Intelligence Corps. At the end of the war he identified a captured German soldier as Heinrich Himmler. On leaving the British Army with the rank of Major in 1947 he returned to Israel and joined the new Israeli army. Herzog served in the 1948 Arab Israeli war and subsequently became head of Military Intelligence. After the army he went into law practice and entered politics. He spent three years as Israel's Permanent Representative at the United Nations. In 1983 Chaim Herzog became the sixth President of Israel.

Chaim Herzog's brother and the other son of Rabbi Herzog was Yaakov Herzog,[197] who became a diplomat. Dublin-born, he helped improve relations with the Vatican after the Six-Day War, and led diplomatic communications with King Hussain of Jordan. He had secret talks with Hussain in a London doctor's clinic both before and after the Six-Day War which paved the way for peace between Israel and Jordan. He was Ben-Gurion's right hand man during the 1956 Sinai campaign.[198] Yaakov Herzog became a personal friend of, among others, John F Kennedy and Eamon de Valera. In 2015 Isaac Herzog, Chaim's son, took over the ZR's Labour Party and became Leader of the Opposition in their DOT, the Knesset.[199]

CHAPTER 8

SELECTIVE AMNESIA:
SEAMLESS CENSORSHIP

Pasternak also proved Stalin right about one thing. If you ease up on absolute censorship, you never know where things might end.

Michael Scammell[200]

The history of the vanquished is written by their conquerors!! From its foundation in 1592 to the present day, Dublin's Trinity College has pursued a policy of hostility to the point of negation, towards the great cultural achievements of the Native Irish before the arrival of the Vikings, Normans, Tudors, Cromwellians, the nefarious Act of Union of 1800 which placed the people of the island at the mercy of an avaricious, bigoted, brutal, cruel, vengeful and vindictive Cromwellian Institute, followed by a century of self-destructive Independence.

Ireland never enjoyed more than a tithe of British privileges and prosperity.

Hugh Brogan[129]

The treatment of Geoffrey Keating's work by Trinity College was the beginning of the campaign. Trinity now claims ownership of the world famous *Book of Kells,* created by our ancestors. This magnificent illuminated manuscript came into their possession shortly after the Cromwellian Invasion of 1649, having been acquired as plunder by Cromwell's cavalry who were occupying Kells. Trinity College even claims copyright of the *Book of Kells* and demands payment for permission to reproduce illustrations!!!

The current Carroll Professor of Irish History at Oxford University, Robert Fitzroy (Roy) Foster, is a graduate of Trinity College Dublin who appears to have brought its prejudices with him. He is editor of the *Oxford History of Ireland,*[201] published by the Oxford University Press, a department of the University of Oxford, a book that yields little information about life before the Christian era. The index contains numerous Norman names: de Braose, de Cogan, de Courcy, de Fréine, de Genville (de Joinville), de Nangle, de Verdon, de Vere, de Vescy in addition to two de Mandivilles, three de Lacys, four de Clares, seven Butlers, eleven Burke/de Burgs, and twenty-four Fitzgeralds. There are no Nolans, O'Nolans, or O'Nuallain, apart from Brian O'Nolan (1911-1966) novelist and satirist who wrote under the pseudonyms Flan O'Brien and *Myles Na Geopaleen*. The two kings Mael Sechnaill Mac Domhnall have Mac Domhnall (son of Daniel) eclipsed to become: Mael Sechnaill. Known descendants of the foremost of the Twelve Tribes of Israel obliterated from history!!! One of Foster's other books: *The Irish Story: Telling Tales and Making it Up in Ireland.*

Oxford University is institutionally anti-Catholic, and has been since the time of Henry VIII. On St Stephen's Day (Boxing Day in England) 2014 the author was browsing a book over coffee in Waterstones. It was about midday and I was vaguely aware of a one-sided conversation between a typical "Oxford Man" and a younger woman, probably a postgraduate, who were opposite. I reacted with surprise when he uttered the word "Islam" rather sharply. On seeing the look on my face he immediately added "and Roman Catholicism". I must have "Pat" written all over me!! Wyndam Lewis:

> A Nineveh hostess, hailing from New Haven, Connecticut, is the possessor of an extremely long upper lip . . . "That lip, Madam," said I, is an *Irish* lip — as you know quite well! . . . Now the religious cleavage, with its connotation *foreign*, where it concerns the Roman Catholic (Rome is after all the capital city of the Italian Mediterranean world) takes with it something else which every would-be student of modern America must note. Catholic also spells *socially inferior* . . . It is the "Old Religion", as they used to call it, I reminded her . . . Has much in its favour. Pretty ritual.
>
> Wyndham Lewis[23]

It is particularly offensive to use the Roman prefix for Irish Christians! It was an English Pope (Adrian) and a Norman king of England (Henry II) who imposed the Roman Church on us. And many of those who persecuted us for being under the influence of Rome were of Norman descent!!! Lady Antonia

Fraser in *Cromwell*: 'it is pleasant to reflect that Oliver Cromwell had at least his dash of Norman blood.'[41] He certainly did!!!

The former Archbishop of Oxford Rt Rev Lord Richard Harries used the BBC's *Thought for the Day* to vent his anti-Papish feelings:

> If it is so, then someone in a representative role for this partnership can, I believe, make an apology, as the Pope did on behalf of the Catholic Church for its treatment of Jews over the centuries.
>
> Richard Harries[202]

The following are two entries in *The New Oxford Dictionary of English*:[203]

> Ford, Henry (1863–1947) American motor manufacturer. A Pioneer of large-scale mass production, he founded the Ford Motor Company, which in 1909 produced his famous Model T. Control of the company passed to his grandson Henry Ford II (1917–1987) in 1945.

> Pius XII (1876–1958), pope 1939; born *Eugenio Pachelli*. He upheld the neutrality of the Roman Catholic Church during the Second World War, and was criticized after the war for failing to condemn Nazi atrocities.

The United States of Amnesia.

> Gore Vidal[160]

Where did Hitler discover his radical views on the so-called international Jewish menace? Answer: Henry Ford.

> Edwin Black[204]

Reading the *The New Oxford Dictionary of English*'s benign micro-biography of Henry Ford the reader would have no idea that his writings were the catalyst for the Holocaust. Ford's anti-Semitic book *The International Jew: The World's Foremost Problem*[205] was first published in November 1920 (Figure 4), and subsequently translated into sixteen languages. Six editions were published

The Ford International Weekly
THE DEARBORN INDEPENDENT

One Dollar   Dearborn, Michigan, May 22, 1920   Five Cents

The International Jew:
The World's Problem

"Among the distinguishing mental and moral traits of the Jews may be mentioned: distaste for hard or violent physical labor; a strong family sense and philoprogenitiveness; a marked religious instinct; the courage of the prophet and martyr rather than of the pioneer and soldier; remarkable power to survive in adverse environments, combined with great ability to retain racial solidarity; capacity for exploitation, both individual and social; shrewdness and astuteness in speculation and money matters generally; an Oriental love of display and a full appreciation of the power and pleasure of social position; a very high average of intellectual ability."

—The New International Encyclopedia.

THE Jew is again being singled out for critical attention throughout the world. His emergence in the financial, political and social spheres has been so complete and spectacular since the war, that his place, power and purpose in the world are being given a new scrutiny, much of it unfriendly. Persecution is not a new experience to the Jew, but intensive scrutiny of his nature and super-nationality is. He has suffered for more than 2,000 years from what may be called the instinctive anti-semitism of the other races, but this antagonism has never been intelligent nor has it been able to make itself intelligible. Nowadays, however, the Jew is being placed, as it were, under the microscope of economic observation that the reasons for his power, the reasons for his separateness, the reasons for his suffering may be defined and understood.

In Russia he is charged with being the source of Bolshevism, an accusation which is serious or not according to the circle in which it is made; we in America, hearing the fervid eloquence and perceiving the prophetic ardor of young Jewish apostles of social and industrial reform, can calmly estimate how it may be. In Germany he is charged with being the cause of the Empire's collapse and a very considerable literature has sprung up, bearing with it a mass of circumstantial evidence that gives the thinker pause. In England he is charged with being the real world ruler, who rules as a super-nation over the nations, rules by the power of gold, and who plays nation against nation for his own purposes, remaining himself discreetly in the background. In America it is pointed out to what extent the elder Jews of wealth and the younger Jews of ambition swarmed through the war organizations—principally those departments which dealt with the commercial and industrial business of war, and also the extent to which they have clung to the advantage which their experience as agents of the government gave them.

IN SIMPLE words, the question of the Jews has come to the fore, but like other questions which lend themselves to prejudice, efforts will be made to hush it up as impolitic for open discussion. If, however, experience has taught us anything it is that questions thus suppressed will sooner or later break out in undesirable and unprofitable forms.

The Jew is the world's enigma. Poor in his masses, he yet controls the world's finances. Scattered abroad without country or government, he yet presents a unity of race continuity which no other people has achieved. Living under legal disabilities in almost every land, he has become the power behind many a throne. There are ancient prophecies to the effect that the Jew will return to his own land and from that center rule the world, though not until he has undergone an assault by the united nations of mankind.

The single description which will include a larger percentage of Jews than members of any other race is this: he is in business. It may be only gathering rags and selling them, but he is in business. From the sale of old clothes to the control of international trade and finance, the Jew is supremely gifted for business. More than any other race he exhibits a decided aversion to industrial employment, which he balances by an equally decided adaptability to trade. The Gentile boy works his way up, taking employment in the productive or technical departments; but the Jewish boy prefers to begin as messenger, salesman or clerk—anything—so long as it is connected with the commercial side of the business. An early Prussian census illustrates this characteristic: of a total population of 269,400, the Jews comprised six per cent or 16,164. Of these, 12,000 were traders and 4,164 were workmen. Of the Gentile population, the other 94 per cent, or 153,236 people, there were only 17,000 traders.

A MODERN census would show a large professional and literary class added to the traders, but no diminution of the percentage of traders and not much if any increase in the number of wage toilers. In America alone most of the big business, the trusts and the banks, the natural resources and the chief agricultural products, especially tobacco, cotton and sugar, are in the control of Jewish financiers or their agents. Jewish journalists are a large and powerful group here. "Large numbers of department stores are held by Jewish firms," says the Jewish Encyclopedia, and many if not most of them are run under Gentile names. Jews are the largest and most numerous landlords of residence property in the country. They are supreme in the theatrical world. They absolutely control the circulations of publications throughout the country. Fewer than any race whose presence among us is so noticeable, they receive daily an amount of favorable publicity which would be impossible did they not have the facilities for creating and distributing it themselves. Werner Sombart, in his "Jew and Modern Capitalism" says, "If the conditions in America continue to develop along the same lines as in the last generation, if the immigration statistics and the proportion of births among all the nationalities remain the same, our imagination may picture the United States of fifty or a hundred years hence as a land inhabited only by Slavs, Negroes and Jews, wherein the Jews will naturally occupy the position of

The article that signalled the beginning of Henry Ford's seven-year hate campaign against the Jews. (Collections of the Henry Ford Museum, Greenfield Village)

in Germany between 1920 and 1922. A large table covered with multiple copies of his diatribe against the Jews would be seen by anyone entering Adolf Hitler's office in the Munich headquarters of the National Socialist German Worker's Party during the winter of 1922.[204] Adolf Hitler's *Mein Kampf* was first published in 1925, much influenced by Ford's thinking. In 1942 the thirty-seventh edition of *Der Internationale Jude* was published.

As a young man Henry Ford visited a mechanised Chicago slaughterhouse, and there got the idea for the assembly line. The animals, suspended upside down from a moving chain, would be dismembered piece by piece, each by an individual workmen, and come out processed and packaged.[206,207,208]

> Henry Ford, who was so impressed by the efficient way meat packers killed animals in Chicago, made his own special contribution to the slaughter of people in Europe – nor only did he develop the assembly-line method the Germans used to kill the Jews, but he launched a vicious anti-Semitic campaign that helped the Holocaust happen.
>
> Charles Patterson[208]

Baldur von Schirach, former head of the Hitler Youth organisation and wartime governor of Nazi-occupied Vienna, testified at Nuremberg:

The decisive anti-Semitic book which I read at the time was Henry Ford's book, *The International Jew*. I read it and became anti-semitic. This book made . . . a great impression on my friends and myself, because we saw in Henry Ford the representative of success, also the representative of a progressive social policy. In the poverty-stricken and wretched Germany of the time, youth looked towards America, and . . . it was Henry Ford who, to us, represented America . . . If he said the Jews were to blame, naturally we believed him.[19,112,204]

Of great concern is the following statement by Bernard Wasserstein in his recently published book *On the Eve: The Jews of Europe before the Second World War*.

> Translated into many languages, the *Protocols [of Zion]* was the most widely disseminated text of the interwar period, second

only to Mein Kampf, and in the late 1920s was reported to be circulating even in the Soviet Union.

Bernard Wasserstein [209]

An astonishing statement by Wasserstein, a historian on the staff of The University of Chicago. He completely fails to mention Ford's *The International Jew*[205] or *Der Internationale Jude*. The Ford Foundation is a benefactor to the University of Chicago, an example of just how appallingly Corrupt and Evil the nefarious practices of advertising, marketing and sponsorship really are!!!

To learn who rules over you simply find out who you are not allowed to criticize.

Voltaire[210]

People often ask why did Pope Pius XII, Eugenio Pacelli, not speak out more forcefully against Hitler. Historian Fr Dermot Fenlon of Birmingham Oratory looks at facts and sets the record straight:[211] The answer is recounted by a former inmate of Dachau, Mgr Jean Bernard, later Bishop of Luxumburg: 'The detained priests trembled every time news reached us of some protest by a religious authority, but particularly by the Vatican. We all had the impression that our warders made us atone heavily for the fury these protests evoked . . . whenever the way we were treated became more brutal, the Protestant pastors among the prisoners used to vent their indignation on the catholic priests: 'again your naive Pope and those simpletons, your bishops, are shooting their mouths off . . . why don't they get the idea once and for all, and shut up. They play the heroes and we have to pay the bill.'

Robert A Graham[211]

Dr Joseph L Lichten, a Polish Jew, and head of International Cultural Department development of the Anti-Defamation league of B'nai B'rith, wrote in 1963: 'The Pope did not speak out more strongly against the Jewish persecutions by the Nazis, because anything he would have said was liable to make matters even worse for the Jews.' . . . Rabbi Herzog's repeated expressions of gratitude after the War seem to prove that he approved of the action taken by the Pope. After 1945 I know of no authoritative Jewish accusation which equated papal reticence with inaction or reluctance to save Jews. On the other hand, there are on record several statements by Jewish leaders similar in tenor to the words of Dr Marcus Melchior, the Chief Rabbi of Denmark, who himself was rescued, together with virtually his entire Jewish community, thanks to silent *unpublished* endeavours: 'I believe it an error to think that Pope Pius XII could have any influence whatsoever on the brain of a madman. If the Pope had spoken out, Hitler would have probably massacred more than six million Jews and perhaps ten times ten million Catholics, if he had had the power to do so. . . ' It is against this background of genocidal indifference and callousness, that the Catholic effort within Nazi stricken Europe must be evaluated. On the one hand, statesmen, diplomats and generals who refused to save Jews, to avoid "embarrassment" or "complications"; on the other hand, peasants, priests, housewives, nuns and workers who, unarmed defied the mightiest juggernaut in modern times, in order to save 800,000 Jews . . . The Germans took revenge in Northern Italy and executed several priests who had helped the Jews.

Italian Catholics—from cardinals to policemen—tried to save Jewish lives by providing shelter, false identity cards, food ration cards, and other papers. Many of these Catholics were arrested by the Nazis and more than a few killed. Giovanni Palatucci, chief of police of Fiume, perished in Dachau for aiding Jews. The seven children of Edoardo Focerini editor of the Bologna Catholic daily *Avvenire d'Italia,* died in a concentration camp because of their father's efforts on behalf of Bologna's Jews . . . He [Monsignor John Patrick Carroll-Abbing the founder of Boys' Towns of Italy and a confidant of Pius XII] stressed that the idea of he and others like him acted in spite of the pope's silence 'is a blatant lie!' 'I spoke many times during the war, in

89

person, face to face and he told me not once but many times to assist the Jews . . . I can personally testify that the pope gave me direct face-to-face orders to rescue Jews.'

Pinchas E Lapide[212]

There may be much imposture, much also of hypocrisy, and no small share of self-delusion amongst *individuals* of every [religious] sect, but sincerity will be found in the *aggregate* of each: prehensions, nay, where *unity* is incompatible with freedom of thought and will, it would more become us, methinks, to make allowance for each other's weaknesses, than to vilify any worship, which, after all, may only differ from our own as to mode. Christianity, beyond a question, does not inculcate such intolerance. The *true* follower of that faith recognizes in every *altar* an evidence of common piety.

Henry O'Brien[115]

Tributes in Dahlin's *The Myth of Hitler's Pope: How Pope Pius Rescued Jews from the Nazis.*[213]

Rabbi David Dahlin has written an admirable defence of Pope Pius XII from a religiously committed Jewish perspective. He effectively answers the vicious, distorted charges that portray Pius XII as a Nazi sympathizer who did nothing to help save Jews from Nazi genocide. Dahlin's meticulous scholarship shows just what an effective enemy of Nazi racism Pius XII really was, both before and during the papacy, and the collective risks he took to rescue as many Jews as he could under the most dangerous conditions imaginable.

David Novak[214]

Courage is contagious, so clutch this book close to your heart. Righting great wrongs requires great courage, and that is what *The Myth of Hitler's Pope* delivers. With devastating effectiveness Dr. Dalin exposes their motives and subdues the assailants who with rashness and folly attempt posthumously to assassinate Pope Pius XII. This restoration of a good man's name is a mitzvah—a Jewish good deed.

Rabbi Daniel Lapin[215]

Pope Pius XII's reputation as a friend of the Jewish people has suffered since Rolf Hochhuth depicted the pontiff as 'silent' in the face of Nazi atrocities in his 1964 play *The Deputy*. Today, Pius is regarded in some circles as an anti-Semite and even a Nazi sympathizer. His most fervent critics have constructed the fable that he was 'Hitler's pope.' In his superb book *The Myth of Hitlers Pope*, Rabbi David Dalin buries this slanderous tale under an avalanche of facts.

Robert P George[216]

Albrecht von Kessel, an official at the German Embassy to the Holy See during the War wrote in 1963:

We were convinced that a fiery protest by Pius XII against the persecution of the Jews would certainly not have saved the life of a single Jew. Hitler like a trapped beast would react to any menace that he felt directed at him, with cruel violence.

Robert A Graham[211]

During the first years of the (Nazi) regime the Gestapo and SD concentrated their surveillance and persecution measures against the churches above all on the Catholics.

Peter Longerich[217]

Virulent German Anti-Semitism goes back to the Soloist Martin Luther's so-called 'Reformation':

In 1543, the leader of the Protestant movement, Martin Luther, published *On the Jews and their Lies*. Luther's solution, because the Jews failed to convert, was to set fire to their to synagogues or schools, their houses also to be razed and destroyed, their rabbis forbidden to teach on pain of life or limb, safe-conduct on the highways be abolished for Jews, and all cash, silver and gold to be taken from them and put into safekeeping . . . For centuries, Luther's solution was resurrected and implemented in part or in whole by various towns and kingdoms when it was useful for the local authorities and the local populace to do so . . . But Adolf Hitler took the theme of local Jew-hatred to a dramatic and odious new low. Luther's solution was advocated by Hitler, not only chapter and verse, but with a new political imperative and rationale.

Edwin Black[204]

The day after the monumental exercise in Hypocrisy in Paris Sunday January 11, 2015, Republican Representative Randy Weber from Texas tweeted: 'Even Adolph Hitler thought it more important than Obama to get to Paris . . .'[218] What Weber failed to tell his fellow twits was that without neo-Nazi neo-Cons Henry Ford and GM's (General Motors) president Alfred P Sloan, Adolf Hitler would not have made it to Paris either!!! If Germany had won World War II, Adolf Hitler would be as much a darling of Capitol Hill as are his fellow genocidal psychopaths, the Roman Marcus Porcius Cato,[86] Cato the Elder (234–149 BC) responsible for the destruction of Carthage "*delende est Carthago*", after whom the Cato Institute[219] is named, and Oliver Cromwell:

> Tony Blankley, the press secretary for Speaker Newt Gingrich, spent yesterday apologizing for some complimentary remarks he made about Oliver Cromwell the day before . . . The article quoted Mr. Blankley as saying that Cromwell was an "intriguing character, a visionary misunderstood in his time and afterward".

Elaine Louie[220]

At 6 am on September 1, 1939, Adolf Hitler launched his motorized *Blitzkrieg* (lightening war) on Europe. Using warplanes, tanks, trucks and command cars the Third Reich moved swiftly to conquer, occupy and destroy much of Europe. Blitzkrieg was a development of "Total War" as advocated by the Prussian General Carl von Clausewitz,[221] based on Napoleon Bonaparte's brutal military tactics. In the opinion of Napoleon, Niccolò Machiavelli's notorious *The Prince*,[153] was the only book worth reading:

> *The Prince* is the only book worth reading . . . I like only those people who are useful to me, and only so long as they are useful.
>
> Napoleon Bonaparte[222]

> Then came the French Revolution and Napoleon. After 1789, for France war became "the business of the people — a people of thirty million, all of whom were considered citizens. Because Frenchmen now identified with the nation, they allowed themselves to be called to arms in greater numbers. Napoleon also discovered that by pursuing defeated troops, giving his cavalry their head, he could significantly magnify the scale of the victory". . . . and so when von Clauswitz came to maturity, war was becoming far more brutal. This (the lesson of Napoleon) too was one of Clauswitz's arguments, was that the defeated feel defeat more keenly than victors enjoy their victory, an observation that was to echo down the nineteenth century and all the way to 1939. Clauswitz and Napoleon were the creators of total war.
>
> Peter Watson[223]

Henry Ford's support for Hitler's Third Reich was not confined to his Anti-Semitism. Ford-Werke, AG was majority owned by the Ford Motor Company USA. By 1941 Ford-Werke Cologne was producing 1,000 trucks per month. More than 60 per cent of the three-ton tracked trucks produced for the German army were made by Ford-Werke, AG. Unlike other American-owned property in Germany Ford-Werke wasn't confiscated by the German government.[204] American troops entering Cologne at the end of the war encountered starving foreign slave-workers behind barbed wire at the Ford-Werke plant; foreign captives, mostly from Eastern Europe had laboured there under Gestapo supervision for 12-hour days with little more than 200 grams of bread and coffee.

Adolf Hitler came to power in January 1933. On March 27, 1933 a million protesters jammed Madison Square Garden in New York and millions more around the world gathered to protest against Nazi brutality. By the spring of

1933, the entire world was beginning to learn about the lawlessness and anti-Semitic savagery of the new Nazi regime at a time when another American motor manufacturer, GM (General Motors), was embarking on a strategic business relationship with the Nazis.[204] GM and its president, Alfred P Sloan, worked continuously during the 1930s to modernise Hitler's army through its German subsidiary Opel. By 1937 GM's Opel was three times the size of Germany's Diamler-Benz. Sales to the German army yielded a greater profit per truck than civilian sales, a hefty 40 per cent more; the company made the three-ton truck specifically for the Blitzkrieg. Opel's Brandenburg plant was converted to an aeroplane engine plant supplying engines for the Luftwaffe's JU-88 bombers. Sloan was not just interested in profit, he despised President Franklin Delano Roosevelt and his New Deal and greatly admired Adolf Hitler.

> The factories and infrastructure that GM built during the 1930s was in fact finally used for their intended purpose – War. Opel-built trucks on the ground, Opel-operated bombers in the sky, and Opel-detonated torpedoes in the seas brought terror to Europe from every direction.
>
> Edwin Black[204]

> The Germans were over this house last night and the night before. It is a queer experience, lying in the dark and listening to the zoom of a hornet, which may at any moment sting you to death. It is a sound that interrupts cool consecutive talk about peace. Yet it is the sound – far more than prayers and anthems – that should compel one to think about peace. Unless we think peace into existence we – not this one body in this one bed, but millions of bodies yet to be born – will lie in the same darkness and hear the same death rattle overhead.
>
> Virginia Woolf[224]

> The battle of the Atlantic was the dominating factor all through the war. Never for one moment could we forget that everything happening elsewhere, on land, at sea or in the air depended ultimately on its outcome.
>
> Winston Churchill[225]

According to a Costello and Hughes, [225] Germany had the largest submarine fleet in the world: 36,000 merchant seamen were killed, 3,500 merchant vessels lost, 175 warships lost, 30,000 u-Boat submariners lost and 783 submarines lost.

> My mother had to leave school early and go to work. Onkel Gerd had no more money once he lost his job as lord mayor. She got a job in the Kempen registry office and had to learn typing and filing names in alphabetical order. She remembers people coming in to find out if their grandfathers or grandmothers had ever been Jewish. She remembers how happy one old woman was, how she had tears in her eyes and put her hand on her heart when she found out that she was one of the lucky ones. Other people were not so lucky. Every day they came to make sure they were not Jewish. Every day, Tia Maria wondered if the Catholics would be next. It wasn't long afterwards that the Nazis closed down the convent in Mühlhausen and wrote dirty words all over the classrooms.
>
> Hugo Hamilton[226]

When the Nazis identified exactly where Jews lived, even those living Christian lives but with Jewish ancestors in their bloodlines, one company knew what was happening. When the Reich persecution machine pinpointed exactly which professors, doctors, art dealers and members of any of a thousand other niches in society were Jews and then ousted them, one company knew. When the banks seized Jewish savings, corporate stock and property, one company knew ... When the Jews, catalogued by numbers and scheduled by precise calculations, were herded into trains and metered into death camps, one company knew. Who knew? Answer: International Business Machines and its president, Thomas J Watson. IBM organised and essentially co-planned the Holocaust with the Nazis.

Edwin Black[204,227]

In the 1880s, a US government census employee Herman Hollerith invented the punch card system and shortly afterwards founded his own company, a company that subsequently became IBM. The new punch card system allowed vastly more information about individuals to be collected and tabulated than merely their age, name and address. By punching a hole in a specified space in a particular column or row, considerable information about individuals could be collected and collated. A small army of people was required to operate the large number of machines required to punch in and read the data. As war became imminent in the late 1930s, Watson passed instructions through the company's office in Geneva, Switzerland, so as to circumvent United States law. IBM's tabulating machines were leased to the Nazis and the company was paid monthly right through the war years. Hitler's Reich was exceedingly profitable for IBM; Watson received a five per cent bonus on every dollar received from the Reich, after tax and dividends were paid.

> With IBM as a partner, the Hitler regime was able to substantially automate and accelerate all six phases of the twelve-year Holocaust: identification, exclusion, confiscation, ghettoization, deportation, and even extermination.
>
> Edwin Black[204,227]

It is frequently stated that World War II was between the Democracies and Nazism. Was Germany not a democracy? Power attracts pathological personalities [PPP].[22] The National Socialists (Nazis) under Adolf Hitler won 43.9 per cent of the vote in the Reichstag elections of 1933.[228] If nothing else, Adolf Hitler's rise to power showed the fickleness of democracy and how easy it is for despots to use it to gain power.

Even before Hitler came to power the German government was working on ways of making Hollywood compliant with their wishes, and stop them making movies that were considered anti-German.[228] In January 1932 Dr Martin Freudenthal, of the German Foreign Office started a year-long visit to the United States, the purpose of which was to encourage Hollywood to make German friendly movies; Germany was one of Hollywood's biggest overseas markets. First Freudenthal met with Carl Laemmle of Universal Pictures who agreed to postpone the sequel of *All Quiet on the Western Front*. Throughout the remainder of the year he met with Laemmle's son, Carl Laemmle Jr, and from then on many movies were made in Germany's favour by Universal Pictures. And so it was with other studies: RKO promised that whenever a movie involving Germany was made they would work "in close collaboration" with the local consul general; Fox agreed to consult with a German representative in all future movies; and even Universal Artists offered "the closest collaboration." These arrangements remained in place throughout the 1930s.[228]

CHAPTER 9

PHYSICIANS AS AUTHORS:
FACT RATHER THAN FICTION, FANTASY,
FAIRY TALES AND LIES

Yet unchecked legend is the greatest enemy of historical truth.

Hugh Brogan[129]

The Book of Tephi[62] was published by physician, antiquarian and poet John A
Goodchild in 1897. Goodchild practiced medicine in Bordighera on the Mediterranean coast of Italy not far from Monaco, seeing mostly expatriate Britons
as patients.[229] His great epic narrative biographical poem about Tephi Queen
of Ireland and Gibralter, was overshadowed by Augusta Gregory's: *Gods and
Fighting Men: The Story of the Tuaatha De Danaan and of the Fianna of Ireland
Arranged and put into English by Lady Gregory. With a Preface by W B Yeats*,[230]
based on mythology. Under normal circumstances Goodchild's *Tephi* would
have been well received but at the turn of the twentieth the "Celtic Revival"
was in full swing and with the strong support of William Butler Yeats, Gregory's *Gods and Fighting Men* was highly acclaimed. Yeats was awarded the
Dynamite Prize for Literature for his poetry, and *Fairy and Folk Tales of the
Irish Peasantry*. At a time of intense anti-Catholic and anti-Semitic bigotry,
there was no market for an epic narrative poem about the Hebrew Princess
who became Queen of Ireland in 583 BC, who had instituted laws based on the
Torah, Brehon Laws, and who ruled Ireland (Hebernia) wisely for 49 years.

Goodchild's *Book of Tephi* is almost unknown compared to Gregory's
Gods and Fighting Men. A survey by the author of the London Library's copies
of both books found that the one copy of *Tephi* had been borrowed four times
in the previous thirty years, compared to over eighty times for the three copies
of *Gods and Fighting Men*, confirming Flinders Petrie suggestion that fiction is
twenty times more popular than fact.[46] The opening lines of *Gods and fighting
Men*:

It was in the mist the Tuatha de Danaan, the people of the gods of
Dana, or as some called them, the Men of Dea, came through the

air and the high air to Ireland. It was from the north they came.

Augusta Gregory[230]

The timing of the publication of *Gods and Fighting Men*, first published in 1904, raises the question as to whether it was specifically written to eclipse Goodchild's *Book of Tephi*. Yeats had been directly influenced by Standish James O'Grady when he first became interested in Irish literature.[231] It was O'Grady's translations of ancient Irish manuscripts and those of Whitley Stokes of Trinity College, whose father and grandfather were physicians, that Goodchild relied on for his epic narrative poem. The "Celtic Revival" may yet prove to have been a criminal conspiracy!!

> For centuries a latent animosity toward the Jews prevented Western scholars from an impartial examination of the evidence in favour of our common descent from the ancient Hebrews.

Robert Latham[232]

The author of the highly acclaimed *The Ethnology of Europe*.[232] Robert Gordon Latham (1812–1888) was lecturer and assistant physician at the Middlesex Hospital London, and Professor of English at University College London. *Ethnology of Europe* was also published at a time (1852) of intense anti-Catholic and anti-Semitic prejudice in England among the ruling elite and it is not surprising that it received so little attention. Latham also published *Norway and the Norwegians* (1840), *The English Language* (1841), *An Elementary English Grammer* (1843) and *A Handbook of the English Language* (1851).

Of Human Bondage[193] by W Somerset Maugham, first published in New York in 1915, is a masterpiece in narrative. Maugham[233] (1874–1965), who had been a medical student at St Bartholomew's Hospital London, became a fulltime author after his first year's practice in the slums of London's East End provided him with material for his first novel, *Lizzy of Lambeth*,[234] and much of the material for his critically acclaimed autographical novel *Of Human Bondage*.[193] Both provide insight into life at the time, particularly the appalling conditions of the downtrodden.

But when at an election the Liberals had written on his garden fence in large blue letters: This way to Rome, he had been very angry, and threatened to persecute the leaders of the Liberal party in Blackstable. He made up his mind now that nothing Josiah Graves said would induce him to remove the candlesticks from the alter, and he muttered Bismark to himself once or twice irritably . . . The masters had no patience with modern ideas of education, which they read sometimes in the *Times* or *The Guardian*, and hoped fervently that King's School would remain true to its old traditions. The dead languages were taught with such thoroughness that an old boy seldom thought of Homer or Virgil in after life without a qualm of boredom; and though in the common room at dinner one or two bolder spirits suggested that mathematics were of increasing importance, the general feeling was that they were a less noble study than the classics . . . Once a man who was strong and in all the power of his manhood came because a persistent aching troubled him and his club-doctor did not seem to do him any good; and the verdict for him too was death, not the inevitable death that horrified and yet was tolerable because science was helpless before it, but the death which is inevitable because the man was a little wheel in the great machine of a complex civilisation, and had as little power of changing the circumstances as an automaton. Complete rest was his only chance. The physician did not ask impossibilities.

"You ought to get some very much lighter job."

"There ain't no light jobs in my business."

"Well if you go on like this you'll kill yourself. You're very ill."

"Do you mean to say I'm going to die?"

"I shouldn't like to say that, but you're certainly unfit for hard work."

"If I don't work who's to keep the wife and the kids?"

Dr. Tyrell shrugged his shoulders. The dilemma had been

presented to him a hundred times. Time was pressing and there were many patients to be seen . . .

The wards were crowded, and the house-surgeon was faced with a dilemma when patients were brought in by the police: if they were sent on to the station and died there disagreeable things were said in the papers and it was very difficult sometimes to tell if a man was dying or drunk . . . people don't commit suicide for love, as you'd expect, that's just a fancy of novelists; they commit suicide because they haven't got any money . . . "Oh, don't talk to me about your socialists. I've got no patience with them," she cried. "It only means that another lot of lazy loafers will make a good thing out of the working classes . . ." With the men the most common ailments were due to the excessive use of alcohol, but with the women they were due to defective nourishment . . . Philip thought of the countless millions to whom life is no more than unending labour, neither beautiful not ugly, but just to be accepted in the same spirit as one accepts the changes of the seasons . . . By listening to the women as they talked and by chance remarks from which he could deduce much that was left unsaid, Philip learned how little there was in common between the poor and the classes above them. They did not envy their betters, for the life was too different, and they had an ideal of ease which made the existence of the middle classes seem formal and stiff; moreover, they had certain contempt for them because they were soft and did not work with their hands . . . his heart was filed with rage against the cruelty of the world. He knew the hopelessness of the search for work and the desolation which is harder to bear than hunger.

W S Maugham[193]

And that was only *Of Human Bondage*. Maugham's output was prodigious; he published 16 books, 20 novels, 189 articles, 25 plays, 16 collections and 11 unpublished plays.[233] Maugham was never awarded the Dynamite Prize for Literature!!

Imagination grows by exercise and contrary to common belief, is more powerful in the mature than in the young.

W S Maugham[235]

In 1884 Anton Chekhov (1860–1904) qualified as a physician and throughout his life considered the practice of medicine his principal profession although he made little money from it, as he treated the poor free of charge.[236] He described his dual professions:

> I feel more confident and more satisfied when I have two professions and not one. Medicine is my lawful wife and literature my mistress; when I get tired of one, I spend the night with the other.
> en.wikipedia.org/wiki/Anton_Chekhov[237]

In *The Cherry Orchard*[238] Chekhov is critical of the upper classes:

> The vast majority of the intelligentsia such as I know seek nothing, do nothing, and are as yet incapable of work. They call themselves the "Intelligentsia," they say "thou" and "thee" to the servants, they treat the peasants like animals, learn nothing, read nothing serious, do absolutely nothing, only talk about science, and understand little or nothing about art. They are all serious; they all have solemn faces; they only discuss important subjects; they philosophise.
> Anton Chekhov[238]

The only real philosophy: – intuition based on common sense, and usually expressed in few words of a sentence or two!! Anton Chekhov became a strong advocate of penal reform following his visit to the penal colony of Sakhalin Island.[239]

Another professional who was critical of the upper classes was General Charles Vallancey FRS[240] of the Royal Engineers who became Surveyor of Ireland about 1770:

> One great evil of this vanity in our Irish gentry is, that you shall hardly meet with any of them, that scorns not to take up any

manual craft, whereby they may earn an honest livelihood, as if like chameleons, they could live on these airy vanities, that thus puff up their minds . . . The landlords of old were, and still are great oppressors of their tenants and followers.

Charles Vallancey[75]

One of the most widely known characters in fiction Sherlock Holmes, was created by physician turned prolific author Sir Arthur Conan Doyle. Born Arthur Ignatius Conan Doyle on May 22 1859,[241] he qualified from Edinburgh University Medical School in 1881. Following ten years of varying success practicing medicine he became a full-time author. His other works include fantasy and science fiction stories, plays, romances, poetry, non-fiction and historical novels. [241] During his time in medical practice Doyle obtained his MD by thesis on *tabes dorsalis*, and published a paper on Gelsemium as a poison in the *British Medical Journal.*[242] (MD is a higher medical degree in the United Kingdom and Ireland)

Doyle questioned the fairness of the legal system and personally investigated two closed cases, leading to two men being exonerated of the crimes of which they were accused. The first was a shy Parsi Indian lawyer George Edalgi who had allegedly written threatening letters and was supposed to have mutilated animals. Doyle had the conviction overturned and Edalgi was released from jail. Partly as a result the Court of Criminal appeal was established in 1907. The second case was the conviction of German Jewish Oscar Slater, a gambling-den operator, for bludgeoning an 82-year-old woman to death in Glasgow in 1908. Doyle became interested because of inconsistencies in the prosecution case and a general sense that Slater was not guilty, and paid most of the costs for Slater's successful appeal in 1928.[241]

An author and physician who highlights the evils of violence and its causes is the American psychiatrist James Gilligan. He quotes Mahatma Ghandi: 'Poverty is the most deadly form of violence'.[243] Gilligan continues:

When I realized that I and all other Americans, were living on and enjoying land that had been stolen from other people, by the simple expedient of killing any who resisted, and this had happened no longer than one lifetime ago, on land my family owned, it set in motion a scepticism about the received conventional notions of crime and punishment, justice and injustice, property and theft, legal and illegal, that I finally found Tolstoy's nineteenth century Russian Prisons, *Resurrection* . . . All violence is an attempt to achieve justice, or what the violent person perceives as justice, for himself of for whoever it is on whose behalf he is being so violent . . . The most powerful predictor of the homicide rate in comparisons of the different nations of the world, the different states of the United States, different counties, and different cities and census tracts, is the size of the disparities in income and wealth between the rich and the poor . . . 50% of perpetrators or victims of murder and other serious violence have alcohol in their bloodstreams . . . He (Sipes) found that societies that played the most combative physically violent games also engaged in the most warfare, concluding that far from serving as mutually exclusive alternatives to, the two forms of violence only reinforced each other. See: Sipes "War, sport and aggression; an empirical test of two rival theories". *American Anthropology 75, 1985 pp 64–86.*

James Gilligan[243]

Interesting when one remembers that Queen Teia Tephi, shortly before she died August 1, 534 BC specified that the Tailtean Games were to be non-competitive!!

Its inhabitants are, as the man once said, "whores, pimps, gamblers, and sons of bitches", by which he meant Everybody. Had the man looked through another keyhole he might have said, "Saints and angels and martyrs and holy men", and he would have meant the same thing.

John Steinbeck[244]

POPULIST AUTHORS: *ILLETTERATO*

> There was a regular supply of inexpensive fiction written to
> order by poor hacks for the consumption of the illiterate.
>
> W S Maugham [193]

> In our day this fact is often obscured, to an extent that would
> have appalled Orwell, by the ease with which semi-literate but
> efficiently-hyphenated authors can become famous – and rich
> . . . *Down and Out* was accepted on condition that certain names
> were changed and all swear words deleted.
>
> Dervla Murphy [245]

At the other end of the spectrum is modern Populism, exemplified by Edna
Obrien's *Country Girl: A Memoir*. O'Brien is shown with a cigarette in her
mouth on the cover of the paperback edition.[246] In *Country Girl* IRA terrorists are portrayed as patriotic heroes and Police are villains, although the term
Police is not mentioned as such, merely "Black and Tans", "English militia",
or "invader". The Black and Tans were made infamous by Irish Republican
propaganda.[247]

O'Brien fails to mention that her family were landlords, the O'Brien Clan
of County Clare:

> By the time I was born we were no longer rich. True, we had the
> large house and two avenues, but the thousand acres or more
> that my father had inherited had been sold off in bits, or given
> away in fits of generosity, or bartered to pay debts. My father
> had inherited a fortune from rich uncles who, when they were
> ordained as priests, emigrated to New England and served in
> the parish of Lowell . . . Not far from our house was the ruin of
> the house, also called Drewsboro, which like many big houses
> had been burnt in order that the English militia, the Black and
> Tans, could not occupy them as a barracks. My father took part
> in that burning and would describe the high spirits with which
> he and the other gallants doused rags in petrol, then went all

around with the petrol cans, soaking walls and woodwork. Scores of matches were struck and the subsequent bonfire, seen for miles around, was another notch of victory over the invader . . . My grandmother would rave on about the hardships she had endured and what proud patriots I was descended from . . . Her son Michael had been chief of the 3rd Brigade [IRA] in East Clare, a fearless soldier on the run from the British army, with a price on his head.

Edna O'Brien[246]

The Irish insurgency was a one-sided war, the guerrillas did most of the killing, and the Police did most of the dying.[247]

The war is romantically referred to as the War of Independence or Anglo-Irish War. Actually, this "War" was a terrorist campaign of murders, arson of private houses, destruction of property and businesses, land seizures, intimidation, and local cleansing of minorities. The actions would today be regarded as squalid atrocities or war crimes, and their ferocity belies romantic tales of flying columns and bold rebel ambushes.

James Dingley[248]

Patriotism was not always a quality associated with the O'Briens!! We have already seen how The O'Brien linked up with the Norman invader William de Burgh during 1199–1202 to plunder Connaught. The O'Brien family virtually owned County Clare along with their relatives the McNamaras. The chiefs of the Clan O'Brien were descendents of the usurper Brian Boru, and were the kings of Thomond until the time of the Tudor Terror when they became Earls of Thomond on submitting to Henry VIII and converting to the Protestant religion; by so doing they were allowed to keep all their lands in Clare. Later they became the Earls of Inchiquin.

A reminder of times past, when fewer windows meant less rent to the English landlords, except that I did not know that then, aged eight or nine.

Edna O'Brien[246]

This term "English landlord" was applied at different times to landlords who were descendants of the Native Irish, Normans, Tudors and Cromwellians, particularly if they were of the Protestant faith.

> Pat. He was an Anglo-Irishman.
> Meg. In the name of God, what's that?
> Pat. A Protestant with a horse.
>
> Brendan Behan[249]

Historians in Ireland frequently refer to the Normans as Anglo-Normans, which is incorrect. They came from Wales and their soldiers were Welsh; they originated in Normandy and French was their language. The descendants of the soldiers often go by the surnames Walsh and Welsh. The term Cambro-Norman is only very occasionally encountered. It was applied to Sir John de Wogan who was Justiciar, chief judicial officer, of Ireland from 1295 to 1313.

> In December 1296 he took office as Justiciar, and organised a two-year truce between the feuding Burkes and Geraldines. In 1296 he organised a force with Richard Óg de Burgh, 2nd Earl of Ulster, Theobald Butler, and John FitzGerald, 1st Earl of Kildare to assist Edward I in his war against the Scots.
>
> en.wikipedia.org/wiki/John de Wogan . . . [250]

It was then that Edward I removed the Stone of Destiny (Liá Fáil) from Scotland to Westminster Abbey. According to Henry O'Brien the Norman invaders of Scotland destroyed much of the old writings, as the Tudors would subsequently do in Ireland.[161] The broadcaster Sir Michael Terence (Terry) Wogan is presumably a descendent of Sir John de Wogan.

It was the Absentee Landlords who lived in London while their agents collected rack-rents and evicted many of those who were unable to pay, who were the most detested. One of the first absentees was Murrough O'Brien, First Earl of Inchiquin!!

> 22 December 1660 . . . At noon I went to the Sun tavern on fish streete hill to a dinner of Capt. Teddimans, where was my Lord

Inchiquin (who seems to be a very fine person), Sir W. Pen, Capt. Cuttance, and one Mr Lawrence (a fine gentleman now going to Algier) and other good company; where we have a very fine dinner, good Musique and a great deal of wine.

Samuel Pepys [251]

In 1642 the President of Munster died and Murrough O'Brien was appointed to the office. O'Brien was educated a Protestant and hated Catholicism.

He was entirely devoid of mercy or pity; was cruel, coarse, brutal and ferocious, one of the cruellest men in times when there were many such. He had considerable energy and ambition, and no small share of military capacity, and desirous of pursuing the war with vigour, and perhaps of neutralising the effect of the fall of Limerick, he made earnest application to England for supplies ... Inchiquin had then to rely on the force under the sons of the Earl of Cork and all he could draw away from the garrisons of Cork, Youghal, and Kinsale, and with those he marched through Cork, and encountered the Irish army at Liscarrol. He had 1,600 men under his command; the Irish had 7,000, and the advantage position; yet they were disastrously and shamefully beaten, with the loss of 700 men killed, three pieces of artillery, 13 colours, 300 muskets and three barrels of powder; while on Inchiquin's side the loss between killed and wounded was no more than forty ... Inchiquin in Munster followed Munroe's example and went over to the Parliament, piqued because the King had appointed Lord Portland to the Presidency of Munster ... There was then no meaning in sending Irish troops to England. Nor ought they leave Ireland, for the cause of the Confederate Catholics was menaced with many dangers. In Munster Inchiquin was again active, and was sweeping through the province, murdering the inhabitants, burning their houses, and destroying their crops.

E A D'Alton [159]

O'Brien would afterwards be known as 'Murrough of the Burnings'. (Irish historians frequently refer to him as Inchiquin even before he was ennobled, presumably reluctant to reveal his Native Irish origins!) O'Brien was responsible for the notorious Sack of Cashel in 1647. The town was held by the Irish Catholic Confederate's Munster army and was besieged and taken by an English Protestant Parliamentarian army under O'Brien. The attack and subsequent sack of Cashel was one of the most brutal incidents of the wars of the 1640s in Ireland.[252]

Equally disastrous was the news from Munster. Muscarry was superseded in the command by Taaffe, but the new general was as ineffective as the old; and Inchiquinn in September first captured Cahir and then Cashel. The garrison of the latter town was offered leave to depart, if they gave Inchiquin £3,000, and left the citizens at his mercy. They refused these terms, and resolved to defend themselves and so made their way to the Rock of Cashel, where they were attacked with fury. The defenders fought well, but numbers told, the place was stormed, and the infuriated Puritans massacred all within, men, women and children. Some soldiers surrendered on condition of their lives being spared, but when their arms were given up they were instantly cut down. The victors entered the church where many of the priests were killed; crucifixes, statues and pictures were broken in pieces; vestments were used as horse cloths, or worn by the soldiers in derision, and Inchiquin himself put on the Archbishop's mitre, boasting that he was governor of Munster and Mayor and Archbishop of Cashel. This tale of horror was soon spread throughout Munster. Indignation was universal at the supineness or incapacity of Taffe, and that general, thus urged, proceeded to measure swords with Inchiquin. The battle was fought at Knockanoss, near Mallow. Taffe, who was much superior in numbers, was aided by Colkitto and MacDonnell, who had so distinguished himself in Scotland under Montrose, and now commanded the right wing of the Confederate army. With a heroism worthy of his record he rushed impetuously on the foe. His men with their dreaded claymores [two edged broadsword] cut down the artillerymen men at their guns and drove the enemy's whole left wing off the field, pursued them

at a good distance, and then returned and took quiet possession of the guns. But Taffe's left wing and centre had behaved
like poltroons, and made little resistance, and were cut down
in hundreds by Inchiquin. After pursuing them a distance he
returned and confronted the heroic MacDonnell, who was soon
killed. The loss amounted to 3,000 men; and arms, ammunition and baggage fell into the victor's hands; and the army of
Munster under Taffe was as effectively wiped out as the army of
Leinster had been under Preston.

E A D'Alton[159]

Murrough had lived up to the motto of the O'Briens!!

Though she [Edna O'Brien's great-grandmother] lived alone,
she would dress each evening for dinner, always in black, with a
white lace ruff, and she drank toddies from a silver-topped horn
cup that bore the questionable motto of the O'Briens – "Might
before Right".

Edna O'Brien[246]

In 1654 Murrough O'Brien was enobled by Charles II as First Earl of Inchiquin
after deserting the Parliamentarians and pledging loyalty to the exiled King.

The most distasteful task for the RIC during the latter half of the nineteenth
century, was attending evictions to protect landlords' agents and bailiffs.
Nearly all the constables and non-commissioned officers were from the same
class as the people being evicted, the peasantry, and they detested this aspect
of Policing. In many cases they would have a collection among themselves for
the unfortunates being evicted.

On September 1, 1920 five RIC officers were cycling from Ballaghaderreen in County Roscommon to Frenchpark Petty Sessions when they were
ambushed by the IRA at Rathmacross. Constable Edward Murphy was killed
outright. Constable Martin McCarthy seriously wounded, died the next day.[253]
McCarthy was from Cloghaninchy in County Clare about three miles south
of the fishing village of Quilty, and had been in the RIC for eight years when

he was killed. Martin McCarthy was the author's first cousin once removed, through my grandmother Martin's sister.

The McCarthy's were a quiet peaceful industrious people, and Martin's achievement in getting into the Police was welcome. One field separated their smallholding from the sea and as a result the soil was poor because of salt water deposited during the winter storms. Martin's brother John, who had spent time in the Chicago Police but returned home to Ireland when he considered it to be getting too dangerous, had a third share in a currach. Each day during the summer, weather permitting, he and his two co-owners would go fishing in the early morning and in the evening. The catch was filleted, salted and put into small wooden casks for storage to use during the winter. On the dust cover of *Clippers: The Ships that Shaped the World*[254] I mention the short trip in John's currach. John's wife Marian baked the most delicious bread in a griddle pan on the open fire.

It so happened that Aunt Lily (Lillian Hegarty) was staying in Clohaninchy when news was received of Martin's murder. Lily, a teacher, was spending time with her relatives before returning to England. A graduate of Liverpool University, Lily taught geography at Wigan Girls' High School, having been a teacher at Wigan Grammar during the Great War when there was a shortage of male teachers. It was from Cloghaninchy that my McCarthy grandmother emigrated in the middle part of the second half of the nineteenth century, travelling to Wigan with two cousins who were sisters. They had left West Clare in the 1850s shortly after the Great Famine, having been evicted with their mother after the death of their father. It was fairly common practice, particularly in the west of Ireland, for landlords to evict widows and their children.

In addition to the killing and maiming of RIC officers there was extensive intimidation of the families of the RIC and anyone who showed sympathy for them:

> . . . early in 1919 the IRA began a campaign of intimidation against officers of the RIC, who were subject to threats, violent attacks and ostracizing of their families from the local community. Others who dared to show support or even sympathy for RIC families thereafter were similarly intimidated.
>
> James Dingley[248]

It would have been difficult for members of Martin's family to attend his funeral because of *Sinn Féin*-IRA and Police roadblocks, and so Aunt Lily volunteered to represent them. Having travelled by train, Lily arrived at Ballaghaderreen the evening before the funeral. Walking towards the town she encountered people coming the other way carrying their belongings. Lily asked them why they were leaving. On being told that a number of lorry loads of Black and Tans had arrived in the town and were preparing to sack the town and burn it to the ground in reprisal for the killing of Constables Murphy and McCarthy, Lily went to where the Auxiliaries were billeted to confront them. The Auxillary Division of the RIC had been formed only a few months earlier and they were called "Tempoary Cadets".[247] The Auxiliary companies were composed of ex-officers and were intended as a mobile striking and raiding force to support the RIC, whereas the Black and Tans were ex-servicemen recruited to the RIC, mostly from an ordinary background.

Lily marched into their quarters and demanded to see the officer in charge. The men were drinking in preparation for the unpleasant task ahead; this would have been a premeditated reprisal in the war between the *Sinn Féin*-IRA and the RIC. Lily, of slight build and medium height, an early advocate of Women's Rights, was undaunted. It must have been quite a surprise for the Auxiliaries to be faced with this young and determined well-spoken schoolmarm! Lily stated her case to the commanding officer: 'The McCarty family wanted no reprisals,' and Lily is reputed to have been given an assurance that there would be none. Leeson's extremely well researched *The Black and Tans*,[247] however, records ten buildings damaged or destroyed in Ballaghdereen on 2 September 1920.

The author feels obliged to declare a possible conflict of interest!! O'Brien's *Country Girl* was awarded the Irish Book Awards Argosy Non-Fiction Book of the Year in 2012. My own *Clippers*:[254] ISBN 978-1-908726-00-1 was submitted for consideration, not only for the above prize, but in two other categories of the Irish Book Awards of that year. E-mail acknowledgements were received for all three, informing me that I would be invited to submit copies if *Clippers* was shortlisted!! No postal address was given and *Clippers* was judged unseen as not being worthy of shortlisting!! And if my recollection is correct the awards were for books published in Ireland!! *Clippers* was also submitted for the BBC's Samuel Johnson Prize for non-Fiction, and probably deserved to be long listed, but it was not so. One can't expect much of the nepotistic BBC unless one is a Celebrity!!

Country Girl was widely reviewed in the Press. Edna O'Brien's publisher or agent, presumably the latter, even managed to have it reviewed in the local *Oxford Times*.[255] It was, however, Anne Enright's approximately 700-word review in the *Guardian*[256] which is of concern, and even more so when we learn that the *New York Times* invited O'Brien to interview *Sinn Féin*-IRA's Gerry Adams:

> In 1994, 30 years after the first furore liberal Ireland was deeply unsettled when O'Brien interviewed the *Sinn Féin* leader Gerry Adams, glowingly for the *New York Times*. She used Michael Collins, hero of the Irish war of independence as a natural point of comparison: 'whereas Collins was outgoing and swashbuckling, Gerry Adams is thoughtful and reserved.' . . . talking to Gerry Adams, like having premarital sex, is now a respectable thing to do.
>
> Anne Enright[256]

Is it?!!! If Michael Collins had preferred women to alcohol and guns we might have been spared a century of terrorism, killing, maiming, intimidation, division, hatred and impoverishment, and we would have been spared Gerry Adams *Sinn Féin*-IRA; and having to talk to him!! Collins even withstood the amorous advances of the lovely Lady Lavery whose portrait adorned the Irish pound note for decades.

> But whatever demons these events ingenerated [in Maximilian Robespierre] manifested themselves mostly in a ferocious work ethic, personal rigidity, and quite possibly a severe case of sexual repression . . .
>
> David A Bell[257]

And the following by Enright is a slight of "the ordinary sensible people" as Sean O'Casey described them:[258] 'The O'Brien's house was a house in decline: the remnants of its grandeur are given as sops to the persecutory peasantry that surround it'.[256] And this in an English newspaper!!

113

Another populist British publication deserves mention, Planter Pakenham Tom's *The Year of Liberty: The Bloody Story of the Great Irish Rebellion of 1798*.[259] In the preface:

> The Irish Catholic peasantry were some of the most wretched in Europe. The country was governed by a grotesque colonial partnership: a weak British viceroy with British staff, bullied by a narrow oligarchy of Irish Protestants of British settler stock . . .
> Tom Pakenham[259]

Quite so!!! Were not the Cromwellians the most recent invaders, and was it not their Settlement, Parliament and Penal Laws that put the Native Catholic People in such dire straits? And had not Oliver Cromwell and his officers such as Captain Henry Pakenham of Abbott's Dragoons brought the great evil known as "Republicanism" to Ireland?

> The most ardent of all was Lord Edward Fitzgerald, the Connollys' nephew and the brother of the Duke of Leinster. He had joined the "United Irishmen", founded by Theobald Wolfe Tone and others in 1991, and was now one of the leaders. Their aim was a complete severance with Britain and the unification of all "hearts" in Ireland under the banner of a French-style republic.
> Eliza Pakenham[140]

> What is one to make of [Theobald Wolfe] Tone: soldier of France, Irish patriot, colonial adventurer, citizen of the world? Daniel O'Connell was impossibly harsh when he described Tone and his friends as "criminals" . . . But it was his persuasiveness, his charm and his optimism about Irish unity that helped decide the French to try their luck in that quarter; and, but for the hopes of French assistance, there would have been no rebellion in Ireland.
> Tom Pakenham[259]

And would not that have been a blessing? George Orwell would have agreed with O'Connell!! Daniel O'Connell was vehemently opposed to violence and speaking *Gaelic*. One of his best known quotes: 'The altar of liberty totters when it is cemented only with blood'.[260] O'Connell was at school in France during the French Revolution, his early schooling had taken place in a "Hedge School," sheltering under a hedge or in a hay barn, as Catholic Irish were prohibited by the Penal Laws from being educated.

But the lessons in philosophy, from which he expected to derive so much profit, were shortly interrupted by the progress of the French Revolution, and in obedience to his uncle's orders he and Maurice quitted Douay in January of the following year. Forced for safety's sake to wear the tricolour stockade, but loathing himself for so doing, Daniel no sooner found himself on the Dover packet than he tore it from his hat and flung it into the sea. How intense, then, must have been his disgust to hear one of his fellow-passengers, a countryman of his own to boot, one John Sheares by name, destined himself a few years later to a traitor's death for his share in the Rebellion of '98, gloating over the details of the execution, which he had witnessed, of the unfortunate Louis XIV! For such brutalities O'Connell had no taste.

Robert Dunlop[261]

France's new republican regime seemed to teeter on the edge of catastrophe threatened by an armed coalition of European powers, and a series of dangerous domestic rebellions. Under these conditions, power passed into the hands of a dictatorial "Committee of Public Safety" that claimed sweeping emergency power. Tens of thousands of political opponents were executed, and many more perished in the repression of the provincial uprisings . . .

David A Bell[257]

Far from attaining Irish unity a successful French invasion would have been extremely divisive. In the Rebellion of 1798 as many as thirty thousand people are reputed to have lost their lives, and bitter divisions were created that last to this day. And it presented the Cromwellian Institute with an excuse to press ruthlessly ahead with its plans for the Parliamentary Union of Britain and Ireland.

THE MEDIA AND THE BOOK TRADE: CRONYISM

> The non-fiction list includes biography, history, reference, current affairs and packaging journalists and celebrities for the book market.
>
> Andrew Lowney Literary Agency, London[262]

It can be extremely difficult to get a book published unless one is a celebrity or a journalist. In my own case I found some of the more established publishers to be the most helpful, although they were unable to take on *Clippers* because they said they would be unable to do it justice. My initial scepticism was proved wrong when I discovered how much legwork it entailed to get the book into print. I was recommended an excellent book designer, which made all the difference. My experience with literary agents I will put down to experience. Of the two recommended one rejected my enquiry outright, while the other told me she might have been interested if my book was about cooking!

Shortly after *Clippers* was published it received a well-written and enthusiastic full-page review by Cian Gallagher in *Inshore Ireland*.[263] Four illustrations were featured: the lovely clipper barque *Spirit of the Age* under full sail; the Australian clipper packet *Sobroan* under full sail; South Street New York in packet days with the ships' bowsprits extending over the road, almost touching the upper floor windows of the offices and houses that line the street; and a lithographic print from the *Illustrated London News* of the City of Dublin Steamship Company's side-paddle steamer *RMS* (Royal Mail Steamer) *Ireland* on her maiden cross-channel voyage between Holyhead and Kingstown in October 1885 when she recorded 21 knots, a record for a steamship in those days.[254] Shortly afterwards I was interviewed by Marcus Connaughton on RTEs (Radio Telefis Eireann) *Seascapes* programme, and since then Marcus has interviewed me about *The Book of Tephi*.[63]

And then the surprises: Having sent a copy of *Clippers* to the literary editors of most of the national newspapers and journals in Britain and Ireland in addition to a number of yachting magazines, a publication that could be considered the ultimate book on the Tall Ships, the people who built them and those who sailed them, it was not reviewed once. In each case I had spoken to the literary editor before sending a copy of *Clippers* with a covering letter.

The biggest surprise was the *London Review of Books*. Having left in a copy of *Clippers* I contacted them to be told by e-mail they were not reviewing it. I then discovered that the *London Review of Books* had a bookshop so I phoned and asked if they sold books that were not necessarily reviewed by them, and was told they did. There the young man who said he was the assistant manager took *Clippers* and looked through it in a perfunctory manner before handing it back to me saying they would not be interested. This was the only case where a bookshop actually handed back a copy of *Clippers* without at least accepting it for perusal. The *London Review of Books* is unlikely to treat the pretentious Norman Grandee Colm Tóibín (Tobin) like that!!

The Irish newspapers were no more interested in a book published in Ireland than their British counterparts. It appears that the *Irish Times* is much more interested in British books. Richard Dawkins, a zoologist masquerading as a scientist, quotes *The Irish Times* in a paperback edition of his *The God Delusion*: 'He is surely one of the finest living writers in the English language.'

> No human inquiry can be called science unless it pursues its path through mathematical exposition and demonstration.
>
> Leonardo da Vinci[264]

When I questioned the lady at the *Sunday Independent* on the phone as to why they were not reviewing *Clippers* I was rather indignantly told 'we only have room for three'. Afterwards it was suggested that I contact the marine correspondent of the *Irish Times*, but when I remembered the larger than life sized mural of the psychopathic serial cop killer Michael Collins, presumably a hero of theirs, on their window in Tara Street Dublin, I thought better of it!!

It was then I decided to approach the *Belfast Telegraph* a second time. Clipper ships were among the first ships built by the Harland & Wolff shipyard, and a number of Belfast shipping companies operated clipper fleets. The largest vessel belonging to the Dublin shipping company of Messrs Richard Martin & Co was the 2,510-ton Harland & Wolff built four-masted barque *Fingal*. Martins' also operated the three-master *Dunboyne* a clipper that made many successful voyages under Captain John O'Neill. *Dunboyne*, renamed *af Chapman*, remains afloat in Stockholm harbor. Many of the captains of the Belfast operated clippers were from Rush and Skerries. The most successful clipper captain of all time was Captain Charles McDonnell of Glenariff, not far from Cushendall, County Antrim. When in command of the Canadian-built *Marco Polo* and Boston-built *James Baines* on the Australian run between Liverpool and Melbourne he logged a record four 24-hour passages of over 400 miles, and set the all-time top speed of a sailing ship of 21 knots.[254] McDonnell appears to have inherited his seafaring skills from his Danite-Phoenician ancestors!! After typing 'marine correspondent *Belfast Telegraph*' for a Google search, up came: "The Nine Pub Prizes of Northern Ireland!!"

When I gave a copy of *Clippers* to the librarian in the Library in Bray his attitude was quite different. He admired the book, commenting on the quality of the binding, print, paper and illustrations and graciously accepted a copy. The manager of the local bookshop Dubray, part of a chain, was not quite as enthusiastic. More recently, in December 2014, two books on display in Dubray's window caught my attention. The largest word of the title on the front cover of one was the vile Darwinist term "Humankind!!" On the front dust cover of the other, three well dressed "Revolutionary" women each with a rifle on their lap were pictured. Bookshops, at least the major ones in the Dublin area, are obsessed with portraying terrorist violence, the killing and maiming of our fellow Human Beings and those who perpetuate it, as laudatory.

> We are not fighting for integration, we are not fighting for separation, we are fighting for recognition as human beings.
> Malcolm X[265]

CHAPTER 10

PARLIAMENTARY UNION OF 1801: ETHNIC CLEANSING BY SLOW STRANGULATION

After a tedious passage of twenty-four hours, landed on the 20th in the morning, at Dunlary, four miles from Dublin, a city which much exceeded my expectation. The front of the Parliament house is grand . . . The apartments are spacious, elegant and convenient, much beyond the heap of confusion at Westminster, so inferior to the munificence to be looked for in the seat of the empire . . . I was struck with all these appearances of wealth which the capital of a thriving community may be supposed to exhibit . . . Dublin harbour crowded with ships moving to and fro to the capital. In Dublin signs of wealth abounded, although the government was inefficient, magistrates corrupt, prisons dens of infamy, and street brawls frequent. Music was cultivated, theatres patronized, newspapers published and booksellers thriving . . . Lord Charlemont's house in Dublin is equally elegant and convenient, the apartments are large, handsome and well disposed, containing some good pictures, particularly one by Rembrandt of Judas throwing money on the floor, with a strong expression of guilt and remorse; the whole group fine. In the same room is a portrait of Cæsar Borgia, by Titian. The library is the most elegant apartment of about forty by thirty, and of such a height as to form a pleasing proportion; the light is well managed, coming in from the cove of the ceiling, and has an exceeding good effect; at one end is a pretty ante-room, with a fine Venus de Medicis and at the other two small rooms, one a cabinet of pictures and antiquities, the other medals. In the collection also of Robert Fitzgerald, Esq., in Merrion Square, are several pieces which very well deserve a traveller's attention; it was the best I saw in Dublin.

Arthur Young[266]

In 1776 Arthur Young toured Ireland for the first time and found Dublin and the rest of the country to be rather prosperous. Young was made aware that even then talk about union with Britain was most unpopular, the great objection being the increasing the number of absentees. By going to England on a regular basis they would become residents; and they would educate their children there. Others would be elected, and thus by degrees, a vast portion of the kingdom now resident would be made absentees, which would be so great a drain on Ireland.[266]

> Had the events of 1798 and 1800 not taken place it is possible that the warring classes and creeds would have been brought together . . . But the horrors of the Rebellion, and the treachery and corruption which accompanied the Act of Union, not only stayed the progress of reconciliation and appeasement, but perpetuated and intensified class hatred and sectarian rancour.
>
> E A D'Alton[267]

The nefarious Act of Union of 1800 was The Great Fraud carried out on the Native Irish by the Cromwellian Institute. When one considers how the members of the Irish DOT were bribed to vote themselves out of existence there can be only one conclusion: The 1800 Act of Union between Britain and Ireland was a Criminal Act!!! Even William Hague in *William Pitt the Younger*[268] admits that Secret Service money was used for bribery.

The Act came into being on January 1, 1801. It was an unmitigated disaster for Ireland. Dublin, one of the leading capital cities of Europe, suffered an exodus of people far in excess of what had been predicted, and Ireland's leading city quickly became a shadow of its former self. The exodus of the landlord class, their servants, professionals and crafts people could be described as a stampede!! And with them went priceless works of art, as well as splendid pieces of gold and silver the work of Irish goldsmiths and silversmiths, as well as fine handcrafted cabinets, furniture and clocks. No 1 the Royal Crescent museum in Georgian Bath is furnished with mostly Irish furniture!!

The value of property plummeted and the fine Georgian houses that adorned the streets and squares of city were soon worthless. An example of how property lost its value was Mornington House, 21 Upper Merrion Street, bought by the Wellesley family in the early 1790s for £5,000. In 1810 it was sold for £500 and shortly afterwards changed hands for even less. Some of the finest Georgian houses were in Gardiner Street where a family of four to six and their servants would have lived comfortably in the 1790s. When it proved impossible to find a buyer for them they were let. By 1840 they had become tenements with up to 200 people living in one house, and remained so for over a century. Gardiner Street would become the synonym for some of the worst slums in Dublin.

Dublin's descent from Georgian splendour to Georgian slums was spectacular. In the closing years of the nineteenth century Dublin had the worst slums in Britain or Ireland, nearly all in former Georgian houses. Today it is difficult to envisage the great splendour that was Georgian Dublin. And the countryside fared no better. With the exodus of the landlord class to London their tenants were increasingly exploited to provide them with the means of living in the style to which they became accustomed. The Irish were represented by 100 MPs, many hostile to the aspirations of the People, helpless against the might of the other 558, most of whom were viciously anti-Catholic and anti-Semitic.

During a speech in the Cromwellian Institute in 1834, Daniel O'Connell listed the reasons why the Union had proved a curse to Ireland: increased indebtedness to Britain, increased taxation, an increase in the number of absentee landlords, the absolute power of tyrannical landlords resulting in an increase in the misery and suffering of the poor, manufacturing decayed, diminished energy in the cities and towns, and less meat was consumed while there was an increase in the number of cattle exports to England. The wretched conditions of the millions of peasants were described by the French writer De Beaumont and the German Kohl as well as in the Dover Commission Report.[267]

The Union was supposed to bring Ireland and Britain closer, but for most of the 19th century competition between the countries increased and it proved difficult to get support or funding from Parliament or elsewhere in Britain for Irish industry and projects. The Great Famine was a disaster waiting to happen, and any help given was too little too late. During the Famine wheat and other foodstuffs were being removed from Ireland, some protected by the military. The excuse was made that Irish peasants did not know how to use grain because they were so dependent on the potato; probably so. And whose fault was that? Was it not ancestors of many of the Native Irish who brought wheat-growing to this part of the world in the first place; our ancestors and their kinsfolk had supplied the Greeks with grain from Scythia. Scythia covered most of what is now known as Ukraine.

The ruling elite in Ireland as well as in any other free-market liberal democracy are completely out of touch with the lot of ordinary people, while blaming the poor for their problems; poverty in Ireland has for centuries been blamed on the priests!!

> If I didn't have red eyes and an Irish accent I could be purely American and I wouldn't have to put up with Professors tormenting me with Yeats and Joyce and the Irish Literary Renaissance and how clever and witty the Irish are and what a beautifully green country it is though priest-ridden and poor with a population ready to vanish from the face of the earth due to Puritanical sexual repression and what have you to say to that, Mr McCourt?
>
> Frank McCourt[128]

The Oxford History Professor Roy Foster and the 8th Earl of Longford Tom Pakenham are judges for the Christopher Ewart-Biggs memorial prize. The opposing Orange Order and *Sinn Féin*–IRA, whose roots can be traced to the 1798 Rebellion, are by far the greatest cause of division in Ireland!!

> The objectives of the prize are to recognize work that promotes and encourages reconciliation in Ireland, a greater understanding between the peoples of Britain and Ireland, or closer co-operation between the partners of the European Community.
>
> www.ewartbiggsprize.org.uk[269]

At the beginning of Her Majesty Queen Elizabeth II's visit to Ireland in 2011 a spokesperson for the British-Irish Association, no doubt republican, interviewed on the BBC's *Today* programme, said the Queen's visit was premature. It was not premature; it was long overdue and proved to be a great success!! The ruling elite have always been out of touch with the People.

…many Gaelic Leaguers were privately active in the celebrations attending the centenary of the 1798 rebellion, nationalists in general were vocally pro-Boer, and Queen Victoria's lamentably ill-timed visit to Ireland in 1900 served to polarise opinion for months before her arrival.

Ruth Dudley Edwards[270]

The Gaelic League and the Gaelic Athletic Association had, like *Sinn Féin*, come under the control of the IRB. It gave this small group of ultra-Nationalists considerable power. Today ruthless revolutionaries like the IRB would be described as Nazi or neo-Nazi. It is Evil to celebrate a rebellion in which such a large number of people died and which generated so much suffering, division and hatred!! As for the Gaelic League, the vast majority of the Irish People had no interest whatsoever in learning what for them would be a new language. "A love of The Language" it is called, words that are nearly always voiced at any event where "Irish" as it is now called, is the medium of communication. Language was used as a political weapon throughout the twentieth century, particularly against the children.[226] If the zealots only loved their neighbour half as much as they loved The Language, Ireland would have had a much more peaceful 20th century!!

Conor Cruise O'Brien boasted that he remained sitting for the Royal Toast when a student at Trinity College Dublin.[271]

> Edward the 6th Earl, displayed a different brand of bravery by refusing to join the Corps at Eton, which no one had apparently done before and he infuriated his fellow Anglo-Irish by refusing to stand for "God Save the King" at Dublin Horse Show and becoming an ardent supporter of the new Irish State.
>
> Eliza Pakenham[140]

> Don't be surprised if I demur, for be advised.
> My passport's green.
> No glass of ours was ever raised
> To toast the Queen.
>
> Seamus Heany[272]

It was the very combination of the monarch's popularity and its official association with the constitution that made it such a perceived threat. The popularity of the monarchy was an embarrassment and had to be refuted. Instead, the hostility to monarchy that nationalist elites vigorously promulgated enforced on the population was shrouded in an ideology in which the monarchy bore the blame for the action of British politicians in Ireland; this was intentionally designed to mirror the admiration for the monarchy in Britain which was esteemed for being synonymous with the imperial success of the nineteenth century.

Queen Victoria visited Ireland on four occasions during her long reign. These visits occurred in 1849, 1853, 1861 and 1900 – she was met with popular enthusiasm that suppressed all expectations and generally unsettled hostile nationalist sentiment. Around four hundred volunteers, including John MacBride (1868–1916) volunteered for military service with the Boers . . . more than seventy times that number 28,000 Irishmen, signed up to fight with the British Army against the Boers. Until the end of WW I a career in the British Army was viewed as an acceptable choice in Ireland.

Richard J Kelly[273]

CHAPTER 11

POLITICIANS: ENEMIES OF THE PEOPLE

The name of a politician – a party man! Less than nothing; a mere
void without as much as a shadow of responsibility – cast into it
from that light in which move the masses of men who work, who
deal in things and face the realities – not the words – of this life.

Joseph Conrad[274]

It is striking that in our supposedly liberal twentieth century the
Government faced with a similar problem had little difficulty in
convincing itself and persuading Parliament to abolish jury trial
for such offences in Northern Ireland. Peel and his colleagues do
not seem to have considered this. They were too deeply rooted
in traditional respect for the right of trial by jury even for a
seditious Irish peasant.

Douglas Hurd[275]

Absolutely outrageous, even for a bigoted former member of the Cromwellian Institute's DOT, and now of its House of Robber Barons. What was
the seditious crime the Irish peasants were judged guilty of? Temperance and
demanding Repeal of the nefarious Act of Union of 1800!!! Hurd continues:

On 24 June [1828] their leader, Daniel O'Connell, announced
that he would stand for County Clare himself . . . The scene
entirely changed. The Irish, like British, elections were famous
for drunkenness, disorder and fraud. Worse, Ireland was full of
murder and all manner of violent crime. By contrast in County
Clare the Catholic Association deployed peaceful strength as a
political machine, powerfully backed by the local priesthood.

Douglas Hurd[275]

In Carrick Street Kells, Kells of the Book, there is a hall with the following
over the door: 'Kells Silver Band, Founded 1843, Hall opened 1847'. The band
was one of many created as part of Daniel O'Connell's and Father Theobald

Mathew's Great Temperance Campaign.[276] The bands were known as Temperance Bands. In 1849 Fr Mathew visited the United States. New York welcomed him on July 2:

> Mayor Woodhull, a non-Catholic, placed City Hall at his disposal. For two weeks the crowds besieged its chambers practically eliminating all city business. Vice-President Millard Fillmore was one of the callers. In Washington, President Zachary Taylor invited Fr. Mathew to dine at the White House. Congress gave the humble Capuchin friar its highest honours. The House unanimously admitted him to a seat on the floor of the House. The Senate admitted him within the bar of the Senate, an honour given previously only to Lafayette . . . For two years, despite grave illness, Father Mathew blazed a trail of success across the United States. Boston, Philadelphia, Cincinnati, Little Rock, New Orleans, and many places in Florida, Georgia, Tennessee, Virginia, Delaware and other areas heard his extortions and were won to the practice of total abstinence. Everywhere there were crowds and enthusiastic receptions. When he left the USA in 1851, strong Temperance societies carried on his work. 'I thank heaven I have been instrumental in adding to the ranks of temperance over 600,000 in the United States.' he wrote. Mathew has a statue dedicated to him in Salem, Massachusetts.
> wikipedia.org/wiki/Theobald_Mathew [276]

Hurd's reference to a seditious Irish peasantry is presumably a reference to the people who attended meetings of the Repeal Association, addressed by Daniel O'Connell, demanding the repeal of the Act of Union. O'Connell argued for the re-creation of an independent Kingdom of Ireland to govern itself, with Queen Victoria as Queen of Ireland.[261] The largest was the "Monster Meeting" held at the Hill of Tara on Tuesday 15 August 1843, the feast of the assumption of the Blessed Virgin in the Catholic Calendar:

> . . . 1,300 carriages paid toll at Phibsborough. There were 10,000 horsemen in attendance. Many camped there the night before. Close to some million people of orderly demeanour, confident,

non-rowdy, gentle, courtesy displayed towards women and children. Music from assembled temperance bands. (Father Matthew's spectacular revivalist Temperance Movement was almost a subsidiary of the Repeal Association)

Robert Dunlop [261]

What does Hurd think "Orange" (Sir John) Peel, as Daniel O'Connell labelled him, should have done to the seditious Irish peasants? It would have required a large concentration camp to house over a million people! And if that had happened it would have predated Andersonville:

The notorious Confederate prisoner-of-war camp known today as the forerunner of the German Concentration camps of the following century, in which Yankee soldiers died like flies under appalling conditions.

James Gilligan [243]

O'Connell arranged an even bigger meeting for Sunday October 8 at Clontarf. Peel made it illegal by issuing a proclamation on the day before declaring it to be an unlawful assembly. O'Connell called it off. His enemies were delighted.

Lord Clarendon, formerly George Villiers saying that under fear of collision or prosecution he will eat dirt and more dirt and try to cram the same unsavoury paludal down the throats of all the followers he can re-dupe. His milk and wateriness and his feder-ation and his anglomania and all the rest of his recent garbage . . . In any other county but Ireland a leader like O'Connell would at once lose all chances of future prestige and profit, but the people were so blarney-ridden and priest-ridden that no such thing would probably occur . . .

When the secret dispatches of Government are one day opened for the public, it will be known what object was to be served in postponing the proclamation till a collision between the military and the people was all but inevitable. With our pres-ent information [1900] it is impossible to avoid the conclusion that those responsible for the manoeuvre really contemplated the perpetuation of another Peterloo on a more extended scale. *"Pour la canaille faut la mitraille,"* hummed Wellington, as he read the Government proclamation with evident satisfaction. [The Duke of Wellington's wife the Duchess of Wellington, was Kitty Pakenham] That such a calamity, to call it by no worse name, was avoided thanks are due alone to O'Connell. Never had he done more to prove his incontestable right to lead the Irish nation, and the sincerity of the doctrines he preached, never more to advance the cause of Irish freedom, and to earn the gratitude of mankind, than he did by his conduct on this occasion.

Robert Dunlop[261]

A week after the cancellation of the Clontarf meeting, Orange Peel followed up his attacks on the Repeal Association when the Cromwellian Institute issued writs for the arrest of O'Connell, his son John, and his chief colleagues, in addition to two unknown parish priests, Father Tyrrell and Father Tierney. They were charged with conspiring to create discontent and disaffection among the liege subjects of the Queen, and with contriving, 'by means of intimidation and the demonstration of great physical force to affect changes to be made in the government, laws, and constitution of this realm'.[261]

Never in the annals of jury-packing in Ireland had the necessity of procuring a conviction led to such an outrageous misuse of the powers reposed in the Crown as on the present occasion . . . On 12th February, [1844] the jury, after a little decent delay, returned a verdict of guilty of unlawful and seditious conspiracy . . . sentence was postponed till the beginning of next term. In the interval O'Connell, after once more appealing to the people not to allow themselves to be tempted to break the peace, but to act peaceably, quietly, and legally, proceeded to London . . . when he entered the House of Commons he was received with an outburst of applause so spontaneous and hearty as must have conveyed to Peel a painful warning of the dangerous ground on which he was standing.

Robert Dunlop[261]

On May 30, O'Connell was sentenced to imprisonment for twelve months, to pay a fine of £2,000 and to find surety for his good behaviour during the next seven years, himself in £5,000 and two others each in £2,500. Later that day he and his fellow "conspirators" were removed to Richmond Bridewell where a surprise awaited them. They were provided with comfortable quarters almost as many visitors as they liked and the best of food brought in by their relatives and friends. An appeal to the House of Lords was successful, with the Law members deciding that the judgement pronounced in Ireland be reversed.

> ... the Lords achieved a victory over their own prejudices deserving the high encomium passed on it by Montalembert. Besides, there can be no question that Lord Denman's remark, 'that if such practices as had prevailed in the case were to continue, trial by jury in Ireland would become a mockery, a delusion, and a snare,' was sound law as well as sound sense.
>
> Robert Dunlop[261]

By 1945, Daniel O'Connell was the most influential and outspoken critic of American slavery, and refused to go to America as long slavery existed. He also refused money for the Repeal association that was in any way tainted by slavery. O'Connell befriended and became a great inspiration to the African-American escaped slave, abolitionist, social reformer, orator and author Frederick Douglass,[277, 278] who published his first autobiography: *Narrative of the Life of Frederick Douglass, an American Slave* in 1845.[279] Douglass's book became a bestseller and was influential in supporting abolition.

> Frederick Augustus Washington Bailey was born into slavery at Talbot County, Maryland . . . Years later, after escaping to the North he took the surname Douglass . . . Douglass's mother died when he was about ten. After [Aaron, overseer in Wye House Plantation] Anthony died, the boy was given to Lucretia Auld, wife of Thomas Auld, who sent him to serve Thomas's brother Hugh Auld in Baltimore. When Douglass was about twelve years old, Hugh Auld's wife Sofia started teaching him the alphabet, although Maryland state law prohibited teaching slaves to read. Douglass described Sofia Auld as a kind and tender-hearted

woman, who treated the boy the way one human being, ought to treat another. When Hugh Auld discovered her activity, he strongly disapproved, saying that if a slave learned to read, he would become dissatisfied with his condition and desire freedom ... In his autobiography Douglass related how he learned to read from white children in the neighbourhood and by observing the writings of men with whom he worked ... when Douglass was hired out to William Freeland, he taught other slaves on the plantation to read the *New Testament* at a weekly Sunday school. As word spread, the interest among slaves in learning to read was so great that in any week more than 40 slaves would attend lessons. For about six months, their study went relatively unnoticed. While Freeland remained complacent about their activities, other plantation owners became incensed about their slaves being educated. One Sunday they burst in on the gathering armed with clubs and stones, to disperse the congregation permanently ...

en.wikipedia.org/wiki/Frederick_Douglass [277]

After he escaped to New York he became involved in the abolitionist movement and because of his oratorical skills became a prominent speaker at their meetings.

Douglass's friends and mentors feared that the publicity would draw the attention of his ex-owner, Hugh Auld who might try to get his "property" back. They encouraged Douglas to tour Ireland, as many former slaves had done. Douglas set sail on the *Cambria* for Liverpool on August 16, 1845. He travelled in Ireland as the Irish Potato famine was beginning.

en.wikipedia.org/wiki/Frederick_Douglass [277]

The feeling of freedom from American racial discrimination amazed Douglass:

Eleven days and a half gone and I have crossed three thousand miles of the perilous deep. Instead of a democratic government, I am under a monarchical government. Instead of the bright blue sky of America, I am covered with the soft grey fog of the Emerald Isle. I breathe, and lo! The chattel becomes a man. I gaze around in vain for one who will question my equal humanity, claim me as a slave, or offer me an insult. I employ a cab—I am seated beside white people—I reach the hotel—I enter the same door—I am shown into the same parlour—I dine at the same table—and no one is offended . . . I find myself regarded and treated at every turn with the kindness and deference paid to white people. When I go to church, I am met by no upturned nose and scornful lip to tell me, *"We don't allow no niggers in here!"*

Frederick Douglass[279]

O'Connell was to be a great inspiration, and in September he attended a Repeal meeting in Dublin. Douglass was mesmerised by O'Connell, saying that he was at his best when he spoke out against slavery saying 'I feel grateful to him, for his voice has made American slavery shake to its center. I am determined wherever I go, and whatever position I may fill to speak with grateful emotions of Mr O'Connell's labours.'[279]

Throughout his life Douglass, had linked that individual experience with social reform, and like other Christian abolitionists, he followed practices such as abstaining from tobacco, alcohol and other substances that he believed corrupted body and soul.

Laurence Fenton[280]

Plaques commemorating Douglass's visit were installed in the Imperial Hotel Cork and unveiled on 31 August 2012, and on the façade of Waterford City Hall, unveiled on 7 October 2013.[280] Probably the greatest tribute to Daniel O'Connell is in Belfast's Folk Museum. It simply says "He was a Pacifist."

Peel was not moved by emotional compassion. He believed in sense, not sentiment. He was not persuaded by the suffering of boys in factories. He showed no interest in the anti-slavery movement. He supported the 1834 Poor Law and the workhouses which it established. He despised the sentimentality of

George IV in pressing for mercy to be shown to criminals facing the gallows.

Douglas Hurd[275]

The Welsh Wizard, David Lloyd George. In late 1920:

Lloyd George began with discussions with Patrick Maylette and soon afterwards had talks with Joseph Clune, Archbishop of Perth (and uncle of the unfortunate Conor Clune who was so brutally done to death by Captain Hardy).These gentlemen soon found Lloyd George to be an extremely slippery character, a will o' the wisp who said one thing one day and the complete opposite the next. One minute he was adamant that he would never talk to rebels unless they surrendered unconditionally; the next day he would negotiate with them on equal terms without preconditions. One day he would deal with Collins; the next he would insist that Collins must be handed over. One day he would be sweetness and light; the next, some slight, real or imagined, would send the fiery Welshman back behind the barricades once more. The news from Ireland was contradictory and confusing, and whenever Lloyd George thought he detected a wavering in the enemy's ranks he would dig in his heels again. The well meaning intervention of *Sinn Féin* pacifists Roger Sweetman and Father Flanagan gave the impression that the rebels were at the point of caving in, and induced the Prime Minister to insist that the Volunteers must surrender their arms before talks could be considered . . . as a result the war would continue for a further six months, escalating in violence and atrocities.

James MacKay[190]

A politician who had a particularly deleterious effect on Ireland was Sean MacBride,[281] son of Major John MacBride, an IRB member, who fought with the Irish Transvaal Brigade alongside the Boers in the Boer War. His mother was the weird Maud Gonne, Yeats's muse. Although not a member of the volunteers he happened to be in Dublin and took part in the 1916 Rebellion.

He signed the Proclamation of the "Irish Republic" and was one of those executed.

Sean MacBride was born in Paris, and French was his first language. He came to Ireland shortly after his father's death and finished his schooling before joining Fianna Eireann and subsequently the IRA. He took a law degree at UCD and resumed his IRA activities in the mid twenties. In 1927 he became the IRA's Director of Intelligence, becoming its Chief of Staff in 1936.[281] In 1946 he founded the republican socialist party *Clann na Poblachta*. Having won 10 seats in the 1948 election he joined a coalition government under the lacklustre lawyer John A Costello, and presumable persuaded Costello to declare an Irish Republic. On Easter Monday 18 April 1949 the Irish Free State became a Republic and left the British Commonwealth of Nations, even though it was unconstitutional by any stretch of the imagination even by Irish political standards, having not even been mentioned in the previous general election. Cardinal D'Alton, Primate of all Ireland, in Armagh apparently pleaded with the politicians not to leave the British Commonwealth. D'Alton was the nephew of Canon E A D'Alton who wrote the authorative six-volume History of Ireland. Although a schoolboy at the time I knew nothing about it. It was only years later that I discovered how Ireland became a Republic against the wishes of the People.

> The moment the dinner [Commonwealth conference of lawyers at Ottawa] was over Costello did a very rash and ill-considered thing. He called the reporters around him and announced that Eire would hereafter be known as the Irish Republic . . . The Dáil ratified Costello's unilateral declaration. We had to. He had made us look foolish enough in the eyes of the world without the stupidity of disavowing our Prime Minister. The reason for Costello's abrupt action has never been completely explained. It probably was the pay-off to MacBride for his support . . . Its tragic consequence was to further postpone the end of Partition as de Valera had foreseen.
>
> Robert Briscoe[165]

Early in June 1921, Tom Casement, brother of Roger, contacted his old friend Jan Christiaan Smuts [who was in London] . . . On

14 June 1921 de Valera met Casement and said he was prepared to meet the South African Statesman if Tom could arrange it. During the conversation Casement told de Valera that Smuts could not stand for an Irish Republic as he was Prime Minister of a Dominion. 'De Valera frankly told me that a Republic was out of the question. All he wanted was a treaty between two nations. I saw that point and told him I would put it to Smuts.' Interestingly de Valera would afterwards deny this. Needless to say, there is no mention of it in de Valera's authorised biography by the Earl of Longford and T.P. O'Nell.

James MacKay[190]

In the second place, it is quite clear, now that Southern Ireland has separated itself altogether from the Crown, that the maintenance of the position of Northern Ireland becomes all the more obligatory upon us. It is evident that a gulf has been opened, a ditch has been dug, between Northern and Southern Ireland which invests partition with a greater permanency and reality than it ever had before.

Winston S Churchill[282]

Churchill had been a staunch supporter of Popular Irish Nationalism: Home Rule. By declaring the Irish Free State a Republic, Costello and MacBride distanced the 26-county Southern Ireland even more from the northern six counties, making further accommodation with the Unionists extremely unlikely. It was a green light for the *Sinn Féin*-IRA men of violence to resume the terror campaign aimed at achieving an all-Ireland Republic. By the late 1950s MacBride had lost his seat in the DOT *Dáil Eireann*. He subsequently became a founding member of Amnesty International and served as its International chairman.[281] An organisation that welcomes a dysfunctional misfit and former terrorist leader as one of its leaders is unfit for purpose!! In 1974 McBride was awarded the Dynamite Peace Prize, and in 1975–1976 the Lenin Peace Prize.

On April 15, 1999 there was a service of Thanksgiving for the life of Oliver Cromwell in the crypt of the Cromwellian Institute. One of speakers was Ian

Paisley who gave one his usual lengthy anti-Catholic, anti-Papist and, on this occasion, anti-Royalist diatribes:[283]

At any great crisis in a nation's history, oftentimes for a time, the evidence of the sovereignty and supremacy of Almighty God is concealed . . . The Jesuits, the shock troops of the Vatican, directed across Europe in the middle of the seventeenth century, brought a resurgence of Popery, recovering part of the ground lost in the Reformation. In Germany, France, the Low Countries, Spain and even Italy the Counter-Reformation of Rome gained or regained ground. It was imagined that the protestant faith would be overthrown in the British Isles, and the liberties of the Reformation would be lost forever. Europe became awash with priests, Jesuits, friars and monks. The fight in Cromwell's day was the battle against the Papacy. The Royal House of the Stuarts sided with Rome and was broken in the conflict . . . Rome always blackens those employed in the furtherance of Heaven's purpose against her . . . No one has suffered more by such diabolical treatment than Oliver Cromwell . . . The years between 1642 and 1669 demonstrated that the alarms of the puritans were solidly based. Charles II, who, as his mother Henrietta Maria declared to Louis XIV, 'had abjured the heresy of his education, and was reconciled to the church of Rome,' composed a treatise to prove that there could be but one Church of Christ upon earth, and that was the Church of Rome . . . After his death and the return of the perfidious Stuarts, Oliver Cromwell was blackened beyond recognition. The Roman Church in Ireland furnished the tarring and feathering process . . . The Protestant Reformation interest was ill-served by the Stuart kings . . . Since the time of the glorious Protestant Reformation, in days of spiritual decline, God has raised up single champions to call the nation back to the old paths of truth and righteousness when the darkness of apostasy has invaded the Church and State. God has not left himself without a witness. Such a one was Oliver Cromwell.

Ian Paisley[283]

Paisley quoted from three apparent book reviews of Antonia Fraser's *Cromwell: Our Chief of Men* in his speech, repeating the most anti-Irish one from the *Sunday Telegraph*. None of the reviews mentioned that Fraser was a descendent of Captain Henry Pakenham of Abbott's Dragoons, raised specially for the invasion of Ireland, and who would have taken part in the massacres at Drogheda and Wexford!! Henry Pakenham is mentioned as a footnote in Fraser's *Cromwell*. Cromwell, himself, left Ireland after Drogheda and Wexford, well before large-scale ethnic cleansing, carried out on his orders and those of Parliament, got under way. Paisley:[283]

> *The Times Educational Supplement*: 'Lady Antonia Fraser has sought to "humanise" Cromwell, to bring out the nature of the man himself rather than seeking to relate him to the "political and social trends of the age." Partly as a result, Cromwell's family plays a far greater role in this life than hitherto, and this, it seems to me is both justifiable and successful. The most notable achievement of this biography is its absolute fairness. Lady Antonia is at her best in the detailed analysis of particular, critical episodes, especially Cromwell's massacre of the Irish Catholics at Drogheda and Wexford in 1649. There is a real attempt to present the man, warts and all, and to judge him by his own values and those of his day. Readers of Cromwell will be rewarded with a book that is clear, scholarly and fair. This book should finally destroy any lingering stereotyped view of Cromwell as the "dissembling perjured Villain", cold, scheming and hypocritical.'
>
> The *Sunday Times* says: 'Lady Antonia wishes us to know that Cromwell was no tyrant, was not ambitious, had a bursting conscious, and was civilized. The evidence she has assembled is overwhelming.'
>
> The *Sunday Telegraph* says: 'Lady Antonia sees, better than anyone has, the complexities of his character, the different strains in it. The author puts forward a cool, and convincing, defence of Cromwell in Ireland, which will be a surprise to Irish readers brought up on the legend rather than the facts.'
>
> Ian Paisley[283]

Paisley repeats the last sentence in another part of the speech. All psychopaths have complex characters!! Telegraph Newspapers have always been blatantly anti-Irish, and no notice should be taken of what their *Illetterato* tell us about Ireland!! A heading in the *Daily Telegraph* April 21, 2015: '*Magna Carta* for every school to teach children about freedom.' As for *The Times Educational Supplement* and the *Sunday Times;* anything to do with Machevil Rupert Murdoch PPP is suspect!! Paisley's real message: He and his Orange Unionists are far more republican than the Green Fenians, who do not even know why they are republican!!!

The Baron and the Ballawán: John Reid, Baron Reid of Cardowan and George Galloway, Ballawán. Reid, born near Glasgow in 1947 of working class parents, joined the Young Communist League at the age of twenty five, the beginning of a political career that would, in time, permit him to tick all the boxes of Cromwellian Totalitarianism: autocracy, bureaucracy, democracy, plutocracy, hypocrisy, militarism, republicanism, capitalism, and communism. At university he [John Reid] became a member of the Communist Party of Great Britain; in 1979 he became a research officer for the Labour Party in Scotland, from 1983 to 1985 he was a political adviser to Labour leader Neil Kinnock, and from 1986 to 1987 he was Scottish Organiser of Trade Unionists for Labour; in 1987 he was elected to the Cromwellian Institute; in May 2007 it was alleged that Reid had given up alcohol as a consequence of having harassed a fellow Labour Member in the early 1990s when drunk; during the Bosnian War, Reid struck up a friendship with the Serb rebel leader, Radovan Karadžić, later to be indicted as a war-criminal. Reid admitted he spent three days at a luxury Geneva lakeside hotel as a guest of Karadžić in 1993. This was during the period (April 1992–July 1995) in which the crimes for which Karadžić was indicted were committed; Reid had seven Cabinet posts [Peoples' Commissar] while Tony Blair was C-in-C, followed by Minister for the Armed Forces, Minister for Transport, Secretary of State for Scotland, Secretary of State for Northern Ireland; Secretary of State for Health; Secretary of State for Defence [War], Secretary of State for the Home Department (Home Secretary), creating 8,000 more prison places within 100 days of starting; in March 2003 Robin Cook resigned as Leader of the DOT due to his objections to the legality of Britain's involvement in the Iraq War. John Reid was appointed to take over on 4 April to ensure continued support for the war, he voted against a motion that the case had not yet been made for war against Iraq.[284]

> In September 2006, Reid addressed Muslims in a run-down part
> of East London, warning them that fanatics were looking to
> groom and brainwash children for suicide bombings. During the
> speech he was confronted and barracked by Abu Izzadeen, also
> known as Omar or Trevor Brooks. Mr Brooks is a leader of the
> UK-banned Al Ghurabaa, an offshoot of the terrorist supporting
> Al-Mujahitoun – a man who many accuse of glorifying terrorism
> and inciting racial hatred.
>
> en.wikipedia.org/wiki/John_Reid[284]

According to George Galloway, Reid is an accomplished singer and guitar player and 'taught a whole generation of Labour activists, including yours truly, the entire IRA songbook'.[285] Astonishing, and inexcusable for anyone to be celebrating the killing and maiming of their fellow Human Beings, particularly politicians celebrating the murder of their slaves: Police Officers. One of the vilest IRA songs is the *Boys of Kilmichael* celebrating the "Macroom Massacre:"

> On November 28, 1920 a patrol of seventeen Auxiliary Police
> Officers and one temporary constable were ambushed at Kilmi-
> chael, not far from Macroom in County Cork. By that evening
> sixteen were lying dead on the road, one was in a coma and the
> remaining survivor was being interrogated by the IRA. Of the
> two cadets who survived the ambush one Frederic Henry Forde,
> was badly wounded with severe fractures of the skull appar-
> ently caused by an axe or rifle butt. The other, Cecil Gutrie, had
> managed to escape and had nearly returned to Macroom when
> he was captured by the IRA. After being held for two days he was
> either shot or died from his wound, and was buried secretly in a
> bog. His pregnant wife was in Macroom at the time. She did not
> recover his body until years later. She never remarried.
>
> Macroom Ambush[286]

The following is a verse from the *Boys of Kilmichael:*

> And here's to the boys of Kilmichael
> Who feared not the might of the foe
> The day they marched into battle
> And laid the Black and Tans low

And it is even worse!! Reid oversaw the final stages of the transformation of the RUC into the Police Service of Northern Ireland.[284] The RUC's punishment for having had the temerity to defend themselves against the IRA!!!

In January 2006 Commissar-in-Chief Tony Blair's Peoples' Commissar for War John Reid, sent 3,300 troops (slaves of the Cromwellian Institute) to Helmund province in Afghanistan saying 'we would be perfectly happy to leave in three years without firing a shot because our job is to protect the construction'.[284] On March 19, 2006 Reid contradicted Iraq's C-in-C Ayad Allawi when he said Iraq was in the grip of civil war.[284] On Wednesday 29 October 2014 an article in the Guardian by Peter McKenna on troop withdrawals from Afghanistan:

> As an anti-war activist, I see no reason to celebrate the British troop withdrawal from Helmand province, although this has happily brought to an end a costly chapter in the 13-year campaign, with the vast majority of 453 troops who died in the conflict losing their lives fighting the Taliban insurgency in Helmund . . . Private security firms, arms dealers, people smugglers, cheque-book journalists and other merchants of war must be bitterly regretting the end of what has been a very lucrative business enterprise.
>
> Peter McKenna[287]

In December 2013 a Royal Marine sergeant was sentenced to life in jail by one of the Cromwellian Institutes legal functionaries for killing a wounded Taliban fighter. Part of the report in the *Guardian* on December 6, 2013:

> Privately in military circles there is unease and frustration that Blackman was given what many would consider a harsh

sentence, and have huge sympathy for him and his family. Blackman's commanding officer, Lt Colonel Simon Chapman, said he would continue to support the marine. He said 'Fundamentally he is not a bad man. In fact, in almost every respect, he is a normal citizen tainted only by the impact of war'.

Steven Morris & Richard Norton-Taylor[288]

Can the same be said about the scheming criminals who sent Blackman and the other troops to Afghanistan? Following the expenses scandal Reid was requested to repay £2,731.88 but chose to pay £7,336,51; a later offer to refund £4,604.63 was accepted.[284] In September 2007 Reid became Chairman of Celtic Football Club. Most appropriate for a man who taught his fellow Glasgow Labourites IRA songs!!!

The author made the mistake of activating the Print icon when viewing Galloway's details on Wikipedia:[285] Out poured 48 pages of verbiage!! Apparently Galloway believes in the "armed struggle", saying that he is a revolutionary and supports the armed struggle where there is no alternative.[289] The ordinary people of Ireland have had enough of "armed struggle" to last them a thousand years, to paraphrase the Vietnamese Ninh Bao who served in the North Vietnamese Army during the Vietnam War:[290]

> After the battle no one mentioned Battalion 27 anymore, though numerous souls of ghosts and devils were born in that deadly defeat. They were still loose, wandering in every corner and bush in the jungle, drifting along the stream, refusing to depart for the Other World. From then on it was called the jungle of Screaming Souls. Just hearing the name whispered was enough to send chills down the spine . . . The life of the B 3 Infantrymen after the Paris Agreement was a series of long, suffering days, followed by months of retreating and months of counter-attacking, withdrawal, then counter-attack. Victory after victory, withdrawal after withdrawal. The path of war seemed endless, desperate, and leading nowhere . . . I'm not afraid of dying, but this killing and shooting just goes on, forever . . . We were up to our ankles in blood, splashing through blood. I used to do anything to avoid stabbing with bayonets or bashing skulls in with my rifle butt,

but now I've got used to it. And to think that as a child I wanted to take orders and go into a seminary . . . But war was a world with no home, no roof, no comforts. A miserable journey, of endless drifting. War was a world without real men, without real women, without feeling . . . Desertions were rife throughout the regiment at the time, as though soldiers were being vomited out, emptying the insides of whole platoons . . . But he knew it wasn't true that young Vietnamese loved war. Not true at all. If war came they would fight. And fight courageously. But that didn't mean they loved fighting . . . No. The ones who loved war were not the young men, but the others like the politicians, middle-aged men with fat bellies and short legs. Not the ordinary people. The recent years of war had brought enough suffering and pain to last them a thousand years.

Ninh Bao[290]

Glasgow seems to make a habit of creating division and hate which spills over into Ireland!!

. . . at an early age Bonar Law became a member of the Glasgow Parliamentary Debating Association which held its meetings at the Assembly Rooms in Bath Street. It was a mock Parliament founded by some enthusiastic young men in 1876 . . . Bonar Law devoted much of his most vigorous invective to an attack on the whole principle of Home Rule . . . Bonar Law threw himself heart and soul into the support of the Ulster cause . . . Bonar Law was now committed to the most extreme course . . . The rally at Blenheim Palace was attended by some forty peers, including – to the fury of the Irish Nationalists – the Duke of Norfolk who was generally regarded as the leading Catholic layman of England.

Robert Blake[186]

The Hewbrew Queen of Ireland Teia Tephi's opinion of debate 2,598 years ago:

Moreover, meseemed that I
Was little advised of these things, lacking strength to descry

Wherein I might choose; and therefore I watched long time their debate,
Till it rose in stormwinds of fury and howled in tempests of hate.[62,63]

As the rich get even richer and the vast majority of the people get poorer, Anton Chekhov's self-styled "Intelligentsia" have a way of justifying their position as the controllers of everyone else: Creative writing and debating!! Debating never solves problems; it merely creates them. Debating causes division and hatred, perpetuates lies, and can be the catalyst for violence. But it keeps the Chattering Class busy!! One of the most successful debating organisations goes by the pretentious name *Intelligence*[2] (Squared)!![291] It should come as no surprise that the London based *Intelligence*[2] is anti-Catholic. They have already had three debates on Catholicism and the Papacy. On November 14, 2012 the title was anti-Papist and pure Evil: ' "Hitler's Pope": Pius XII did too little to save the Jews from the Holocaust.' And it featured the anti-Catholic John Julius Norwich as the principal speaker. Norwich is one who has been made aware of Henry Ford's Anti-Semitism; a copy of Ford's *The International Jew* in the London Library is shelved: Jews – Anti-Semitism. Some of *Intelligence*[2] other debates: "Burgandy vs Bordeaux." "Western Liberal Democracy would be wrong for China." Agreed – it is wrong anywhere!!! And the mind boggler: "How to look Hot at 100!!" Anyone with a thinking mind should give *Intelligence*[2] a wide berth.

C-in-C Cameron is reported to have said that multiculturalism has not worked. He is absolutely right. A procession of burning crosses takes place each year on November 5 in the Deep South (of England) in an anti-Catholic parade that draws huge crowds to Lewes, Sussex. An effigy of the Pope and others is carried and subsequently burned on the bonfire.[292]

> Neither a borrower nor a lender be,
>   For lending oft loses both itself and friend,
> And borrowing dulls the edge of husbandry.
> William Shakespeare[293]

On May 28, 2012 Cameron and Lord Young announced plans to provide £80 million of taxpayers' money for 18–24 year-olds to gain access to Start-Up loans and expert personal support to help develop business plans and access training. Business and Enterprise Commissar Mark Frisk:

. . . By investing in young people now, we have a great chance of creating entrepreneurs who can become tomorrow's success stories. However, it is not just about money. It is about creating the whole package for young entrepreneurs, training, mentoring, business planning and help to access finance. StartUp loans will help young people achieve all of these goals and give them an early and exciting chance to realise all of their personal and business potential.

www.gov.uk/. . . 80-million-start-up-loans-for-new-
businesses[294]

In the early 1930s America was in the depth of the Great Depression. There were more people out of work in the United States, both proportionally and actually, than in any other nation on earth. Thirteen million unemployed represented a quarter of the workforce in an age when, in most families, only the men held jobs. Now those millions stood in bread lines and queued up at soup kitchens waiting for their next meal.[134]

The collective misery was simply the result of laissez-faire capitalism gone wild, the maniacal exuberance of Wall Street financiers who had stoked an express train until it careered off the tracks, leaving others to pick up the pieces of the wreck while the guilty fled the scene.

Irving Howe & Lewis Coser,[295] Tim Tzouliadis,[134]

Beside them, little pot-bellied men in light suits and panama hats; clean, pink men with puzzled worried eyes, with restless eyes. Worried because formulas do not work out; hungry for security and yet sensing its disappearance from the earth. In their lapels the insignia of lodges and service clubs, places where they can go and, by weight of numbers of little worried men, reassure themselves that business is noble and not the curious ritualised thievery they know it is; that business men are intelligent in spite of the records of their stupidity; that they are kind and charitable in spite of the principles of sound business; that their lives are rich instead of the thin tiresome routines they know; and that the time is coming when they will not be afraid any more . . . 'I talked to good sound business men out there (California). They don't see a chance till we get rid of this chap in the White House'.

John Steinbeck[296]

And the "chap in the White House", Franklin D Roosevelt had something to say about the moneybags in big business:

> The rulers of the exchange of mankind's goods have failed, through their own stubbornness and their incompetence, have admitted their failure, and abdicated. Practices of the unscrupulous moneychangers stand indicted in the court of public opinion, rejected by the hearts and minds of men . . . a host of unemployed citizens face the grim problem of existence, and an equally great number toil with little return. Only a foolish optimist can deny the dark realities of the moment . . . the money changers have fled from their high seats in the temple of our civilization. We may now restore that temple to the ancient truths. The measure of the restoration lies in the extent to which we apply social values more noble that mere monetary profit.
>
> Franklin D Roosevelt [134]

> We know now that government by organized money is just as dangerous as government by organized mob. Never before in all our history have these forces been so united against one candidate as they stand today. They are unanimous in their hatred for me and I welcome their hatred.
>
> Franklin D Roosevelt [204]

Three years before his death, Henry Ford had had sent a message to Joseph Stalin, brought to the Kremlin by Eric Johnston, the young head of the American Chamber of Commerce. From the record of the meeting, preserved in the Russian state archives, we know that on the evening of 26 June 1944, Eric Johnston told Stalin that he had talked to Henry Ford in Detroit before his departure and that Henry Ford had requested him to pass along his personal greetings to the Soviet Leader. Stalin replied that he had not expected to receive greetings from Henry Ford: 'We owe Henry Ford a lot, he helped us to construct automobile plants'. At this point, Johnston conveyed Henry Ford's willingness to help the Soviet Union again in the future, to which Stalin answered that 'the Soviet Union would repay Ford for his help' just as it had done in the past. The Soviet stenographer then recorded that Johnston then complimented Stalin: 'In his opinion J. V. Stalin is in fact a real businessman.' To which Stalin replied that, 'if he was born in America and lived there he would probably have really become a businessman'.

Tim Tzouliadis[134]

The [European] Commission said that relieving the Royal Mail of the pension costs would ensure it did not "suffer from structural disadvantages in comparison with competitors" . . . the deal to allow the state to take over Royal Mail's pension fund also adds £37.5 billion of liabilities to the national debt.

Christopher Hope[297]

The Cromwellian Institute, under the command of C-in-C Cameron, and the European Commission are partners in Grand Larceny and a Ponzi scheme!!! The state pension scheme is a Ponzi scheme as pensions are paid from the taxpayers' contribution to the Exchequer and not from accumulated funds. A Ponzi scheme is any financial adventure in which the depositors can only be paid by using the money of other investors.[298] Apparently many local authority pension schemes in Britain are no different!! The £37.5 billion of pension liabilities absorbed into the state pension scheme is a burden on future taxpayers who will have to pay the Royal Mail workers pensions, in addition to those of retired state employees. And all this to bring in private sector investment, the euphemism for profit extorted from the People by the banks, or by the banks going into debt by borrowing funds. In the latter case when the banks cannot meet their debts they become insolvent, and have to be bailed out by the ever suffering taxpayer!!!

A recent example of a Ponzi scheme was the one operated by Bernie

Madoff under the guise of a hedge fund. When it ended in 2008 investors had accumulated losses of $18 billion, considered to be the largest financial fraud in United States history.[298] In 2009 Madoff was sentenced to 150 years in jail.

> Last year, the 54 billionaires said to work in Britain were esti-mated to have paid just £15m tax on earnings of £126 billion. Four thousand City employees received bonuses of £1m or more, and if any of them paid the 40% tax the rest of us pay they are mugs.
>
> Robert Preston[299]

> Families fork out an average of almost two thirds of a million pounds in tax over a 55-year "lifetime", a study has found. The typical household pays £656,000 in direct and indirect taxes during its members' working lives and retirement – including more than £250,000 in income tax and £101,000 in VAT [Value Added Tax].
>
> Daniel Martin[300]

> David Cameron last night promised to put promoting UK banks and defence companies at the heart of Britain's foreign policy … Mr Cameron said he would personally lead efforts to promote Britain's financial and defence sectors around the world.
>
> John Kirkup[301]

Anyone who believes that usury and weapons of war are the way forward will believe anything!!

The BBC's Chief Sneer Leader John Humphries: 'If we can't trust the Police who can we trust'.[302] An excellent question, albeit rhetorical!

> Why, there has always been something charming in the relation of women to me. What they principally liked in me was the skilful doctor. Ten or fifteen years ago, you remember, I was the

only decent *accoucheur* in the whole province. Besides, I was an honest man.

Anton Chekhov[303]

A retired colleague told me how in the late 1950s, as a registrar training in surgery she was advised by her father never to trust politicians: 'Every time there is an opinion poll, doctors come top the list as being the most trustworthy, and politicians come bottom; and they don't like it.' Opinion poll findings have remained much the same ever since. The heading reporting an Ipsos MORI Poll published on June 27, 2011: 'Doctors are the most trusted profession – politicians least trusted in 2011'.[304] Doctors were trusted to tell the truth by 88% of people whereas politicians were trusted by only14%, journalists by 19% and bankers by 29%. Teachers were trusted by 81% of people, not far behind doctors.[304]

> . . . giving money to government is like giving whiskey and car keys to teenage boys . . . When you looked at the Republicans, you saw the scum off the top of business. When you looked at the Democrats, you saw the scum off the top of politics . . . What does any person without a PhD in economics know about the budget and we have copious evidence that persons with those PhDs don't know anything about it either.

P J O'Rourke[15]

In the opinion polls, journalists are only marginally ahead of politicians in trustworthiness, with about 20% or less of the public trusting them to tell the truth. Nowhere is corrupt cronyism more rampant than in the media:

> Is the English press honest or dishonest? At normal times it is deeply dishonest. All the papers that matter live off their advertisements and the advertisers exercise an indirect censorship over news.

George Orwell[146]

And who enables the media to make a fortune out of advertising? Answer: The politicians. Margaret Thatcher, two years after the election that put her into 10

Downing Street had lunch with the Machevil Media Mogul Rupert Murdoch at Chequers, the Prime Minister's county residence. The meeting only came to light thirty years later. Thatcher enabled her guest to avoid a reference to the Monopolies and Mergers Commission, even though Murdoch, already the owner of two newspapers with the biggest sales, the daily *Sun* and the Sunday *News of the World,* intended buying out the biggest selling quality newspapers the *Sunday Times* and the *Times.*[305]

> Thatcher listened to Murdoch enthuse about the commercial aspects of the *Sunday Times:* '. . . even at the depths of the recession, this newspaper was turning down advertising . . .' and ' . . . the market clearly permitted an increase in advertising rates'. Thatcher should have given an ear to the competitors but did not as she was more interested in helping her ally avoid the Monopolies and Mergers Commission. 'He had stood by me in the dark days she told an official.'
>
> Harold Evans[305]

> Andrew Neil, then the editor of the *Sunday Times,* said on Radio 4's *The Media Show* this week (April 2013) that Thatcher played a crucial role in the publisher's victory, and not just by outlawing secondary picketing. Rupert Murdoch had told him that he had squared Mrs Thatcher as far as the police were concerned, and that he'd had a guarantee from her that enough police would be available to keep the company going about its lawful business.
>
> Torin Douglas[306]

According to Sir Harold Evans who was Editor of the *Sunday Times* 1967–1981 and the *Times* 1981–1982, successive governments of both parties have done no better in dealing with Murdoch.

> Thatcher unleashed the United Kingdom's advertising sector assisted by Saatchi and Saatchi . . . which helped her into Downing Street with its "Labour isn't Working" poster – and grew to be the world's largest advertising group. The advertising

business reaped millions of pounds from the privatization of companies like British Telecom and British Gas.

Torin Douglas[306]

The Leveson Inquiry was a judicial public inquiry into the culture, practices and ethics of the British press following the News International phone hacking scandal; a series of public hearings held throughout 2011 and 2012. When Rupert Murdoch appeared before the enquiry panel the following was read out from Sir Harold Evans's *Good Times: Bad Times* – last six lines on page 534: 'In my year as editor of the Times, Murdoch broke all these guarantees. He put his point of view very simply to the home editor of the Times, Fred Emery, when he summoned him from holiday on 4 March to his office shortly before asking for my resignation.' [Mr Jay to Murdoch] This is 4 March 1983. You apparently said this: 'I give instruction to my editors all round the World, why shouldn't I in London?' Another quotation from the book was read out by Mr Aitken regarding the phone hacking: 'How much Murdoch knew and when he knew it may not be pinned down because he exercises what the sociologist Max Weber defined as "Charismatic Authority" where policy derives from how the leader is perceived by others rather than by instructions'.[307]

Evans gave evidence over video link to the inquiry on the afternoon of May 17, 2012. 'In the first six months, Mr Murdoch was just the kind of owner one would like: involved, not bullying. He came into a few things – for instance, when he suggested I attack the Royal Family in the first budget because they had got the civil list increased, I didn't mind him suggesting that. When I investigated the facts, I found it was completely wrong, he'd misread it. That evening I went to the *Sun* newspaper and told the editor – the editor said, 'I'm doing a blast on the Royal Family,' I said, 'Just a minute, those figures you've been given are not right because you're misreading the calendar years', and I told Mr Murdoch too. But the *Sun* continued with the false story and I didn't do it in the *Times* and he never said a word about that.'[308]

Mr Jay 'The lunch that Mr Murdoch had with Baroness Thatcher on 4 January 1981, you point out that the existence of that did not enter the public domain until March of this year; is that right?' Sir Harold:

Correct. It was an astonishing piece of news. It wasn't even known to the Cabinet at the time that Mrs Thatcher had had a secret meeting with Mr Murdoch and Mr Murdoch kept it secret to the point of telling the official historian of the time Mr Graham Stewart, no such meetings took place during that period . . . What happened in 1981 is entirely relevant today because it's a manifestation of the culture of too close a connection between a powerful media group and politicians. Evens quoted Murdoch: 'I want the Business News for the revenues. Business advertising. You worry about the editorial. I'll worry about the revenues. Sport, sport!' He sent for the elderly and academic Mr Hickey, who went in tremendously to be told by Mr Murdoch, 'your leaders are too long, too complex. You should be attacking the Russians more.'

Harold Evans[308]

The Western media, the Gutter Press of the world, is completely controlled by advertising. Rupert Murdoch, an Oxford graduate in PPP, is the most powerful media mogul. In the past he was very hands-on, particularly with his tabloid the *Sun*. Murdoch even told the Leveson inquiry: 'If you want to judge my thinking, look at the *Sun*.'[307]

Oliver Cromwell was a usurper, and at no time since his dictatorship was the Cromwellian Institute sanctioned by the People. Parliament remains usurping government with no divine, ethical, constitutional, legal or moral right to even exist. And the same goes for its legal functionaries, the Courts of Law. The great majority of people have little trust in politicians. Which begs the question: Why should we be ruled by thieves, liars and drug pushers (purveyors of tobacco, alcohol and gambling)?

Political language is designed to make lies sound truthful and murder respectable, and to give the appearance of solidarity to pure wind.

George Orwell[180]

CHAPTER 12

STATE TERROR:
THE NOTORIOUS ADVERSARIAL LEGAL
SYSTEM

> . . . for if Hell is half as diabolical as the cells of an English gaol
> on the day before an assize, it is a terrible place indeed.
>
> Ian Pears[34]

The Poor had No Lawyers

Andy Wightman[309]

The corrupting practices of the adversarial legal system are despicable. Its inadequacies are brought to mind in a book with a most appropriate title: *The Poor had No Lawyers:* by Andy Wightman. [309] Wightman tells how the Scottish monarchy and landowners stole land belonging to the Church, helped by the Law and lawyers, even before the widespread land-grab of Henry VIII and Thomas Cromwell during the Tudor Terror.

> Besides, it must not be forgotten that O'Connell [Daniel], lawyer though he was, had small respect for the mummeries of the law, and laughed heartily at the legal virtues of horse-hair wigs. Doubtless the laugh was full of bitterness. For he could not forget that he was an Irishman, and that the honours open to the descendant of a French Huguenot were inaccessible to him – a Catholic and a Native.
>
> Robert Dunlop[261]

> The nearest place he could think of was Lincoln's Inn Fields. The atmosphere there was foul, a miasma of laws.
>
> Samuel Beckett[310]

If he tells the plumb truth no one will believe. First, just as it is important to mix truth with falsity, if falsity is to be accepted, so it is important to mix falsity with truth, if truth is to be accepted. All lawyers know this. Indeed, it may be called one of our Rules of Law. But the lawyers can say this for themselves, at least, that their trade is advocacy, and that they do not so much as pretend the truth. There is no concealment. We are not deceived . . . The former president of the Law Society, one of the most respected solicitors of his generation, said that you could never tell which way a jury, and more so a judge was going to jump. Cases are not always won on rights or wrongs – all too often they are lost on the personal prejudices or the minor dislikes of jurors and judges.

Hiliare Belloc[311]

. . . if England and Venice differ in many ways, they are alike in one, which is that lawyers have an insatiable love of money . . . One would have thought that a learned judge would have been sufficient as it is everywhere else, but this is not the case. For having appointed such a person, they give all his power to a group of twelve men, chosen at random and utterly ignorant of all law. What is more they are inordinately proud of their most bizarre system and hold this jury in awe as the bedrock of their liberties. These men listen to the arguments in court and vote about the verdict . . . for the awful majesty of the law needs sacrifice . . . And there is no place better for making a name than the Inns of Court, and no profession more suited for amassing wealth than the law.

Iain Pears[34]

And the origins of the adversarial legal system? Answer: Rome.

The Goddess of Justice goes back to antiquity. She was referred to as Ma'at by the ancient Egyptians and often depicted carrying a sword with an ostrich feather in her hair (but no scales) to symbolize truth and justice. Ancient Rome adapted the image of a female goddess which it called Justitia. To the ancient Greeks she was known as Themis. Justicia was often portrayed as evenly balancing both scales and a sword and wearing a blindford.

en.wikipedia.org/wiki/Lady_Justice[312]

The Romans seem to have simply added the Scales of Justice emblem of the Tribe of Dan[106,107] (Figure 2) without acknowledgement, creating a plagiarised version which would accompany Roman Rule of Law as it spread throughout the world. So much so, that the plagiarised images represent the judicial system in nearly every country of the world. The Romans, themselves, created little except human sacrifice, plunder, laws to protect their loot, and straight roads!!! Physicians to the Roman ruling elite were mostly Greek, presumably Danaan.

THE GOGGLEBOX EXTORTION FEE

Each year a large number of people are criminalised and a number jailed in Britain for failing to pay the TV (Television) Licence Fee. About £5 billion is spent annually by the BBC on its services, of which about £3.6 million comes from the licence fee. All the annual fee entitles one to do is watch television at home even if one never looks at the BBC. According to the *Huffington Post* British courts jailed 107 people between January 2011 and March 2013, who had failed to pay fines of up to a £1,000 each for not having a TV licence fee of £145.[313] More than 3,000 people come before the courts each week with about 1,500 being convicted. A move by the DOT to decriminalise it was blocked by their cronies the Robber Barons!! And it would only have decriminalised non-payment of the TV Licence Fee, with cases being dealt with in the civil courts instead. The Fee is enforced by detection vans that are supposed to carry equipment for detecting television sets in use, and by inspectors who trick their way into private houses without a search warrant. In England there has been no similar intrusion of the privacy of the home without a search warrant since Cromwell's soldiers invaded homes on Christmas Day and threw out any meat that was cooking.[32] Oliver Cromwell had abolished Christmas.

The BBC is merely the mouthpiece of the Cromwellian Institute, and as such, it is both anti-Royalist and anti-Papist. Terry Wogan deserves to be congratulated for Outing the arch-Republican John Humphries who '. . . put a damper on the happy day [the opening of the new BBC studios] by asking Her

Majesty if she was aware that she shared her birthday with Fiedel Castro'[314] The BBC obediently publicises Cromwellian Institute propaganda such as describing the Dutch invasion of 1688 as "The Glorious Revolution", when in fact it was the overthrow of King James II by an invading Dutch army led by William Prince of Orange at its head, having been invited by the Parliamentarians. The invading army was unwelcome, but after the horrors of the English Civil War the people were in no mood for more bloodshed.[315]

> One of the few flashes of resistance was sparked by a man with an abundance of fighting spirit was an Irish Catholic Life Guards officer. Berwick called him 'a man of amazing stature, utterly devoid of sense, very good natured and very brave.' He met an Anglo-Dutch detachment at Wincanton on 20 November. When its officer declared that he was for the Prince of Orange, [Patrick] Sarsfield declared: 'God damn you! I'll prince you', and promptly pistolled him. He had the better of the fight, but pulled back after enemy reinforcements appeared.
>
> Richard Holmes[316]

The Crown became subservient to Parliament and remains so to this day. Britain became a *de facto* Republic, and has been so since, with the Cromwellian Institute having control of Britain's armed forces, their own standing army with which to wage war whenever and wherever they wish. Not everyone considered the Revolution glorious:

> In the civil wars the Egremonts, pricked by their Norman blood, were cavaliers, and fought pretty well. But in 1688, alarmed at the prevalent impression that King James intended to insist on the restitution of the church estates to their original purposes, to wit, the education of the people and the maintenance of the poor, the Lord of Marney Abbey became a warm adherent of "civil and religious liberty," the cause of which Hampden had died on the field, and Russell on the scaffold, and joined the other Whig lords, and great lay impropriators, in calling over the prince of Orange and a Dutch army, to vindicate those popular principles which, somehow or other, the people would never

154

support . . . [And if the invasion had not taken place] . . . we might have been saved from the triple blessing of Venetian politics, Dutch finance, and French wars.

Benjamin Disraeli[29]

Shortly afterwards the Dutch introduced gin, to the delight of the parliamentarians who taxed it, but to the horror of people like William Hogarth.[317]

During the recent visit of His Holiness Pope Francis to Palestine and the Zionist Republic the BBC was particularly harsh in its condemnation of Pope Pius XII, a Person who in fact had done so much for the Jewish people during their dreadful ordeal. 'Israel also remains deeply suspicious of the reluctance of the Vatican to open its World War Two archives regarding the attitudes of Pope XII towards the Holocaust,' David Willey is reported to have said on May 22, 2014. While the BBC spends millions snooping on other people it would claim to be completely unaware of the *Sinn Féin* Rabbi who repeatedly thanked Pius XII for what he had done for the Jews, whose son Chaim became President of the ZR, and whose grandson, Chaim's son, is now leader of the Opposition in the ZR's DOT. And the BBC would also claim to be completely unaware of the roles Henry Ford and IBM in the Holocaust!!!

The less well off pay for the delights of the more comfortably off. The following in the BBC's *In Our Time* is nonsense:

> Mervyn Bragg and his guests discuss Max Weber's book *The Protestant Ethic and the Spirit of Capitalism*. Published in 1905, Weber's essay proposed that Protestantism had been a significant factor in the emergence of capitalism, making an explicit connection between religious ideas and economic systems. Weber suggested that Calvinism, with its emphasis on personal asceticism and the merits of hard work, had created an ethic which had enabled the success of capitalism in Protestant countries.
>
> www.bbc.co.uk/programmes/b03yqj31[318]

Capitalism has nothing to do with a work ethic; it is all about exploitation!!!

> It is that the Capitalist has found a slave that has supplanted
> the labour and ingenuity of man. Once he was an artisan: at the
> best, he now only watches machines; and even that occupation
> slips from his grasp to the woman and the child. The Capital-
> ist flourishes, he amasses immense wealth; we, sink lower and
> lower; lower than the beasts of burden; for they are fed better
> than we are, cared for more. And it is just, for according to the
> present system they are more precious. And yet they tell us that
> the interests of Capital and of Labour are identical . . . and father,
> too, said the wife. 'He has been a very good father for you all; and
> I never can understand why one who works so hard should earn
> so little; but I believe it is the fault of these machines. The police
> ought to put them down, and then everybody would be comfort-
> able' '. . . I wish there were no such thing as coal in the land,' said
> his wife, 'and then the engines would not be able to work; and
> we should have our rights again.'
>
> Benjamin Disraeli[29]

Is that not what should be done with the oil wells? Cap them!!!

Day after day, week after week, month after month and year after year go by
with the BBC only occasionally mentioning a WHO (World Health Organisation) bulletin. But when the multi billionaire Bill Gates gives a small fraction
of his massive wealth for some health project he has to be interviewed by the
BBC. The BBC frequently behaves as though it is a commercial channel. It
promotes alcohol; and we were recently told that "Gaming," the euphemism
for gambling, is now an "Industry" worth nearly £2 billion!!! It is no industry and the BBC is totally irresponsible in promoting gambling. It is certainly
no industry for the people and their families who are being asset stripped to
provide profit for the bookmakers the owners of casinos, and on-line gambling
strenuously advertised and promoted on the internet.

CHAPTER 13

CRONY CAPITALISM: OLIGARCHS AND MONEYBAGS

... we have already seen how strong an influence was economic greed, and this affected peoples as well as rulers. The English and the Dutch alike dragged their governments behind them as they pressed into every corner of the world looking for profit.

Hugh Brogan[129]

For what was all working for a living but a procuring and a pimping for the money bags, one's lecherous tyrants the money bags, so that they might breed.

Samuel Beckett[310]

The real difficulty is with the vast wealth and power in the hands of the few and the unscrupulous who represent or control capital. Hundreds of laws of Congress and the state legislatures are in the interests of these men and against the interests of workingmen. These need to be exposed and repealed. All laws on corporations, on taxation, on trusts, wills, decent, and the like, need examination and extensive change. It is government of corporations, by corporations, and for corporations.

Rutherford B Hayes [19th President of the United States][319]

The greatest evil after human sacrifice and conquest is corrupt cronyism. And it started with Cromwell's Parliament:

The prejudices against employing gentlemen rapidly declined after the fall of Charles I. The Company [East India] had to appease the voracious appetites of the Parliamentary oligarchs by enrolling as many as possible among the shareholders and finding jobs for their stupid nephews.

Dennis Kincaid[320]

Four weeks after the Conservatives were re-elected on April 2, 1992 for a fourth term [Sir Richard] Branson asked to meet John McGregor, the new transport minister . . . Branson also mentioned rail privatization, an important pledge in the Conservatives election manifesto. Despite Branson's refusal to endorse any political party, the transport minister was enthusiastic for Virgin's participation in the proposed privatisation of the rail network.

Tom Bower[321]

No Mafioso Godfather ever had it so easy!!! That is how the People of Britain had their Heath-Robinson transport system taken from them, and handed over to a gang of ruthless oligarchs. Fares rose sharply to fund elaborate computer systems for issuing tickets and installing "Cattle Counters", individual computer controlled barriers to check tickets. Cattle Counters were installed in most stations, often requiring more staff to man them than had previously been the case with manual ticket checking. Tickets are nearly always checked again on board train. The oligarchs and top managers pay themselves huge salaries, topped up by indecent bonuses; legalised embezzlement!! And pity the ordinary person trying to go to work by train. There are penalties in the form of even higher fares before nine, or nine-thirty in London, for ordinary people wishing to use this "public transport" system to get to work.

And that does not include scams like the Gatwick Express one. It works like this: on arriving at Victoria Station the traveller is faced with a ticket machine. Having purchased a ticket at the exorbitant price of £30 for a single trip to the nearby Airport, one struggles through the Cattle Counter. In this case no one is supervising. The entrance to 1st Class is strategically placed in front of the entrance, and the unsuspecting luggage-laden passenger gets onto the train, is pleased to find space for luggage, and sits down. The signs indicating 1st class are so obscure that the passenger does not notice them. Why is it a scam? Because about six minutes into the journey two heavies, one carrying a camera, arrive and demand to see tickets. On the morning the author fell for the scam there were three of us in the carriage, all on the standard tickets. In what was obviously a carefully rehearsed routine all the tickets were collected before we were told we were in a 1st class carriage and another £20 was demanded, making it £50 for a single trip from Victoria

Station in Central London to Gatwick Airport. In my case there was further harassment. As I was struggling to get my luggage off the train a third man, obviously an official of the train company, arrived to meet the two heavies, and find out how well they had done on the trip. Within earshot he said 'of course they knew it was 1st class.' This third person had no identification, was not wearing a uniform, and refused to identify himself. In trying to find out who owns Gatwick Express one is confronted with a bureucaratic conundrum!!

Trains were not the only gift to Branson. Nearly all Branson's money-making rackets are gifts from his cronies in the Cromwellian Institute, including Virgin Media and the slots at Heathrow or Gatwick Airports. No previous experience required!! According to Bower, Branson told a couple of his pilots that he would one day be running train services. When asked whether they would be diesel or electric, he is said to have replied that he did not know.[321] An answer reminiscent of the Ukranian-American billionaire Leonard Blavatnik, who made his fortune from the privatization of the Soviet Union's resources, when he told his partners at the Irkutsk Aluminium Plant in Siberia:

> I don't know how aluminium is being made, but I know how money is made. Therefore it will be your task to make aluminium and mine to multiply money.
>
> Connie Bruck[322]

Connie Bruck described Blavatnik's lavish lifestyle in *The New Yorker*:[322]

> His fortune has been estimated at nearly eighteen billion dollars. He owns a mansion on Kensington Palace Gardens, which he bought, in 2004, for forty-one million pounds. Since renovated, it has thirteen bedrooms, a cinema, an indoor-outdoor swimming pool, and armored-glass windows—a display of grandeur that makes the nearby Russian Embassy look like a humble dacha . . . Another friend described one of Blavatnik's lavish parties: 'Rupert Murdoch was going out as I came in. There were Argentinean tango dancers, and great music performers, and young, scantily clad Russian girls playing tennis'. . . . Warner [Music] throws substantially more parties

than it did before Blavatnik took over, and a social "concierge" has been hired. According to former employees, Blavatnik has said that he wants lots of beautiful women at the events, and not too many men.

Connie Bruck[322]

Branson's parties are more downmarket:

> The climax (bonding sessions including weekends in foreign hotels) was glorious mayhem. Television sets were thrown out the windows, fire extinguishers were squirted around bedrooms and buildings were trashed.
>
> Tom Bower[321]

> ... Pyotr Aven, the first Minister of Foreign Economic Relations during Boris Yeltsin's Presidency, described aspects of the programme [privatisation] as 'pure stealing of Russian property' ... Zell found the climate extraordinarily difficult. 'We were making small investments, doing a lot of different things to see if we could function there,' Zell said of his company. 'We concluded we could not.' The reason? 'Start with the Foreign Corrupt Practices Act and go from there.'
>
> Connie Bruck[322]

Blavatnik donated $117 million to the University of Oxford, who described his gift as "one of the most generous in the University's 900-year history". The money is being used to create the Blavatnik School of Government. Andrew Hamilton, Vice-chancellor of Oxford University, at its launch in September 2010:[322]

> Leonard Blavatnik is a man who truly lived the American Dream,' [and Blavatnik]: 'What we'd like to do—and I think the university and myself share this vision—is to build the school of government for the twenty-first century,' he said 'and my hope is that—' He paused, venturing off his script for a moment. 'I don't know if it's eight hundred years from now'—he laughed,

beaming at the thought. 'But, hopefully, one hundred years from now, the Blavatnik School of Government will be recognized as one of Oxford's most esteemed institutions, and the university will be proud of it'.

Connie Bruck[322]

Is this costly Blavatnik School of Government really necessary? After all Common Sense costs nothing!!! Did not Aristotle consider Carthage to have had one of the best systems of government? And it was based on Common Sense!! At this point the author feels obliged to declare a possible conflict of interest: In 1998 I was denied a Professorship by the University of Oxford having applied through the proper channels and been told by the Medical Director of the John Radcliffe Hospital: 'You will deserve it more than most'. Probable reason for refusal? Oxbridge anti-Catholic intrigue!

The fastest route to personal enrichment is political office.

Richard Sakwa[74]

Ireland's Peter Denis Sutherland, lawyer, oligarch and darling of Corporate America, is a law graduate of UCD (University College Dublin) the author's *Alma Mater*. He was called to the Irish Bar in 1969.[323] In 1973 Sutherland was a candidate in the general election, standing for Fine Gael in Dublin's North–West constituency. According to Wikipedia he received 1,969 votes (6.2%), about one fifteenth of the total. Nevertheless, eight years later at the age of 34 C-in-C Garret FitzGerald made Sutherland Ireland's Attorney General. In politics nothing succeeds like Failure!! And that was only the beginning. Wikipedia again:[323]

> Four years later he was appointed to the European Commission and had responsibility for competition policy; he was Chairman of the Committee that produced the Sutherland Report on the completion of the internal market of the EEC; he was the youngest ever European Commissioner and served on the first Delors Commission, where he played a crucial role in opening up competition across Europe, particularly the airline, telecoms, and energy sectors; subsequently he was Director General of the

General Agreement on Tariffs and Trade (now the World Trade Organisation). Later Mickey Kantor, the US Trade Minister, credited him with being the father of globalization and said that without him there would have been no WTO; the Uruguay round of global trade talks, concluded in December 1993 with Sutherland as the chair of GATT, produced a 'comprehensive, rules-based and global trade regime' which was the biggest trade agreement in history and established the World Trade Organisation [WTO]; Sutherland is non-executive Chairman of Goldman Sachs International; he was a director of the Royal Bank of Scotland until he was asked to leave the board when it had to be taken over by the UK government to avoid bankruptcy . . . ; he was Chairman of the Board of Governors of the European Institute of Public Administration (Maastricht) from 1991 to 1996 . . . ; in 2005, he was appointed as Goodwill Ambassador for the United Nations Industrial Development Organisation; in Spring 2006 he was appointed Chair of London School of Economics Council commencing in 2008; Sutherland also served on the International Advisory Board of IESE, the graduate business school of Spain's University of Navarra; in January 2006 he was appointed by United Nations Secretary General Kofi Annan as his Special Representative for Migration . . . ; On 5 December 2006, he was appointed as Consular of the Extraordinary Section of the Administration of the Patrimony of the Apostolic See (a financial adviser to the Vatican) . . . ; in 2010, *The Tablet* named him as one of Britain's most influential Catholics . . . ; Sutherland is also co-Chairman of the High Level Group appointed by the Government of Germany, Great Britain, Indonesia and Turkey to report on the conclusion of the Doha Round and the future of multilateral trade negations, Report issued in May 2011. . . ; outside banking, Sutherland in early 2010 finished a 13-year stint as chairman of BP, Europe's largest oil company, at one time valued on the stock market at £236 billion, making £42 million a day profits; in 2013, University College Dublin Law School was renamed the Sutherland School of Law in his honour, following his financial contribution to the newly completed law teaching facility.

en.wikipedia.org/wiki/Peter_Sutherland[323]

WTO has become a weapon of the big hitters:

> . . . it's nearly impossible to describe the ubiquity of soft drink ads in Mexico, with Coke's logo painted on houses and buildings along the road at least every hundred feet . . . 'These three years in many ways define the future of the child, and it is when malnutrition and diabetes can be prevented,' says the group's director, Dr. Marcos Arana. 'If babies are exposed to a high intake of sugar, they will be conditioned to depend on sugar for the rest of their lives.' While breast-feeding is still the norm for younger children, says Arana, there are still instances of mothers putting Coca-Cola into baby bottles. Anecdotally, Arana says he has seen a steady increase in obesity and diabetes in the communities he serves . . . Arana is part of a group of doctors who pushed for a soda tax to curb consumption nationwide. In 2002, in fact, the country imposed a 20 cent tax on all soft drinks made with high-fructose corn syrup, affecting Coke and Pepsi but not local sodas made with sugar from sugarcane . . . When the tax was passed, however, the United States promptly filed a dispute on Coke's behalf with WTO, arguing it was discriminatory against American products. WTO ruled in favour of the United States in 2005 and again in 2007, after which Mexico repealed the tax.
>
> Michael Blanding[324]

Competition in the telecom sector was the excuse for privatisation the air surrounding the planet: "The Great Airwaves Robbery!!" The EU (European Union) is just another DOT, and although latecomers, it has not taken them long to learn Grand Larceny. Telecom companies like Vodafone are worth billions and are making massive profits, at the expense of the People:

> June 7 (Bloomberg) – Vodafone Group Plc Chief Executive Officer Vittorio Colao saw his 2013 pay drop 30 per cent on a cut in bonus from the carrier's long-term incentive plan. Colao's

total compensation for the year ended March 31 amounted to £11 million ($17.1million), compared with £15.8 million a year earlier, according to the Newbury, England-based company's annual report released today.

bloomberg.com[325]

The [Cromwellian Institute's] Treasury came under fire to urgently review its tax laws that allowed Vodafone to avoid paying tax on its massive £84 billion windfall from selling its [the Peoples'!!] stake in the American mobile giant Verzon.

Andrew Grice[326]

We are constantly being asked to conserve water even though we only use a fraction of the amount that falls to earth because is so poorly harvested. There is no such problem with oil. The more oil we use the better for the oil companies. Any increase in demand is satisfied by drilling more oil wells, even if it means going to more than 400 metres below the surface of the sea. The price per litre of petrol (gasoline) is frequently twice the price of milk. We are never asked to conserve fuel, instead we are exhorted by advertising to buy even more. Petrol requires at least an equivalent volume of fresh water to be refined. Industrial use of water particularly by the unsightly refinery across the lagoon has been responsible, in part, for Venice's sinking problems. We need water to survive – we could do without oil if we had to!!

Following Sutherland's appointment as financial adviser to the Vatican at the end of 2006 it could be said that the Vatican's "Credo" had become "In Goldman, Sachs we Trust", the title of a chapter in John Kenneth Galbraith's *The Great Crash*,[327] which ends as follows:

Years later, [after the 1929 Crash] on a grey dawn in Washington, the following colloquy occurred before a committee of the United States Senate.
SENATOR COUZENS: Did Goldman, Sacks and Company organize the Goldman Sachs Trading Corporation?
MR SACHS: Yes, sir.
SENATOR COUZENS: And it sold its stock to the public?
MR SACHS: A portion of it. The firms invested originally in ten

per cent of the entire issue for the sum of $10,000,000.

SENATOR COUZENS: And the other ninety per cent was sold to the public?

MR SACHS: Yes, sir.

SENATOR COUZENS: At what price?

MR SACHS: At 104. That is the old stock . . . the stock was split two for one.

SENATOR COUZENS: And what is the price of the stock now?

MR SACKS: Approximately 1¾.

The pages that follow tell the greatest cycle of speculative boom and collapse in modern times – since, in fact, the South Sea Bubble. There is merit in keeping alive the memory of those days. For it is neither public regulation nor the improving moral tone of corporate promoters, brokers, customer's men, market operators, bankers, and mutual fund managers which prevents these recurrent outbreaks and their aftermath. It is the recollection of how, on some past occasion, illusion replaced reality and people got rimmed.

John Kenneth Galbraith[327]

Peter Sutherland recently announced he is to retire at the end of June (2015), in order to devote more time to his role as the special representative of the Secretary General of the United Nations for migration and development.[328] A memo to staff indicated that he would continue to provide strategic advice to Goldman Sachs on global business opportunities.

Another Oil Baron who hails from Dublin is David J O'Reilly[329] former chairman and CEO of the giant Chevron Corporation, rated as America's third largest corporation. Chevron makes massive profits. O'Reilly is a UCD graduate in chemical engineering; in 2002 he was awarded an honorary doctor of science degree by his *Alma Mater*. O'Reilly joined Chevron in 1968, the year he graduated. In 2000 he became he became chairman and CEO of Chevron and retired in 2009. His salary in 2007 was $31,543,200. Condoleezza Rice was a member of the Board of Chevron; a 129,000-ton Chevron oil tanker was named "Condoleezza Rice".[330] In 2010 O'Reilly joined the Board of the engineering and construction giant Bechtel Corporation; the same year he was a appointed a director on the board of Saudi Amaco, the national oil company of

Saudi Arabia; he is vice chairman of the National Petroleum Council; O'Reilly is a member of the Business Council, J P Morgan International Council, the Economic Forum's International Business Council, and the American Society of Corporate Executives; O'Reilly serves on the San Francisco Symphony Board of Governors; in April 2002 O'Reilly received the Order of Kurmet from Kazakhstan President Nursultan Nazarbaev.[329]

William Henry "Bill" Gates is one of the world's richest men as a result of the simple expediency of hijacking the alphabet. He was co-founder, with Paul Allen, of Microsoft, the World's largest PC (personal computer) software company.[331] Gates personal fortune is estimated at about $80 billion. As one of the World's richest he is a regular performer at the World Voodoo Forum's annual meeting in the Swiss ski resort of Davos.

Success in business is the ability to practice Machevillism in the right political climate. Machevillism is an essential subject in humanities, advanced business schools and Voodoo institutes:

> Dr Hannah Dawson, an ex-Cambridge historian of striking looks, whose big curly hair and expressive face gave her something of Helen Bonham Carter, was teaching Machiavelli's Prince with great enthusiasm.
>
> Joshi Hermann[332]

John Kenneth Galbraith a close confident of JFK, and a strident opponent of the Vietnam War warned of impending financial collapse. [327] The Great Crash of 1929 has been described as a derailment capitalism's gravy train, when it ended in pieces; it was only put together again by the actions of three of the twentieth century's worst despots: Henry Ford, Joseph Stalin and Adolf Hitler, acting together and against each other in igniting World War II, a war that left over 60 million people dead, millions displaced, and millions emotionally destroyed. As Galbraith forecast, the gravy train of capitalism is on course to hit the buffers because massive debt will have caught up with the poker players who play and gamble away the People's money: bankers, oligarchs, arms manufacturers, warmongers, politicians, media barons and their legal functionaries.

CHAPTER 14

DRUG BARONS: ANGELS OF DEATH

On February 10, 2011 Ian Paisley, speaking in the Cromwellian Institute's DOT:

> The Hon. Gentleman is absolutely right to say that choosing four years as the threshold is far too generous. I wonder whether members have reflected on what that really means. It means 4,370 drug dealers getting the vote.[333]

What Paisley did not seem to realise was that he was in one of the most notorious drug trafficking establishments in history.

OPIUM

> Oh! a dreadful man! A Scotchman, richer than Crœsus, one McDruggy, fresh from Canton, with a million of opium in his pocket denouncing corruption, and bellowing free trade.
> Benjamin Disraeli[29]

And who was the drug baron that Disraeli was referring to? Answer: Sir James Nicholas Sutherland Matheson who with William Jardine founded the Jardine Matheson Company that traded with China. Matheson bought Stornoway Castle on Lewis, one of the islands comprising the Outer Hebrides, and retired there. The Jardine Matheson Company's most lucrative trade was supplying opium to the Chinese market. By 1838 the number of opium addicts in China had grown to between four and twelve million. The Emperor demanded action and in 1839 his officials impounded and burned opium belonging to British traders. And what was the Cromwellian Institute's response to this Outrage? Send in the gunboats and the troops!!! This resulted in a number of skirmishes that became known as the "Opium War", a conflict that lasted until the Emperor Daoguang agreed to a treaty. The Treaty was signed on 29 August 1842 on board *HMS Cornwallis,* anchored mid-river on the Yangtze Kiang at Nanjing, following two weeks of negotiation between Sir Henry Pottinger representing the Cromwellian Institute, and Mandarin Qiyang on behalf of the Emperor. It was a humiliating defeat for the previously powerful Chinese Empire; Huang Ti, known as the Yellow Emperor, is said to have founded Chinese civilization 3,500 years earlier.[254]

The Treaty of Nanjing allowed the West to trade with the cities of Amoy, Canton, Foochow, Ningpo, and Shanghai, afterwards referred to as the five Treaty Ports; Westerners could live in these cities with the privileges of diplomats. The island of Hong Kong was given to Britain in perpetuity; and the Chinese agreed to pay Britain $21 million compensation, mostly for opium that had been confiscated and burned. Payment was made in the form of 65 tons of silver, which was shipped to England and minted into coins. Other countries, particularly the United States, France, Germany, Japan, and Russia, benefited from the Treaty; the Stars and Stripes was the first foreign flag to fly in Shanghai after the Treaty was signed.[254] Hong Kong was returned to China in 1997 amid great rejoicing.

Visitors to China are strongly advised not to wear a poppy in their buttonhole even on Remembrance Sunday, as the Chinese do not take kindly to being reminded of their humiliation at the hands of the Cromwellian Institute!!!

TOBACCO

Cotton-growing exhausts the soil as badly as tobacco.

Hugh Brogan[129]

What drug has replaced opium as the darling of the moneybags, the Cromwellian Institute and the smugglers? Answer: Tobacco.

The number of smuggled cigarettes seized by customs in Hong Kong shot up by 41% last year from 2012. The Customs and Excise Department said yesterday that more than 38 million illicit cigarettes were seized in the year to November, 11 million more than the total for 2012. One in every three cigarettes smoked in Hong Kong in 2012 was illicit – the second highest proportion in 11 Asian countries – Tan said, citing a British study.

Jennifer Ngo[334]

King James I of England and VI of Scotland in 1604:

Have you not reason then to bee ashamed, and to forbeare this filthie noveltie, so basely grounded, so foolishly received and so grossly mistaken in the right use thereof? An your abuse thereof sinning against God, harming yourselves both in persons and goods, and raking also thereby the markes and notes of vanitie upon you: by the custome thereof making your selves to be wondered at by all forraine civil Nations, and by all strangers that come among you, to be scorned and contemned. A custom loathsome to the eye, hateful to the Nose, harmful to the braine, dangerous to the lungs, and in the blacke stinking fume thereof, nearest resembling the horrible Stigian smoke of the pit that is bottomless.

en.wikipedia.org/wiki/A_Counterblaste_to_Tobacco[335]

The ramifications of the tobacco industry and its relationship with the Cromwellian Institute are frightening!!

According to HM Revenue and Customs (HMRC), the typical price of a pack of 20 cigarettes was £6.83 last year [2012]. Of this, a full £5.61 was tax, including tobacco duty and VAT. So 82% of the price of a pack is tax which goes to the Treasury.

fullfact.org . . . smoking_cost . . .[336]

Described as the world's most international tobacco group, BAT (British American Tobacco),[337] one of the world's five largest tobacco companies, operates in about 180 countries, is a market leader in over 50 countries, and is the sixth-largest of any company listed on the London stock exchange.[337] BAT has market capitalization of £65.6 billion. BAT has found many ways over the years of keeping its cigarette brands in the public eye. In 1996 it sponsored the Cricket World Cup naming it "Wills World Cup" and as a result achieved a high level of brand recognition in India where the young fans were the key marketing target. In 1996 BAT purchased the Tyrrell motor racing team for £30 million and renamed it British American Racing. In 1998 the team was used to advertise its cigarette brands particularly Lucky Strike and State Express 555.[337] Lucky Strike's last year of sponsorship in motor racing was 2006. In 2008 BAT spent £700,000 lobbying the EU (European Union).

In the late 1980s, competition between Hong-Kong based rival traders smuggling BAT cigarettes into China became so intense that bribes were paid to the local BAT director whose job it was to deal with them. After one jilted trader exposed the system to Hong Kong's anti-corruption commission, former BAT (HK) export director Jerry Lui was extradited from the United States. BAT itself was not charged with any offence. The case against Lui nearly floundered after the chief witness against him Tommy Chui was murdered on March 29, 1995. His body was found floating in Singapore Harbor, stuffed into a garbage bag with tape over his mouth. Another potential witness committed suicide.[337] In 1998, Jerry Lui was convicted and sentenced to three years and eight months imprisonment. Experts testified that Chui's murder had all the hallmarks of a Triad killing. The three diving belts with four, five and six lead weights, plus the pattern in which the keys had been placed next to the abduction car were Triad warnings to anyone who might consider talking to police about cigarette smuggling.[337] Many countries where BAT operates execute petty traffickers if caught smuggling drugs!!!

Deputy Chairman and a director of BAT (1998–2007) was longstanding member of the Cromwellian Institute's DOT Kenneth Clarke, who was also a long serving Peoples' Commissar. Clark's career is an example of the Revolving Door moving between politics and BAT. Kevin Baron, the chairman of the all-party group on smoking in the DOT:

> Ken Clark holds his position within BAT because of his past office of chancellor and health secretary.
>
> Kevin Baron[338]

. . . Shortly after she left 10 Downing Street, in a deal brokered
by her son, Mark, Britain's first woman prime minister became
a shrill for the tobacco industry, specifically Philip Morris . . .
The deal was sealed on November 10, 1992 when Philip Morris'
General Counsel, Murray Bring, wrote Thatcher Foundation
representative Robert Higdon pledging $750,000 to be split
over three years beginning that year. Documents state that the
contribution was just part of a larger financial arrangement that
Philip Morris had with Thatcher . . . Michael O'Connor was a
civil servant in charge of tobacco policy from 1987 to 1989. He
said yesterday he was saddened to hear of the talks. 'Margaret
Thatcher made the strongest anti-smoking speech ever made by
a prime minister . . . I know because I wrote it. In the interests
of future generations of children she shouldn't be supporting an
industry that is going to kill many of them.' . . . Lady Thatcher's
discussions are thought to involve advising on resisting European Community moves to ban tobacco advertising, and on
controversial expansions of markets in the Third World and
Eastern Europe.

Peter Costello[339]

Amid a dust-up that has seen the duo at the top of the headhunters Odgers Berndtson resign their own board seats from
the listed OPD Parent, the firm led by Richard Boggis-Rolfe
and Lady Bottomley is still filling high-profile roles. The latest
recruitment of a BAT chairman was regarded by some other
board specialists as a tougher-than-usual task, due to the qualms
some candidates might have about the tobacco industry. But
Lady Bottomley, a former health secretary, has filled previous
roles on the BAT board, and is a trustee of *The Economist*, whose
board is chaired by a former BAT director Rupert Pennant-Rea.
As Odgers holds on to its status as a top earner among UK Search
firms, it has also landed the role of replacing UKFI Chief Executive John Kingman, which will be advertised this week, with
Odgers Financial services practice head Simon Mee involved. At
the same time it is filling Sir Christopher Hogg's boots as chair-

man of the Financial Reporting Council, has placed Rob Holden as Crossrail chief executive and former John Lewis chairman Sir Stuart Hampson as chairman of Crown Estate. Enough to justify Mr Boggis-Rolfe and Lady Bottomley being paid £755,000 and £562,000 respectively last year.

Emiliya Mychasuk, & Emiko Terazono[340]

Virginia Hilda Brunette Maxwell Bottomley, Baroness Bottomley of Nettlestone is yet another who appears to owe her success in the corporate sector to political office, confirming Richard Sakwa's observation in *Frontline Ukraine: Crisis in the Borderlands*[74] that it is the fastest route to personal enrichment. From 1992 Bottomley was deputy Peoples' Commissar for ill-health before becoming Peoples' Commissar in 1989, and serving until 1995.[341] Bottomley was a member of the supervisory board of the Dutch multinational AkzoNobel from 2000 to 2012. AkzoNobel[342] is active in decorative paints, performance coatings and specialty chemicals employing 47,000 people while trading in more than 80 countries; sales in 2014 amounted to Euro 14.3 billion. From 2007 to 2013 Bottomley was a non-executive director of the private British healthcare company BUPA, operating in 190 countries. And is currently a non-executive director of Smith & Nephew,[343] a British multinational medical equipment manufacturing company whose products are sold in more than 90 countries.

And what was the tough recruitment challenge facing the headhunters Odgers? Answer: Finding a new chairman of BAT in 2009. Bottomley led the "search" and the man who had been chief executive of Irish Distillers Richard Burrows, became chairman of BAT on December 9, 2008.[344] Burrows is well qualified for the job, having been in the business of marketing and selling poisonous substances for the previous thirty years. In addition to being CEO of Irish Distillers from 1978 to 2000, he had been Co-Chief Executive of Pernod Richard from 2000 to 2005 based in Paris, and held board positions with Carlsberg and Rentokil. Between 2005 and 2009 Burrows was Governor of the Bank of Ireland, a bank that had to be seek fresh capital from the state (the ever suffering taxpayer) during the Irish financial crisis. Burrows was forced to apologise to the bank's investors for the loss of value of their stock and for the cancellation of dividends.[344] He apparently got the job at BAT because of his international experience and knowledge of marketing and branding, particularly the successful selling of Jamieson Whiskey world-wide!! BAT presumably expects him to do the same with for their cigarettes!! Headhunters typically take about one-third of the placed executive's first year's salary in fees, and the individual headhunter responsible for the placement will take a third of that as a bonus. Burrows remuneration was about one million Euros, including 138,000 Euros in perks. Thus in the Burrows BAT case over Euros 200,000 would have gone to the firm Odgers Berndtson led by Boggis-Rolfe and Bottomley, with over Euros 100,000 going directly Bottomley. The latter amount is more than many highly skilled artisans and professionals would earn in a year!!

C_2H_5OH: ALCOHOL

On a Sunday morning in April 2014 the author was in an Oxford taxi travelling to catch a bus to the airport. When passing through George Street at about six o'clock the taxi driver said: 'three hours ago this was like a war zone, I feel sorry for the Police, a judge said that people can swear at the Police'. About the time 24-hour public house opening was introduced I tried to discuss my concerns with one of the local councillors in Oxford. The conversation ended abruptly when I had: 'Prohibition didn't work,' barked at me!! Not long afterwards Tesco applied for permission to sell alcohol from six in the morning until twelve at night six days a week in the former Borders Bookshop (books giving way to booze!). An Oxford City Council notice displayed on the site of the proposed new supermarket stated that any organisation or person could object. However, if an individual objected and it was found to be false they could be liable to prosecution and a hefty fine! In Ireland it is necessary to have a doctor's prescription to purchase 75mg Aspirin tablets while the much more dangerous C_2H_5OH is widely available in unrestricted amounts nearly 24 hours a day.

Anton Chekov, Russian physician and author, warned about the dangers of alcohol and tobacco:

> Wine and tobacco rob us of our individuality. After a cigar or a glass of vodka you are no longer Peter Nikolayevitch but Peter Nikolayevitch plus somebody else. Your ego evaporates, and you

think of yourself in the third person; not as "me" but as "him".

Anton Chekov[303]

We didn't know what to say to each other in the presence of this man on the couch, husband and father. I had my memories of him, mornings by the fire in Limerick, his stories and his songs, his cleanliness, neatness, sense of order, the way he helped us with our homework, his insistence on obedience and attention to our religious duties, all destroyed by his payday madness when he threw his money around the pubs buying pints for every hanger-on while my mother despaired by the fire knowing the next day she'd have to stick out her hand out for charity.

Frank McCourt[128]

Nothing stimulates crime so powerfully as legalizing and advertising those drugs that stimulate violence and cause injury and death: alcohol & tobacco

James Gilligan[243]

Alcohol rots the brain, hardens the liver and breaks the heart.[40] Even socially acceptable levels of alcohol consumption may cause long-term brain damage.

In the tax year 2013/2014 the UK (United Kingdom) Government collected approximately £10 billion in duty from the sale of the widely available drug C_2H_5OH.[345] Alcohol is blamed for a 40 per cent rise in liver disease deaths in the 12 years to April 2014. The changes in public house opening hours and higher levels of alcohol consumption are directly linked to the 'rapid and shocking' increase in the death rates, according to Professor Julia Verne who led the researches for Public Health England.[346] Not only was there an increase of about a third in the incidence of alcoholic liver disease since the public house opening hours were extended in 2005, but also substantial increases in other disorders caused by this dangerous drug C_2H_5OH.

In 2013 Police chiefs branded round-the-clock pub opening a terrible mistake.[347] It was not a mistake; it achieved its purpose, with over a 30 per cent increase in alcohol sales the Cromwellian Institute has had a similar increase in revenue. And their Cronies in the advertising, sponsorship and alcohol trades welcomed similar increases. The equivalent of about one trillion US

174

Dollars is spent annually throughout the world on alcohol. The attitude of the EU and Cromwellian Institute to the sale of alcohol is tantamount to criminal negligence at the very least. Equally, their local functionaries have no qualms about the damage alcohol does to young peoples' health, and seem to be unconcerned about the high level of violence associated with heavy drinking. Twenty-four-hour drinking requires a large Police presence in the middle of the night in the vicinity of night clubs and pubs while their masters the politicians, are safely tucked up in bed at home!!

Being teetotal would have enormous and widespread benefits for the individual and society, and a no-smoking society would be a major additional contribution to health. We could do no better than follow the advice in the Old Testament:

> Let us be given vegetables to eat and water to drink. Then see how we look in comparison the other young men who eat from the royal table, and treat your servants according to what you see. He agreed to this request, and tested them for ten days; after ten days they looked healthier and better fed than any of the young men who ate from the royal table.
>
> Daniel[348]

> I have some thoughts of joining the Total Abstinence . . . We will never get our rights till we leave off consuming excisable articles; and the best thing to begin with is liquors.
>
> Benjamin Disraeli[29]

CHAPTER 15

THE MACHEVIL EMPIRE:
ROME REINCARNATE: NORSE AMERICA

Not since the Thirty Years' War has the conscience of mankind
been so distressed as it is today by the deployment and use of
power within the State and in the community of nations.

Daniel P O'Connell[349]

Malcom X following his pilgrimage to Mecca: 'The white man
is not inherently evil, but it's American political, economic and
social atmosphere.'

James Gilligan[243]

I complain about the United States not being Athens. I certainly
say we are a very good Roman Republic, and the lies are based
upon the most advanced techniques of advertising, which is the
only art form my country has invented – the television commercial – and we sell soaps and presidents in the same fashion.

Gore Vidal[160]

The spirit in which the Golden door was slammed shut was
lucidly expressed by Senator Andrew Johnson, of Washington
State, a sponsor of the 1924 Act, who explained that 'the foreign-
born flood' was a threat to the happiness of individual Americans
and to American institutions and liberties. Of course neither
Senator Johnson nor anyone else foresaw the tragic consequences that this Act would begin to have nine years later. He
was simply enjoying himself, in the ancient fashion of Congress,
giving his prejudices the force of law . . . Congress responded by
setting up an Immigration Commission chaired by one William
P Dillingham, to investigate the immigrants and make recom-
mendations. The resultant Dillingham report was published in
1911; it consisted of forty-two volumes of tendentiously orga-

nized data to draw a distinction between the "old" immigrants from the West and North of Europe and the "new" immigrants from the South: naturally it found that the new immigrants were deeply unsuited to life in the free, Protestant, Nordic American Republic . . . A library of books like Madison Grant's *The Passing of the Great Race* (1916) warned Americans that they could not safely continue to admit members of inferior races to their country and assessed that all races were inferior to the glorious Nordic race. In the South a new Ku Klux Klan began to arise, as viscous as the old and intent on attacking Jews and Catholics as well as blacks.

Hugh Brogan[129]

The Passing of the Great Race had a profound effect on Adolf Hitler's thinking. 'Hitler was so steeped in American race science; he even wrote a fan letter to American eugenic leader Madison Grant. *Der Führer's* letter called Grant's eugenics book *The Passing of the Great Race*, "my bible".

Edwin Black[204]

But his parentage was German and Scotch and English, with remote strains of Danish and French blood giving him the temperament of a Puritan and an insatiable imagination of conquest.

Joseph Conrad[350]

The professor is saying the Pilgrims left England to escape religious persecution and that puzzles me because the Pilgrims themselves were English and the English were always the ones who persecuted everyone else, especially the Irish . . . Andy talks about the Puerto Ricans all the time. He says they're the only people who know how to live in this goddam tight-ass city, that it's a tragedy the Spaniards didn't sail up the Hudson instead of the goddam Dutch and the goddam limeys . . . he spends most of his time in the lavatory or smoking with Digger Moon the carpetman who claims he is a Blackfoot Indian and can lay carpet faster and tighter than anyone in the US of A unless he has had a few and then watch out because he remembers the suffering of his people.

Frank McCourt[128]

The Greeks and Romans accused the Carthaginians, and indeed all Asiatics of a servile attitude towards those in authority. But this was merely an exaggeration of over-refined Oriental politeness. It was a sign of civility.

en.wikipedia.org/wiki/Carthage[81]

Even after the alien invaders had brought untold misery upon their country, simple country-folk [Russian] sometimes displayed a human sympathy for afflicted and suffering of Axis soldiers which moved them. Corti (Lieutenant Eugenio) wrote: 'During halts on those marches many of our compatriots were rescued from frostbite by the selfless, maternal care of poor women.' Corti recoiled from the spectacle of Germans massacring Russian prisoners, though he knew the Red Army often did likewise to its own captives. 'It was extremely painful – for we were civilised men – to be caught up in that savage clash between barbarians' . . . Some Americans responded brutally to such docility (of Italians they took prisoner); in two separate incidences on 14 July, an officer and an NCO of the US 45th Division murdered large groups of Italians in cold blood. One, Sergeant Horace West, who killed thirty-seven with a Thompson sub-machine, was convicted by a court-martial, but later granted clemency. The other, Captain John Compton, assembled a firing squad which massacred thirty-six Italian prisoners. Compton was court-martialled but acquitted, and was later killed in action. Patton, whose military ethic mirrored that of many Nazi commanders, wrote that 'in my opinion these killings have been thoroughly justified'. He agreed to the court-martial only under pressure. Disclosure of both incidences was suppressed, because Eisenhower feared enemy reprisals against Allied prisoners. If Germans had been responsible, they would have been indicted for war crimes in 1945, and probably executed.

Max Hastings[351]

Killing Japanese didn't bother me at the time . . . I suppose if I had lost the war, I would have been tried as a war criminal.

en.wikiquote.org/wiki/Curtis_LeMay[352]

Curtis LeMay was in charge of all strategic air operations against the Japanese Islands, and switched to low-altitude night time incendiary attacks on Japanese targets. Japanese cities were built mostly constructed of materials such as wood and paper. He commanded B-29 Superfortress operations against Japan. Massive incendiary attacks were carried out against 67 Japanese cities. The most notorious was the firebombing of Tokyo on the night of March 9–10, 1945, the single most destructive bombing raid of World War II.[353]

For the first attack LeMay ordered the defensive guns removed from the 325 B-29s and loaded each plane with incendiary clusters, magnesium bombs, white phosphorous bombs and napalm. The pathfinder planes arrived over Tokyo just after midnight and marked the target area with a flaming "X." During a three-hour period 1,665 tons of incendiary bombs killed about 100,000 civilians, destroying 250,000 buildings, and incinerating 16 square miles of the city.[353] The firebombing campaign directed by LeMay between March 1945 and the Japanese surrender in August 1945 may have killed more than 500,000 Japanese civilians and left more than five million homeless.[353] Robert McNamara described LeMay as the finest combat officer of any service he came across in war. 'But he was extraordinarily belligerent, many thought brutal.'[353]

The Korean War was a war for humanity . . . The United Nations forces led by the Americans, used their firepower to bomb the North, the Soviets and the Chinese to the negotiating table, dropping more explosives on North Korea than they had on Nazi Germany. The effect was to flatten the North. Only three buildings survived intact in Pyongyang. Hundreds of thousands of civilians died in the bombing . . . One picture of Pyongyang looks like Hiroshima or Nagasaki after the atomic bombs . . . the suffering of the people was hideous.

Andrei Lankov[354]

In Holland, during the War when I heard at night the heavy drone of hundreds of RAF (Royal Air Force) planes overhead on their way to Germany, the sound had been like a song to me. Now when I saw the enormous grey hulks of the American bombers sweeping low to drop their deadly load over the small defenceless Korean villages huddled against the mountainside; when I saw the villagers, mostly women and children and old people – for the men were all at the front – being machine-gunned as they fled to seek shelter in the fields, I felt nothing but shame and anger.

George Blake[355]

We went over there and fought the war and eventually burned down every town in North Korea anyway, somehow or another, and some in South Korea too . . . over a period of three years or so, we killed off – what – twenty per cent of the population of Korea as direct casualties of war, or from starvation and exposure.

en.wikiquote.org/wiki/Curtis_LeMay[352]

. . . My solution to the problem would be to tell them [the North Vietnamese Communists] frankly that they've got to draw in their horns and stop their aggression or we're going to bomb them into the Stone Age. And we would shove them back into the Stone Age with Air Power or Naval Power – not ground forces.

en.wikiquote.org/wiki/Curtis_LeMay[352]

I don't know about World War III but I know that World War IV will be fought with sticks and stones.

Albert Einstein[18]

What I find most terrifying is not Curtis LeMay with his cheerful suggestion that we bomb everybody back into the stone age, but rather the calm disquisitions of the political scientists on just how much force will be necessary to achieve our ends, and just what will be acceptable to us in Vietnam. What I find terrifying is the detachment and equanimity with which we view and discuss an unbearable tragedy. We all know that if Russia or China were guilty of what we have done in Vietnam, we would be exploding with moral indignation at their monstrous crimes.

Noam Chomsky[356]

Over dinner Col Groves shocked Rotblat when he said in March 1944: 'You realize that the main purpose of this project is to subdue the Russians'. . . . he left the Manhattan project [building the atomic bomb] when it was discovered that Germany had abandoned atomic bomb research in 1942.[19]

IN MARCH 1944 I experienced a disagreeable shock. At that time I was living with the Chadwicks in their house on the Mesa, before moving later to the "Big House"; the quarters for single scientists. General Leslie Groves, when visiting Los Alamos, frequently came to the Chadwicks for dinner and relaxed palaver. During one such conversation Groves said that of course, the real purpose on making the bomb was to subdue the Soviets. (Whatever his exact words, his real meaning was clear.) Although I had no illusions about the Stalin regime – after all, it was his pact with Hitler that enabled the latter to invade Poland – I felt deeply the sense of betrayal of an ally. Remember, this was said at a time when thousands of Russians were dying every day on the Eastern Front, tying down the Germans and giving the Allies time to prepare for the landing on the continent of Europe. Until then I had thought that our work was to prevent a Nazi victory, and now I was told that the weapon we were preparing was intended for use against the people who were making extreme sacrifices for that very aim.

Joseph Rotblat [357]

Sir Joseph (Józef) Rotblat KCMG CBE FRS was a Polish physicist, and the only physicist to leave the Manhattan Project on grounds of conscience, although others refused to work on atomic bombs after the defeat of Japan.[358] At the beginning of 1939 he was a physicist working in the Radiological Laboratory in Warsaw. Its director was Ludwick Wertenstein, who had been a pupil of

Marie Curie in Paris, and who was a pioneer in the science of radioactivity in Poland. Later in 1939 Rotblat moved to Liverpool to work with James Chadwick, who had discovered the neutron, before joining the Manhattan project at the Los Alamos Laboratory in New Mexico. He returned to Liverpool and became acting director of research in nuclear physics in Liverpool, before moving to London as Professor of Physics at St Bartholomew's Hospital Medical School. Rotblat became one of the most prominent critics of the nuclear arms race. He worked with organisations connected to nuclear physics, and apparently arranged the 'Atom Train', a major travelling exhibition for schools on civil nuclear energy.[358]

After hearing of the bombing of Hiroshima and seeing an impending nuclear arms race Rotblat remarked that he 'became worried about the whole future of mankind.'[359] Rotblat's work on contamination caused by fallout from nuclear explosions resulted in the Partial Nuclear Test Ban Treaty signed by the governments of the Soviet Union, United Kingdom and United States in the autumn of 1963.[360] Rotblat campaigned ceaselessly against nuclear weapons throughout his life. In an interview shortly before the 2004 presidential election in the US he expressed the belief that the Russell–Einstein Manifesto still had 'a great relevance today, after 50 years, particularly with the election in the United States,' and above all, with the prospect to the pre-emptive use of nuclear weapons.[358]

The Russell-Einstein Manifesto was issued in London July 9, 1955 by Bertrand Russell. It highlighted the dangers of nuclear weapons and called for world leaders to seek peaceful resolution to international conflict. Albert Einstein was among the eleven prominent intellectuals and scientists who signed the manifesto. The manifesto was released during a press conference at Caxton Hall, London, chaired by Joseph Rotblat. The manifesto called for a conference where scientists would assess the dangers to the survival of humanity by weapons of mass destruction.[359] The first conference was held in July 1957 in London, and they became known as the Pugwash conferences because a Canadian philanthropist who had known Russell since 1938 had offered to finance the first conference in his hometown of Pugwash, Nova Scotia.

The author had the privilege of hearing Rotblat speak on the proliferation of nuclear weapons at a scientific meeting in London in the 1980s. It was a superb presentation. Using bar charts Rotblat convincingly showed how the build-up of nuclear weapons was led by the Americans, whose aim was always to stay well ahead of the Soviet Union in its stockpile of weapons and means of delivering them. Rotblat's lecture was never published as might have been expected, as it was considered "political" by the authorities. Professional medical and scientific societies in Britain are designated as "Charities" because they are non-profit making and not taxable. As a condition of their status the Cromwellian Institute insists that they agree to be non-political!!!

JFK (John Fitzgerald Kennedy) used a speech on June 10, 1963 to announce his own unilateral suspension of atmospheric nuclear tests and proposed negotiations in Moscow aimed at drafting a treaty banning nuclear testing in the atmosphere, underground, underneath the oceans, and in outer space.

> He blamed both sides for the arms race, calling on Americans to 're-examine our own attitude – as individuals and as a Nation', acknowledged Russia's wartime sacrifices, declared that 'no government or social system is so evil that its people must be considered lacking in virtue,' and reminded Americans that they and the Soviet people breathe the same air, 'cherish our children's future' and 'are all mortal,' expressing these truths so eloquently that one British newspaper called the address 'one of the greatest state papers of American history.' Soviet newspapers reprinted its entire text and Soviet leader Nikita Khrushchev praised it as the best speech by an American president since Roosevelt... Wadsworth (James, former US ambassador to the United Nations) warned that retired military officers and Dr Edwin Teller, the developer of the hydrogen bomb and a lifelong conservative who was an implacable foe of limiting nuclear testing, would argue that fallout was not dangerous and the Soviets were likely to violate the treaty.
>
> Thurston Clarke[20]

In 1961 Nikita Khrushev threatened to cut off access to Berlin and the East Germans erected a wall dividing Berlin into East Berlin and West Berlin. The Pentagon's reaction was to recommend to Kennedy that he should consider using nuclear weapons to maintain Western rights in the city.

During the crisis he arrived two hours late for a small White House dinner party. His hands shook as he said, 'God, I hope you've been enjoying yourselves over here because I have been over there in that office, not knowing whether the decisions I made were going to start a war and send the missiles flying.'

Thurston Clarke[20]

LeMay was still furious with Kennedy for refusing to provide air cover support for the Cuban rebels, and after going off the record (To Knebel co-author of *Seven Days in May*) he accused him of cowardice . . . The Cuban Missile Crisis started late in 1962 when the Soviet Union began installing missiles in Cuba. JFK was urged by his civilian and military advisers to bomb the sites and invade the island, a course of action that would probably have resulted in a nuclear exchange. Air Force Chief of Staff Curtis LeMay recommended surrounding Cuba with warships and sending Strategic Air Command bombers to bomb it with nuclear weapons. JFK told John Kenneth Galbraith that he had no intention of doing so.[20]

During the 1961 Berlin crisis . . . Chairman of the Joint Chiefs Lyman Lemnitzer had stated that their assumption was a surprise attack [with nuclear weapons] in late 1963 predated by a period of heightened tensions – a scenario resulting in the deaths of more than a hundred million Americans. The CIA director, Allen Dulles, said such a strike would be less effective until the end of 1962, but that his agency and the Pentagon believed that between then and end of 1963 the United States should enjoy a "window of superiority" in land-based missiles. Kennedy had turned to Rusk afterward and, with a strange look in his face and said, 'And we call ourselves the human race.' Rusk believed that the 1961 NES briefing had convinced him that waging a nuclear war was inconceivable, writing, 'To see it all laid out vividly confirmed Khrushchev's warning 'In the event of a nuclear war, the living would envy the dead.' . . . Khrushchev wrote in his 1970 memoirs that during a secret meeting between Robert Kennedy and Ambassador Dobrynin, Robert Kennedy had said, 'The President is in a grave situation, and he does not know how to get out of it. We are under very severe stress. In fact we are under pressure from our military to use force against Cuba.' Considering this, he said, the president 'implores Chairman Khrushchev to accept his offer.' He also warned that although the president was 'very much against starting a war over Cuba, an irreversible chain of events could occur against his will. If the situation continues much longer, the President is not sure that the military will not overthrow him and seize power. The American army could get out of control.'

Thurston Clarke[20]

William Fulbright told Kennedy it (Dallas) was 'a very dangerous place,' adding, 'I wouldn't go there . . . Don't you go.' Next day (Oct 3) he met in the White House with Governor Connelly of Texas, who was less enthusiastic than Fulbright about his Texas trip.[20] Texas has had a chequered history:

> On 16 January 1917, German Foreign Minister, Arthur Zimmermann, informed his ambassador in Mexico that Germany intended to begin unrestricted submarine warfare on 1 February. If as a result of this the USA ceased to be neutral, Germany offered the Mexican government an alliance, a joint declaration of war on the USA and help for Mexico to recover the states of Texas, New Mexico and Arizona, which it had lost in the mid-nineteenth century.
>
> Keith Jeffery[169]

On Friday November 22, 1963 John Fitzgerald Kennedy, the 35th President of the United States was assassinated in Dallas, Texas. The official report into the assassination was a crude government whitewash designed to hide the real truth.[361] President Nixon confessed that the Warren Report was the biggest hoax ever perpetuated on the American public. Lee Harvey Oswald was unlikely to have been a lone gunman. Colonel John Hughes-Wilson in *JFK: An American Coup D'Etat: The Truth Behind the Kennedy Assassination*[361] is of the opinion that the murder of John Kennedy was, like the murder of Julius Caesar 2,000 years before, nothing less than a bloody coup d'etat by his political enemies, a conspiracy to remove a leader who was threatening the power and the money of the ruling establishment. Pointing the finger at Lyndon Johnson, the CIA and the Mafia, Hughes-Wilson joins Jackie and Bobby Kennedy in their conclusion that the assassination of JFK was far more complex than a deranged attack by Lee Harvey Oswald, the 24-year-old ex-Marine.[361]

> I switch the radio on. It is halfway through the P2's morning news. Russian grenades are pouring down on Grozny. They are at it again. But they will never win, not in the long run, that goes without saying. Tolstoy knew it already in *Hadji Murat*, and that book was written a hundred years ago. It is really incomprehensible that the great powers cannot learn the lesson that in the end it is they themselves who will disintegrate. But of course the whole of Chechnya can be demolished. That is rather more possible today than a hundred years ago.
>
> Per Petterson[362]

On my last visit to America I was horrified to see the Stars and Stripes on the altar in a Catholic Church.

> [Enter] Machevill.
> Albeit the world thinke *Machevill* is dead,
> Yet was his soule but flowne beyond the *Alps*, ...
>
> And let them know that I am *Machevill*,
> And weigh not men, and therefore not mens words:
> Admire'd I am of those that hate me most.
>
> Though some speak openly against my books,
> Yet will they read me, and thereby attain
> To *Peters* Chayre.
>
> Christopher Marlowe[151]

Americans will only get their Rights when they end their adoration of the Stars and Stripes. British Secret Service opinion of Norse America: 'The U.S.A.' minuted Vivian [Deputy head of MI6] 'is the home of crank societies

– most of them semi-social and semi-political – but practically all devoted to the generation and release of hot-air.'[169] An empire built on hot air will either explode, implode, or evaporate. Let us hope it is the latter!!!

CHAPTER 16

THE CONGO DEBACLE:
BELGIUM, THE CIA AND MI6

The greatest purveyor of violence in the world today. My own
Government. I cannot be silent.

Martin Luther King[363]

Between 2140 and 2143 on the night of January 17, 1961 the first prime minister
of the newly independent African state of the Congo Patrice Lumumba, who
had been deposed after only two-and a half months in office, was executed
by firing squad in the breakaway province of Katanga[364] Two of his ministers
Maurice Mpolo and Joseph Okita were executed with him. They were lined
up against a tree and shot one at a time. The death squads were commanded
by a Belgian, Captain Julien Gat. Another Belgian, Police Commissioner
Verscheure was in overall command of the execution site. Earlier that day the
three had been brutally beaten and tortured by Belgian and Katangan officers.[364] Written orders from the Belgian government requesting Lumumba's
execution and documents on various arrangements for the execution came to
light afterwards. President Tshombe of Katanga and two of his ministers with
four Belgian officers under the command of the Katangan authorities were
present at the execution. They were buried nearby but the following day the
Belgians and Katangans dug up and dismembered the bodies, then dissolved
them in sulphuric acid, before grinding down the bones and scattering them.
Again on the afternoon and evening of January 21, Police Commissioner Soete
and his brother dug up Lumumba's corpse for the second time, cut it up with
a hacksaw and dissolved it in concentrated sulphuric acid. Years later in 1999,
on a Belgian television programme on the assassination of Lumumba, Soete
displayed a bullet and two teeth that he boasted he had saved from Lumumba's body.[364] In February 2002, the Belgian government apologized to the
Congolese People, and admitted "moral responsibility" and "an irrefutable
portion of responsibility in the events that led to the death of Lumumba".[364]

Eleven days after the former Belgian Congo became independent on

June 30, 1960 the province of Katanga declared independence under Moïse Tshombe, supported by the Belgian government and mining companies such as the powerful Union Minière. Lumumba'a death was only announced on Katangan radio three weeks after his execution, stating that he escaped and was killed by enraged villagers. Almost immediately there were protests worldwide. In Belgrade, the capital of Yugoslavia, protesters stormed and sacked the Belgian embassy. In London there was a march from Trafalgar Square to the Belgian embassy where a letter of protest was delivered. A demonstration at the United Nations Security Council became violent and spilled over into the streets of New York.

Both Belgium and the United States had actively worked to have Lumumba killed, and there had been previous CIA plots to kill him. A CIA attempt to poison Lumumba may have been ordered by the American President Dwight Eisenhower, who thought he was a communist, which he was not. Lumumba favoured a united Congo and opposed division of the country along ethnic or regional lines. In September 1960 a CIA chemist brought a vial of poison to the Congo with plans to place it on Lumumba's toothbrush, but the local CIA Station Chief Larry Devlin refused permission for it to proceed.[364] It subsequently transpired that Devlin had urged the elimination of Lumumba and is said to have directed the search to capture Lumumba for his transfer to his enemies in Katanga. Recently declassified documents revealed that Eisenhower had said something to CIA chief Allen Dulles to the effect that Lumumba should be eliminated. In December 2013 the US State Department admitted that President Eisenhower authorized the murder of Lumumba.[364] Wikipedia quotes a letter in the *London Review of Books* in which Lord Rea reported having discussed Lumumba's death with Baroness Park of Monmouth shortly before she died in March 2010. Park had been an MI6 officer posted to Leopoldville at the time of Lumumba's death. When Lea mentioned the "uproar" surrounding Lumumba's abduction and murder and how it was suggested that MI6 may have had something to do with it, Baroness Park replied: 'We did, I organised it'.[364]

The apparent haste in eliminating Lumumba was because John F Kennedy was being sworn in as US President on 20 January. Kennedy was expected to liberate Lumumba and establish a closer alliance with the Pan African countries. The White House photographer Jacques Lowe described having seen JFK horror-struck with head in hand, receiving the first news of Lumumba's death by telephone on February 13.[365] Thomas Kanza in *The Rise and Fall of Patrice Lumumba:*

> 1960 was election year in the USA. John F Kennedy was the Democratic candidate, standing against the Republican, Richard M Nixon, Eisenhower's vice-president. Lumumba asked me which one I thought would win. I recalled to him what President Roosevelt's widow had said in 1958 in Boston, when she introduced me to Senator John F Kennedy: 'Here is the future President of the United States of America.' . . . In any case it seemed to me that given the tragic situation in the Congo, it was essential for Lumumba to go there. The West had labelled him a supporter of communism ever since his speech on 30 June – an impression fostered assiduously by Belgian propaganda. Up till then, Lumumba had a lot of sympathizers in America . . .
>
> Three days before Kennedy's official entry into the White House, we heard the tragic news of the transfer of Lumumba, Okito and Mpolo to Katanga. It was on 17 January . . . From the moment of my arrival in the country I had done everything I could to make clear to Americans and everyone else the fear we 'Congolese nationalists' felt for our leader's fate if he remained in the hands of his political enemies without the supervision of the UN. The 20th of January was *the* day. If Lumumba was still alive after that date, he would be safe, and might even be approached by the UN with a view to helping solve the political crisis in the Congo.
>
> Thomas Kanza[366]

Thomas Kanza the Congo's representative at the United Nations was a close associate of Patrice Lumumba. The CIA had targeted Lumumba a few years earlier when Kwame Nkrumah convened the first All-African Peoples' Conference in Accra on December 5, 1958.

> Lumumba met many leaders from other African countries at the Conference. He was able to have long conversations in Swahili, which he spoke fluently, with Tom Mboya of Kenya who was

the chairman. Observers and agents from Eastern and Western countries were also present, and some of them made offers of various kinds to Lumumba. An American who spoke very good French offered his services as an interpreter to Lumumba, who spoke no English, and the offer was accepted. Nkrumah later discovered, however, that this "interpreter" was, in fact, a CIA agent; and Lumumba may have told him more than was advisable. Lumumba vented his anti-colonialist and anti-Belgian feelings in a way he had never been able to express to his Belgian friends, ...

Thomas Kanza[366]

CHAPTER 17

THE WAY FORWARD: A COOPERATIVE UNDER THE CROWN, AND TO HELL WITH CROMWELLIAN TOTALITARIANISM

Dan shall achieve justice for his people as one of the tribes of Israel.

Jacobs Testament[104]

To avoid everything petty, everything illusory, everything that prevents us from being free and happy, that is the whole meaning and purpose of life.

Anton Chekhov[238]

Sometimes, as I lie in bed, I think: 'O Lord, you have given us mighty forests, boundless fields and immeasurable horizons, and we living in their midst, ought really to be giants . . .' Mankind marches forward, perfecting its strength. Everything that is unattainable for us now will one day be near: but we must work; we must help with all our force those who seek the truth.

Anton Chekhov[303]

For the people, and truly I desire their liberty and freedom, as much as anybody; but I must tell you, that their liberty and freedom consists in having the government whose laws by which their lives (the peoples) and their goods might be most their own.

Royal Martyr King Charles 1 on the scaffold 30 Jan 1649[367]

Under the Brehon Laws no one in early Irish Society needed to fear illness. Not only were they assured of treatment and hospitalisation, but the society would not let them or their dependents lack food or means of a livelihood.

Peter Beresford Ellis[120]

Thus, the idea of cooperation was central to Indian [Native American] life, as competition is to ours.

Hugh Brogan[129]

We cannot hope to build a better world without improving the individual. Towards this end, each of us must work towards his own highest development, accepting at the same time his share of responsibility in the general life of humanity—our particular duty being to help those to whom we feel we can be most useful . . . Engaging with the people should replace ruling them.

Marie Curie[368]

At the same time, I remember people suddenly started discussing the Emperor Nicholas II. The only believer in absolute monarchy in our family was Nanny. She always wept whenever she talked about Alexander II's assassination, and looked in awe at portraits of the most august family. My grandmother Liza was also a strong supporter of the monarchy, as she had grown up in similar environment where the Tsar was venerated . . . The only person who did not share our enthusiasm [for the abdication of Nicholas II on 28 February 1917] was Nanny. She sat on a stool and wept bitterly. When people finally asked her what the matter was, she sobbed the same thing over and over again: 'Woe unto you all, woe! You have raised your hand against the Tzar, God's anointed! You will all live to regret it!

Catherine Andreyev[369]

Macedonia's system was monarchy, the most stable form of government in Greek history. It persisted from about 650 to 167 BC and only stopped because the Romans abolished it.

Robert Lane Fox[370]

The notion that there is only one right solution in politics would not only to Mussolini's fascism, but also to communism and any totalitarian political system. Indeed it remains with us today in the Western belief that free-market liberal democracy is the 'answer' to the world's problems.

Paul Strathern[154]

Surely the time has come to rouse the sleeping gods of our hearts and consciousness, to stir the spirits of the Tuatha Dé, to bring light from the darkness, and to restore the glory of forgotten kings, so that once more we might find our path in the world.

Anthony Murphy[76]

If war is the continuation of politics by other means, why politics? The best inheritance we can give our children and grandchildren is a Future. And the best way to ensure a Future is with the simple sound and honest Peasant Principles of Cooperation, Self-sufficiency and Self-reliance. No one can look after the People better than they, themselves.

INTERNATIONALISM

I believe most firmly that this war has been a death-blow to Internationalism, and it has proved an opportunity for a renewal of the slackening sense of Nationality.

Edwin Montague[178]

Patriotism is the cruel tradition of an outlived period, which exists not merely by its inertia, but because governments and ruling classes, aware that not only their power only, but their very existence, depends upon it, persistently excite and maintain it among the people, both by cunning and violence.

Lev Nikolajevic Tolstoy[371]

Youll never have a quiet world til you knock the patriotism out of the human race.

George Bernard Shaw[372]

The greatest disaster of the twentieth century was the demise of internationalism, finally phased out at the beginning of the century by The Great War. It was replaced by nationalism, ultra-nationalism, which can be described as Neo-Nazism, Nazism and patriotism.

Internationalism will replace nationalism and patriotism. Ireland, also to be known as Hebernia, will be a Cooperative under the Crown. The island will be one of the North Atlantic islands of Britain and Ireland. There will be no parliaments, no debating, no representative bodies, no committees, no civil service and no diplomatic service. Experienced and knowledgeable professionals will replace useless and work-shy parliamentarians and their legal functionaries, oligarchs, cronies, mandarins, commissars, bureaucrats and sycophants. The flag of Ireland will be King David's harp on a royal blue background occupying the middle panel, with the top quarter Phoenician purple and the lower quarter a rich green.

> Blue, green and tawny, of Egypt; and the Prophet said, 'Let the blue that is always before thee lead thee to seek the gift that is new.'
>
> John A Goodchild & Daniel J Nolan[62,63]

The new flag or its colours will not be allowed to be used as a national or political symbol in any way. The Union Flag, flying above the Cromwellian Institute, the DOT and House of Robber Barons, is NOT the Royal Flag and will be abolished. The Union Flag includes St Patrick's saltire, the original flag of Ireland; degraded, demeaned and diminished.

CODES OF PRACTICE

Brehon Law as practiced by our Hebrew ancestors was based on the Torah and instituted by the Hebrew Princess Teia Tephi following her Coronation as Queen of Ireland on the Stone of Destiny, Jacob's Pillar *Liá Fáil* on June 21, 583 BC.

Whereon were the things brought forth from the House of

the Lord when we fled, The Stone of Jacob our father, the Seat
wherein Yahveh dwells . . .

John A Goodchild & Daniel J Nolan[62,63]

Brehon Law prevented exploitation, completely unlike our present draco-
nian and vindictive adversarial Romano-Norman legal system, operated by
corrupt governments empowered by violence, cronyism, intimidation, and
punitive taxation systems. Under the new system Codes of Practice, Rules
and Common Sense will replace the present discredited legal system along
with the latest tyranny: European Law. Appropriate mental care will replace
jail for the mentally ill. Psychiatrists and psychiatric nurses will replace judges,
lawyers, criminologists and psychologists. Nearly all others who inhabit our
jails are there because of circumstances such as poverty, ignorance, unem-
ployment, idleness, lack of education, alcohol or drug related violence, and
violence resulting from exposure to gratuitous violence, gun crime and
pornography as portrayed on television.

> Rampant jobless among the less skilled is a terrible plight. It
> is the major cause not only of poverty but of crime, substance
> abuse, alienation, and despair as well, not just for the adults
> who are marginalized . . . but also for the children. The lock
> 'em up strategy for dealing with crime long ago hit the wall of
> diminishing returns, and the human toll of ensuing overkill has
> been tremendous — not only for the people inside the system
> but also for their families and wider communities. The idea of
> prison as rehabilitation has lost any connection with reality;
> time in prison undermines future prospects for both work and
> marriage, disrupts the lives of children, and ultimately precedes
> more crime with sky-high recidivism rates.
>
> Lindsey Brink[373]

Using the cops to crack crime is like taking Aspirin for a brain
tumour.

Raymond Chandler[374]

ADMINISTRATION

> We do not inherit the earth from our ancestors we borrow it
> from our children.
>
> Native American Proverb[375]

The county system will be abolished and the island divided into five provinces
as of old: Connaught, Leinster, Meath, Munster and Ulster. Each province
will have a Provincial Governor, and engineer who will monitor and report on
infrastructure and structure. Private ownership of land will cease – land and
houses will be bought in and the land of Ireland invested in the People through
Hebernian Estates, and managed as small family plots, cooperative farms and
other means. Estates that are already being well managed will be offered back
to the owners on a 999-year lease, should they wish to become part of the new
system. A canal system for transport and irrigation will be constructed. It is
proposed that everyone will have an opportunity to grow their own food, and
cultivation of the soil will replace cattle rearing.

> The Persian economic system (based in dynamic urban centres
> supported by intensive irrigation agriculture, which permitted
> the maintenance of a large population) provided the model used
> by the Arabs in the economic development of the conquered
> areas. The infrastructure was composed of a mixture of land and
> maritime communications, with characteristic links between
> them.
>
> Thomas F Glick[376]

Accommodation will be mostly in spacious well appointed apartments:
Skyscrapers, built of the finest brick, stone, aluminium, steel, gunmetal and
other materials to the highest specifications. Fittings will be of the finest quality. The best locations will be chosen for the building of homes so the occu-
pants have commanding views of the countryside, sea, lakes, hills, mountains
and forests; more pleasing aspects than urban sprawl, Central Park, or the
Hudson River:

The gullet of New York swallowing the tonnage of the world.

Arthur Miller[377]

The apartment will be owned by the occupiers who will pay ground rent to Hebernian Estates for services provided and the upkeep of common areas. They will replace the second-rate housing and the ubiquitous bungalows that blot the landscape. Libraries, art galleries, museums, theatres, concert halls and opera houses will replace the corporates' citadels of glass, office blocks and football stadia. And there is no point in saying that the Native Irish are not up to it. Was it not our engineering forbears who, three thousand years ago, built the round towers, some of the tallest buildings before the American skyscrapers, with the exception of the Great Lighthouse of Alexandria? The round towers are still standing with the exception of those that fell down, or partly fell down, during the earthquake of 401 AD.

A new capital city will be built, probably around Carlingford Lough and named New Carthage or Carthage. And a fitting memorial will be built to our kinsfolk the Carthaginian Phoenicians who suffered terribly when their great city state was destroyed, and its inhabitants killed or taken into slavery by the Romans in 146 BC. Particular attention will be paid to developing the West of Ireland including Donegal with its tremendous potential. It is proposed to enlarge Shannon Airport because of its strategic position, and in time service it with a high-speed rail link to a tunnel under the Irish Sea from Wexford to Wales and across Southern England to link with the Channel Tunnel.

The Engineering Corps of the RHC will be responsible for the infrastructure and structures of the island.

> The name engineer was created in the 18th Century, from the French word "genie" meaning ingenious. The hallmark of an engineer is indeed ingenuity, and he also needs to be creative and innovative, whether a Civil Engineer involved in the design and construction of power stations; a Mechanical Engineer designing and building machinery; an Electrical Engineer working on lighting systems and electronic components; or a Mining Engineer.
>
> Ray Chadwick & Martin C Knights[378]

An Auditor-General, Surgeon-General and Surveyor-General will replace the Attorney-General. The unit of currency will be the Shekel. The Governor-General will be the Chief Executive Officer. The Chief of Finance will be in overall charge of finance, and will report to the Governor-General through the Auditor-General. Medical Examiners will replace coroners and report directly to the Surgeon-General, or deputy, who like the Auditor-General and Surveyor-General will publish an annual report.

Taxing toil converts it into slavery. Under the proposed Codes of Practice there will be no income tax, no National Insurance, no VAT (value added tax), no poll tax, no community tax, no property tax, no stamp duty, no gogglebox extortion fee, no death duties, and no other form of taxation aimed at the individual or the family. The legal system is a giant protection racket administered by the ruling elite: governments and their cronies in the corporate sector who almost daily create new laws to protect their interests and ruthlessly exploit the masses, creating an ever widening gap between a small elite of super-rich getting even richer by the day, while the vast majority of People throughout the world are becoming increasingly impoverished. This is particularly so in Europe, mostly due to the imposition of new European Laws which demand that basic resources, infrastructure and necessities are transferred into the hands of ruthless oligarchs. The media, whose very existence depends on mass advertising, provide a smokescreen by promoting their invidious cult of personality known as Celebrity:

> Professional footballers are hardly on a par with clerks, sales people, engineers and other, more mundane careers. They are more akin to celebrities.
>
> Ramona Depares[379]

In the suggested cooperative future there will be a sales tax fixed at a rate of ten per cent on goods and services with the exception of basic food, footwear, clothing, books, scientific instruments and educational material. Manufacturing will be encouraged. In future there will be no role for business or the corporate sector, whose sole purpose is to transfer goods and services from the producer to the retailer or customer while making a huge margin of profit.

A courier, parcels and mail service will be operated by a single authority, probably known as Royal Mail, in conjunction with the transport system.

An island wide integrated, mostly subterranean rail network in conjunction with a tram system HIMT (Hebernian Integrated Mass Transport), will be constructed. Modern technology makes tunnelling relatively easy compared to previous times; one tunnel-boring machine costs about the same as 2,500 cars. The system may take time to construct but the maintenance costs should be much less than for surface railways, motorways, motorway interchanges, level crossings, flyovers, underpasses, bridges and ferries. An annual ticket at the same price for everyone regardless of where they live would increase efficiency and reduce costs in addition to allowing the money to be spent on operating the system. Giving a service will replace the necessity of making a profit!

The success of trams and railways is based on the fundamental scientific fact:

> Steel wheels rolling on steel rails achieves the most frictionless movement – short of levitation, yet devised, a train can move more tonnage per unit of traction, per unit of fuel consumed and per staff involved in transit than any other medium.
>
> Christian Wolmar; Geoffrey Freeman Allen[380, 381]

> . . . but the transport trucks thundered by at intervals and put little earthquakes in the ground.
>
> John Steinbeck[296]

Electricity will be mostly produced from nuclear energy, generated in underground locations. Cabling for electricity, telephones, television and internet will be tunnelled underground whenever possible. Broadcasting will be from a single television station (Hebernia International) and there will be a single radio station, Hebernian Radio. There will be no mass advertising and no commercial or local television or radio.

LEARNING

> Knowledge is the pathway from slavery to freedom.
>
> Frederick Douglass[279]

The only thing that interfered with my learning was my education.

Albert Einstein [18]

Learning will replace education. Children should, from a very early age be encouraged to learn and explore their new world, and this encouragement should continue throughout childhood and early adulthood. Everyone should learn the alphabet, arithmetic, reading and writing as early as possible. In addition two modern languages, English and French, should be encouraged from an early age. Tutors would replace teachers and tutorial groups will replace classes. Much early learning could take place at home and in small informal groups, with school beginning at the age of seven or eight leading to a qualification at about age twelve that confirms a basic knowledge of arithmetic, algebra, writing, English, French and geography. Learning will be the way of the Tuatha Dé: Encouragement; as opposed to the Roman and Puritan way: Fear and punishment. The only competition in learning will be with oneself: The Pursuit Excellence.

The following are the core subjects to be taught at school for those aged twelve to sixteen leading to a qualification to be known as the Baccalaureate: English, French, arithmetic, bookkeeping, geometry, trigonometry, geography and science (basic physics and chemistry). Core subjects suggested for the final two school years, sixteen to eighteen, leading to the Baccalaureate (Honours): Italian, applied mathematics, basic astronomy and navigation, physics, chemistry and plant sciences. Attendance at secondary school, normally between ages twelve to eighteen would be for three days a week, boys and girls on alternate days, to allow more efficient use of facilities such as science laboratories. This would enable the student ample time to pursue learning and have a reasonable amount of time for recreational activities. During time at secondary school there should be exposure to craft such as sketching, woodcraft, metallurgy and basic mechanics.

It is our moral obligation to give every child the very best education possible.

Desmond Tutu [6]

Personally, in my own intellectual pursuits, I have never felt the need to choose between the arts and sciences. I grew up in a harmonious household in which these 'two cultures' coexisted peacefully.

Lisa Jardine [382]

Basic arithmetic has never been a priority in Britain.

4 July 1662. Up by 5 a-clock; and after my Journall put in order, to my office about my business, which I am resolved to fallow, for every day see what graound I get by it. By and by comes Mr. Cooper, Mate of the *Royall Charles*, of whom I extend to learn Mathematiques; and so begin with him today, he being a very able man and no great matter, I suppose, will content him. After an hour's being with him at Arithmetique, my first attempt being to learn the Multiplicacion table, then we parted till tomorrow . . .

Samuel Pepys: [251]

Whereas in other places much basic arithmetic was self learned at an early age. Marya Sklodovski, later Marie Curie, relates her five-year-old brother's learning:

And at Marki, the torrid grannery where Joseph used to go to learn his multiplication tables . . .

Marie Curie [368]

The universities as we know them will be abolished and replaced by a Mathematical Institute and Medical School. Universities were first created about 800 years ago by the Norman Barons and their ecclesiastical and legal functionaries, and from the beginning were: of the ruling elite, for the ruling elite and by the ruling elite. Subjects taught have become more ridiculous with time. David Day in *Conquest* [383] relates how he broached the subject of Vietnamese refugees in Ireland with his University tutorial group in Dublin. Having asked when the new arrivals should be considered as Irish he describes how a young woman, whose red hair suggested Scandinavian origins, fixed him with a steely stare and declared: 'Never.' [383] First to be abolished will be All

Souls College Oxford and Trinity College Dublin. All Souls is perfectly located to become part of Oxford's "Jewel in the Crown," the Bodleian Library.

The proposed Mathematical Institute will include the following faculties: Astronomy and navigation; mathematics; art, archaeology and architecture; naval architecture, boatbuilding and shipbuilding; physics, chemistry, metallurgy; and engineering: civil, electrical, mechanical, structural, chemical, mining, tunnelling and nuclear. The medical school will incorporate dentistry and there will be an associated school of veterinary medicine.

RHC (ROYAL HEBERNIAN COASTGUARD)

The RHC (Royal Hebernian Coastguard) will replace a standing army. There will be no guns or other weapons of war whose only function is to kill, maim and destroy; and there will be no ceremonial swords or daggers. No toy guns, war games, horror movies or violent movies will be permitted. The Coastguard will be organized along naval-military lines with elite Engineering and Medical Corps, closely integrated with the Mathematical Institute and the Medical School. The Engineering Corps will be responsible for the structure and infrastructure of the Island, while the Medical Corps will provide medical care through a structured, ordered and unified system. Preventative Medicine is by far the most urgent priority and should not concern the RHC as the proposed Codes of Practice are intended to combat poverty by eliminating the availability of alcohol, tobacco, gambling (gaming), junk food, idleness and lack of opportunity in return for a relatively busy, interesting and rewarding lifestyle. Physicians should be free to concentrate on the three main components of patient care in a cooperative and non-competitive system: diagnosis, treatment and rehabilitation. State-of-the-Art hospitals will be specialty based. There will be no general hospitals. Patients with Infectious diseases who are unable to be treated at home by visiting physicians and nurses should be admitted to a specialist centre that can be rapidly expanded in the event of an epidemic.

Two other important corps will be created by the Coastguard: music and catering. The RHC College of Music will oversee music teaching to children from an early age with each child encouraged to learn two instruments, not to include the banjo, guitar or ukulele.

CRAFT

Never forsake the work of your hands!

Psalm 138:8[384]

The only creative thing in the world is the individual.

John Steinbeck[244]

The population is still increasing, whereas the number of people who are willing to use their hands to create a work of art is steadily decreasing.

J L Sellink[385]

Between the extremes came the great bulk of the citizens, 'the middling' sort, the intelligent, energetic, thriving artisan class, the real beneficiaries of America, who gave the city (Philadelphia) its character and did most to exploit the opportunities.

Hugh Brogan[129]

Let every artisan among you come and make all that the Lord has commanded: the tabernacle, with its tent, its coverings, its clasps, its frames, its bars, its columns and its pedestals; the ark with its poles, its cover and the curtain veil; the table, with its poles and all its utensils, and the showbread; the menorah, with its utensils, the lamps, and the oil for the light; the altar of incense, with its poles, the anointing oil, and the fragrant incense; the entrance curtain for the entrance to the tabernacle; the altar for burnt offerings, with its bronze grating, its poles and all its utensils; the basin, with its stand; the hangings of the court, with their columns and pedestals, the curtain for the gate of the court; the tent pegs for the tabernacle, and for the court, with their ropes; . . .

Genesis[386]

Craft will replace graft. Craft is the lynchpin of a civilized society; mass production and built-in obsolescence are its antithesis. Everyone will be encouraged to join the Coastguard for four years after leaving school, although there will be encouragement to join or rejoin at any later age. The first sixteen weeks will mostly consist of basic training with the aim of establishing a good level of physical fitness. The first two years will be a cadetship to be followed by two years as an ensign before qualifying as an officer. During this initial four years the Coastguard will act as a finishing school by combining learning and training in crafts, in addition to including a requirement to do ordinary work. Ample time will be allocated for recreational activities. Most craft training should be complete within four years. If not it should be completed afterwards, hopefully by remaining in the service. There will be no compunction to leave the service, with encouragement to remain in the Coastguard on a full-time or half-time basis. Those working a shift of two or three days per week will be considered half-time, leaving them free to pursue other interests outside the coastguard for the other four or five days. On leaving each person will be encouraged to join the Reserve RHC. Service medals, bronze, silver and gold will be awarded to those completing ten, twenty-five and forty years of full-time or equivalent service.

Crafts will include the following: engraving, art, sculpture, goldsmith, silversmith, watchmaking, coach building, cabinet making, woodcarving, and other woodcraft, model-making, stone mason, bricklaying, shoemaking, harness making, wheelwright, plastering, glassblowing and hand-cutting of glass. Others such as tailoring, dressmaking and embroidering, while being recognized as master crafts, will be reserved for those in the older age groups. Everyone should become proficient in at least one craft throughout their lifetime.

> Moses said to the Israelites: See the Lord has singled out Bezalel son of Uri, son of Hur, of the tribe of Judah, and has filled him with a divine spirit of skill and understanding and knowledge in every craft: in the production of embroidery, in making things of gold, silver, or bronze, in cutting and mounting precious stones, in carving wood, and in every other craft. He has also given both him and Oholiah, son of Ahisamach, of the tribe of Dan, the ability to teach others. He has endowed them with

skill to execute all types of work: engraving, embroidering, the making of variegated cloth of violet, purple and scarlet yarn and fine linen thread, weaving and all other arts and crafts.

Artisans[387]

WORK

An extended day of 4am to 10pm is suggested to replace the present 6am to midnight, with six working days, Sunday to Friday, normally divided into 35-hour shifts of three-days each. There should be proper facilities for staff, including a canteen dining area and a main meal in the middle of the day. Saturday will be a day of rest. The work pattern will be different in hospitals where continuity of patient care will be of paramount importance. Nurses, physiotherapists, radiographers and laboratory staff will work one forty-eight shift each week, to be on duty for up to 14 hours each day. This will enable them to work two days a week with five days free. For the medical staff it will be a three-day working week. This will enable doctors to give their undivided attention to patient care. Clinics, operating theatres and other departments will operate for up to fifteen hours a day. Police officers will also work one 48-hour shift each week, giving them ample time to learn new skills, for recreation, and for looking after children. The period of service will be for 10–15 years unless promoted to a higher rank.

There will be seven holidays each year: St Patrick's Day on March 17, three days in the middle of the year, June 19, 20 and 21 to celebrate Queen Tephi's arrival and ascent to the Throne of David; Chrismas Eve, Christmas Day and St Stephens Day; and on the first of January a half day to welcome the dawn of a New Year. There will be no Bank Holidays. Four weeks annual leave will be the norm.

DE-INDUSTRIALIZATION

The nineteenth-century Atlantic world paid for its numerous leisured classes by merciless exactions on everybody else. The story of industrial workers in England (or, a little later, in

Pennsylvania) was as bad as anything which could be told of the plantations, as defenders of slavery liked to point out . . . (in nineteenth-century Europe) new industries stimulated new wants and destroyed the self-sufficiency of peasant households and the saleability of peasant products . . . as early as 1925, 25,000 people were killed by cars in one year – 17,500 of them pedestrians.

Hugh Brogan[129]

For well over a century we have become increasingly controlled by machines. If the Human Race is to make any progress it would be better if we were to rid ourselves of most of them. The internal combustion engine alone brought few real benefits while creating nothing less than: "Hell on Earth." Nothing has contributed more to death, serious injury and destruction in peace and war than petrol and diesel engines. During the twentieth century hundreds of thousands of civilians, remote from the front line, have been killed in wars, many the victims of violence rained down from the sky. And civilians caught in the front lines have died in their millions, and many more made homeless because of the mechanization of war.

> (10 May 1940) German spearheads were rolling up the Dutch army. Meanwhile south-westwards some 134,000 men and 1,600 vehicles, of which 1,222 were tanks, began threading their way through the Ardennes to deliver the decisive blow of the campaign against the weak centre of the French line . . . before peace came accidents in the blackout [in Britain] killed more people than did the Luftwaffe: in the last four months of 1939 there were 4,133 deaths on the roads, 2,657 of those pedestrians, a figure almost double that for the same period in 1938.
>
> Max Hastings[351]

Katie Alvord in her aptly titled book *Divorce your Car: Ending the Love Affair with the Car*:

> In 1882, German engine-builder Karl Benz took his fledgling internal combustion carriage out for a spin on the streets of Stuttgart. He was promptly arrested. Benz, though, did not let

apprehension by the law stand in his way . . . about the same time and also in Germany, engineer Gottlieb Daimler began pursuing his own dalliance with the car building four prototypes between 1885 and 1889. Benz was first to announce a car for sale, advertising his gasoline-powered three-wheeler in an 1888 prospectus claiming the vehicle posed "no danger whatsoever." French agents, entranced by automobility, soon started selling Benz buggies and cars with Diamler engines to wealthy Parisians who used them for status-displaying promenades along the Champs-d'Elysees . . .

Cable cars and then electric trolleys came to cities in the 1870s and 1880s, soon carrying loads of urban passengers. When bicycles showed up around the same time, the public marvelled at the personal freedom they allowed.

Katie Alvord [388]

The diesel engine was idea of Rudolf Diesel a French-born German engineer.[389] In the late 1880s Diesel published a treatise on his experimental work, following which he obtained a patent for his compression–ignition engine. In his engine, fuel was injected at the end of compression and ignited by the high temperature resulting from the compression. From 1893 to 1897, Heinrich von Buz, the director of MAN AG in Augsburg, gave Diesel the opportunity to develop his ideas. Diesel obtained patents for his design in Germany and other countries, including the United States.[389]

Up to the time I went to Eton I had only once or twice been in a motor-car: and up to his death my father refused to own what he termed 'an invention of the Devil'.

R V C Bodley[390]

The motor-car never replaced horses in the affections of the polo-playing former cavalry officer [Sir Winston Churchill].

David Eisenhower[391]

The internal conflict was evident even in the types of metaphors used to describe the problem. Unlike the first motorists, who saw only the vast potential of automobility and likened the opportunity to the rubbing of Aladdin's lamp, many soon came to see the car as a demon unleashed. Some described this evil as a Frankenstein's monster – a mechanical nightmare created by the vanity of mankind . . . More writers, possibly less comfortable with Victorian science fiction, preferred the metaphor of conflict. Fresh from their experience of World War 1, Americans understood both the inevitable and avoidable aspects of mortal combat.

David Blanke[392]

Eventually the car became the author of ruin as well as happiness, when its insatiable need for petrol outstripped even the abundant supply of American oil and, by oversetting the US balance of payments and putting crucial amounts of wealth and power in the hands of foreign suppliers, upset not only domestic tranquillity but the prospects of peace in the world.

Hugh Brogan[129]

The toll from death and injury on the roads of the world since the first cars, 'Anarchy on wheels', a hundred and twenty years ago years ago has been horrific. According to WHO approximately 1.24 million deaths occurred on the world's roads in 2010.[393] Nearly half of all orthopaedic beds in hospitals are occupied by road accident victims. And our almost constant use of the car is one of the main causes of premature ageing. The financial cost is horrendous and is one of the main causes of impoverishment of the masses. Clearing the roads of powered vehicles would enable people to walk and cycle in peace. And horse drawn vehicles could return. I, myself, have walked, cycled and used public transport whenever possible throughout my life, and I do not feel any the worse for it.

Ironically, while GM was mobilizing the Reich, the company was also leading a criminal conspiracy to monopolistically undermine mass transit in dozens of American cities that would help addict the United States to oil . . . At the centre of the conspiracy was National City Lines, a shadowy company that suddenly arose in 1937, ostensibly run by five barely-educated Minnesota bus drivers, the Fitzgerald brothers. Yet the Fitzgeralds miraculously marshalled millions of Dollars to buy up one failing trolley system after another. Soon through a patchwork of subsidiaries, the brothers owned and controlled transit systems in more than 40 cities. Generally when National City Lines acquired the system, the tracks were pulled up from the street, the beloved electric trolleys were trashed or burned, and the whole system was replaced with more expensive, unpopular and environmentally hazardous motor buses that helped addict America to oil.

Edwin Black[204]

The National City Lines were a front for General Motors, in league with Mack Truck, Phillips Petroleum, Standard Oil of California and Firestone Tires, with GM and Mack trucks dividing the bus manufacturing and sales market between them. Transit systems in sixteen states were taken over. In 1947 the offending companies were charged with criminal conspiracy. They were convicted and fined derisory sums: $5,000 to each corporate defendant except Standard, which was fined $1,000.[204]

Tractors and other powered farm machinery are costly, extremely inefficient, and for the most part unnecessary. We would be better off without them. Horse drawn ploughs can be used where appropriate. It would be nice to think that at some time in the future horses would, to a large extent, replace horsepower! Traditional fishing will replace trawling and fish farming. Reuse will replace recycling. These simple measures alone should significantly reduce waste. Machines that take money such as ticketing machines, vending machines, gaming and cash dispensers are not only expensive but unnecessary. The only coin-operated machines permitted will be public telephones. And the ubiquitous "Cattle Counters" that we have to check through to use rail transport can be dispensed with.

HEALTH

It's wonderful to me what the human body can achieve if you treat it right.

William Boyd[394]

The general health of the population has progressively deteriorated as a result of government policies deliberately put in place to promote profiteering by their cronies, and make those who are already wealthy, even richer. The health of the people will be an absolute priority. Future policy will be aimed at reversing the trend towards absolute ill-health. A lot of time and research is spent on trying to formulate healthy diets. Reverting to the age old custom of having our main meal of proper food in the middle of the day dinner, and ending grazing and snacking as well as avoiding alcohol, tobacco, and drinks made from sugar-rich syrup mixed with water, should go a long way to reducing obesity and the increasing incidence of Type II diabetes.

Markets and ordinary old-fashioned shops will replace supermarkets, superstores, shopping centres, chain-stores, franchises and department stores; looking for good ordinary plain food in a supermarket is like looking for a needle in a haystack! Ice cream parlors, coffee shops, cafés, tea rooms, juice bars and restaurants, owned by individuals, families or small cooperate groups, will replace pubs, drinking clubs, nightclubs, betting shops, gambling dens, casinos, pawn brokers and tattoo parlors. There will be no lottery. Cooperative and mutual banks and building societies will replace corporate banking and loan sharks.

TRADITIONALISM

Traditionalism will replace modernism. Progress, measureable progress, will replace 'moving with the times'.

> Modernism is a totalitarian ideology which, like all dogmatism, is based on improbable symptoms. It is unable to tolerate let alone accept opposition, contradiction or refusal. If you accept such fantastic assumptions you necessarily abandon your own cognitive capacities, and blind yourself to overwhelming evidence, in spite of interior and exterior contradiction. Modernism's declaration of war against tradition was not just a rejection of absolute tradition but it included all knowledge and know-how which does not fit its reductive vision of humanity, history, technology, politics . . .
>
> Leon Krier[395]

EPILOGUE

IRELAND IN THE SEVENTH CENTURY: PRINCE ALFRID'S ITENERARY THROUGH IRELAND[296]

To Ireland, the land of Saints and Scholars, came many foreign nobles and princes to receive an education not to be had in their own countries. Prince Alfrid, a Saxon Prince afterwards King of the Northumbrians, was one of those students, and was in Ireland according to Ven Beade about the year 684. His original poem, of which this is a translation, is still extant in the Irish language.

> I found in Innisfail the fair,
> In Ireland, while in exile there,
> Women of worth, both grave and gay men,
> Many clerics and many lay men.
>
> I traveled its fruitful provinces round,
> And in every one of the five I found,
> Alike in church and in palace hall,
> Abundant apparel, and food for all.
>
> Gold and silver, I found, and money,
> Plenty of wheat and plenty of honey;
> I found God's people rich in pity.
> Found many a feast and many a city.
>
> I found in Armagh the splendid,
> Meekness, wisdom, and prudence blended,
> Fasting, as Christ hath recommended,
> And noble councillors untranscended.
>
> I found in each great church moreo'er,
> Whether on island or on shore,
> Piety, learning, fond affection,
> Holy welcome, and kind protection.

I found the good lay monks and brothers
Ever beseeching help for others,
And in their keeping the holy word
Pure as it came from Jesus the Lord.

I found in Munster unfettered of any,
Kings and Queens, and poets a many –
Poets well skilled in music and measure,
Prosperous doings, mirth and pleasure.

I found in Connaught the just, redundance
Of riches, milk in lavish abundance;
Hospitality, vigour, fame,
In Cruachan's land of heroic name.

I found in the country of Connall the glorious,
Bravest heroes, ever victorious;
Fair-complexioned men and warlike,
Ireland's lights, the high, the starlike!

I found in Ulster, from hill to glen,
Hardy warriors, resolute men;
Beauty that blossomed when youth was gone,
And strength transmitted from sire to son.

I found in the noble district of Boyle
(*MS here illegible*)
Brehon's Erenachs, weapons bright,
And horsemen bold and sudden in fight.

I found in Leinster, the smooth and sleek,
From Dublin to Slewmargy's peak;
Flourishing pastures, valour, health,
Long-living worthies, commerce, wealth.
I found besides, from Ara to Glea,
In the broad rich country of Ossorie,

Sweet fruits, good laws for all and each,
Great chess players, men of truthful speech.

I found in Meath's fair principality,
Virtue, vigour and hospitality;
Candour, joyfulness, bravery, purity,
Ireland's bulwark and security.

I found strict morals in age and youth,
I found historians, recording truth;
The things I sing of, in verse unsmooth
I found them all – I have written sooth.

CONCLUSION

Life should be a learning experience. If everyone does their share of learning, menial tasks, ordinary work and craftwork there will be no need for autocracy, bureaucracy, democracy, plutocracy, hypocrisy, militarism, republicanism, capitalism or communism.

Equality causes no wars
Plutarch

SUGGESTED FURTHER READING

Police Casualties in Ireland 1919–1922. Richard Abbott.

Divorce your Car: Ending the Love Affair with the Automobile. Katie Alvord.

Henry Ford and the Jews: The Mass Production of Hate. Neil Baldwin.

Nazi Nexus: America's Corporate Connections to Hitler's Holocaust. Edwin Black.

The Coke Machine: The Dirty Truth Behind the World's Favorite Soft Drink. Michael Blanding.

Hell on Wheels: The Promise and Peril of America's Car Culture, 1900–1940. David Blanke.

Longman History of the United States of America. Hugh Brogan.

A History of the English-Speaking Peoples. Winston Churchill.

JFK's Last Hundred Days: An Intimate Portrait of a Great President. Thurston Clarke.

Madame Curie. Eve Curie.

The Myth of Hitler's Pope: How Pope Pius Rescued Jews from the Nazis. Rabbi David G Dalin.

Sybil or *Two Nations.* Benjamin Disraeli.

Daniel O'Connell and the Revival of National Life in Ireland. Robert Dunlop.

Hell or Connaught! The Cromwellian Colonisation of Ireland. Peter Beresford Ellis.

The Great Crash 1929. John Kenneth Galbraith.

Violence: Our Deadly Epidemic and Its Causes. James Gilligan.

The Book of Tephi. John A Goodchild. Daniel J Nolan, Editor.

JFK: An American Coup D'Etat: The Truth Behind the Kennedy Assassination. Colonel John Hughes-Wilson.

MI6: The History of the Secret Intelligence Service 1909–1949. Keith Jeffery.

The Rise and Fall of Patrice Lumumba: Conflict in the Congo. Thomas Kanza.

The Last three Popes and the Jews. Pinchas E Lapide.

The Black and Tans: British Police and Auxiliaries in the Irish War of Independence, 1920–1921. D M Leeson.

Of Human Bondage. W S Maugham.

'Tis. A Memoir. Frank McCourt.

Clippers: The Ships that Shaped the World. Daniel J Nolan.

Power to the People: And to Hell with Cromwellian Totalitarianism. Daniel J Nolan.

Hell or Barbados: Ethnic Cleansing of Ireland. Sean O'Callaghan.

An Instance of the Fingerpost. Iain Pears.

Frontline Ukraine: Crisis in the Borderlands. Richard Sakwa.

The Gulag Archopelago. Aleksandr Solzhenitsyn.

The Untold Story of the United States. Oliver Stone & Peter Kuznick.

In Siberia. Colin Thrubon

The Forsaken: From the Great Depression to the Gulags: Hope and Betrayal in Stalin's Russia. Tim Tzouliadis.

The Collaboration: Hollywood's Pact with Hitler. Ben Urwand.

BIBLIOGRAPHY AND SOURCES

1   Rahe, Paul A. *Republics Ancient and Modern*. The Wilson Quarterly. 2004:28;68–84.

2   Purkiss, Diane. *The English Civil Wars: A Peoples History*. London: Harper Press, 2006.

3   *Psalm 37:14* In: Hartgdegen, Stephen J., Ceroke, Christian P., O'Boyle, Cardinal Patrick., Habig, Marion., O'Donnell, Cletus F. *The New American Bible*. Nashville – Camden – New York: Thomas Nelson, 1978.

4   Ellis, Peter Beresford. *Hell or Connaught! The Cromwellian Colonisation of Ireland*. London: Hamish Hamilton, 1975.

5   www.brainyquote.com/quotes/authors/f/francis-of-assisi.html

6   www.brainyquote.com/quotes/authors/d/desmond_tutu.html

7   Ackroyd, Peter. *Civil War: A History of England. Vol III*. London: Macmillan, 2014.

8   Howard, Michael & Paret, Peter. Eds. *On War*. New Jersey: Princeton University Press, 1984.

9   Markham, James M. *NANTES JOURNAL: In a Corner of France, Long Live the Old Regime*. New York Times: June 17, 1989.

10 de Villiers, Philippe. *Open Letter to the Choppers of Heads and Liars of the Bicentenary*. In: Markham, James M. *NANTES JOURNAL: In a Corner of France, Long Live the Old Regime*. New York Times: June 17, 1989.

11 Karsten, Peter. *Cromwell in America*. In: Howell, Roger & Richardson, R C. *Images of Oliver Cromwell*. Manchester: Manchester University Press, 1993.

12 Smith, Harriet Eleanor. Ed. *Autobiography of Mark Twain: The Complete and Authoritative Edition. Volume 1*. Los Angeles & London: University of California Press, 2010.

13 Bramley, Serge, *Leonardo: the Artist and the Man*. London & New York: Michael Joseph, 1992.

14 Gandi, Mahatma. *Non-Violence in Peace and War. Vols I & II*. Ahmedabad: Navajivan, 1948–1949.

15 O'Rourke P J. *Parliament of Whores: A Lone Humorist Attempts to Explain the Entire US Government.* London, Picador, 1991.

16 www.gutenberg.org Roosevelt, Theodore. *The Winning of the West. Volume One. From the Alleghenies to the Mississippi 1769–1776.* New York: G P Putnam's Sons, 1889.

17 Roosevelt, Theodore. *Oliver Cromwell.* London: Archibald Constable, 1900.

18 Isaacson, Walter. *Einstein: His Life and Universe.* New York & London: Simon & Schuster, 2007.

19 Stone, Oliver & Kuznick, Peter. *The Untold Story of the United States.* New York: Simon & Schuster, 2012; London: Random House, 2012.

20 Clarke, Thurston. *JFK's Last Hundred Days: An Intimate Portrait of a Great President.* London: Allen Lane, 2013.

21 Bush, Laura. *Spoken from the Heart.* London: Simon & Schuster, 2010.

22 Herbert, Frank. *Chapterhouse: Dune.* www.notable-quotes.com/h/herbert_frank.html

23 Tomlin, E W F. *Wyndham Lewis: An Anthology of his Prose.* London: Methuen, 1969.

24 Dickens, Charles. *Dictionary of Political Quotations.* Speech at Birmingham and Midlands Institute: September 27, 1869. Oxford: Oxford University Press, 1996.

25 Sand, Shlomo. (Translated by Jeremy Forman) *The Invention of the Land of Israel: From Holy Land to Homeland.* London & New York: Verso, 2012.

26 O'Casey, Sean. *Purple Dust: A Wayward Comedy in Three Acts.* London: Macmillan, 1940.

27 Duff, Tim. *Plutarch's Lives: Virtue and Vice.* Oxford: Clarendon Press, 1999.

28 MacDonough, Giles. *After the Reich: From the Liberation of Vienna to the Berlin Airlift.* London: John Murray/ Hodder Headline, 2007.

29 Disraeli, B. *Sybil* or *Two Nations.* London: Henry Colburn, 1845.

30 http://en.wikipedia.org/wiki/Herodotus

31 Griffiths, John W. *Treatise on Marine and Naval Architecture or Theory and Practice Blended in Ship Building.* 4 ed. New York: D Appleton; London: John Weale, 1854.

32 Churchill, Winston. *A History of the English-Speaking Peoples. Vol 2. The New World.* London: Cassell, 1956.

33 Trevor-Roper, Hugh. *History of the Enlightenment.* New Haven & London: Yale University Press, 2010.

34 Pears, Iain. *An Instance of the Fingerpost.* London: Cape, 1997.

35 *Taking Liberties: The Struggle for Britain's Freedom and Rights.* Exhibition. London: British Library, 2009.

36 http://en.wikipedia.org/Charles_I_of_England

37 http://en.wikipedia.org/wiki/British_Library

38 Jordan, Thomas E. *Sir William Petty, 1623–1687: The Genius Entrepreneur of Seventeenth-Century Ireland.* New York, Toronto & Ceredigion, Wales: Edwin Mellen Press, 2007.

39 Hughes, J Trevor. Miraculous Deliverance of Anne Green: An Oxford Case of Resuscitation in the Seventeenth Century. *British Medical Journal.* 1982:285;1792-1793.

40 Nolan, Daniel J. *Power to the People: And to Hell with Cromwellian Totalitarianism.* Bray, County Wicklow: Malbay, 2014.

41 Fraser, Antonia. *Cromwell: Our Chief of Men.* London: Weidenfeld & Nicolson, 1973.

42 O'Callaghan, Sean. *Hell or Barbados: Ethnic Cleansing of Ireland.* Dublin: Brandon, 2013.

43 Lecky, William Edward Hartpole. *A History of Ireland in the Eighteenth Century.* London: Longman Green, 1913.

44 http://en.wikipedia.org/wiki/John_Philip_Nolan

45 Orwell, George. *Nineteen-Eighty-Four.* London: Secker & Warburg, 1949.

46 Petrie, W M Flinders. *Neglected British History.* London: Proceedings of the British Academy 1917:8:251–278.

47 Murphy, Paul. *Ancient Rock Art is Discovered at Teltown.* The Meath Chronicle. September 22, 2005.

48 Churchill, Winston. *A History of the English-Speaking Peoples. Vol 1.* London: Cassell, 1956.

49 Keating, Geoffrey. *Keating's General History of Ireland. Translated from the original Irish, with many Curious Amendments taken from the Psalters of*

Tara and Cashel, & Co by Dermod O'Connor. Dublin: James Duffy, Sons & Co, 1854.

50 Lythgoe, Jane E. www.Yehweh.org/profiles/blogs/english-alphabet-shaped-by

51 Capt, E Raymond. *Missing Links Discovered in Assyrian Tablets: The Remarkable Discovery of Assyrian Tablets that Reveal the Fate of "The Long Lost Tribes of Israel."* Muskogee, Oklahoma: Artisan, 2012.

52 Davidy, Yair. *Lost Israelite Identy: The Hebraic Ancestry of the Celtic Races.* Jerusalem: Russell-Davis, 1996.

53 *Genesis. 38: 27–30.* In: Hartgdegen, Stephen J., Ceroke, Christian P., O'Boyle, Cardinal Patrick., Habig, Marion., O'Donnell, Cletus F. *The New American Bible.* Nashville – Camden – New York: Thomas Nelson, 1978.

54 D'Alton, E A. *History of Ireland: From the Earliest Times to the Present Day. Vol 1.* London: Gresham Publishing, 1912.

55 www.ldsfreedomportal.net/HISWORD1b.doc Andrews, Darren. *A Synopsis of World History: Being an Overview of Some of the Most Significant and Influential Events of the Past Six Thousand Years.* 2003

56 http://en.wikipedia.org/wiki/Phoenicia

57 Robinson, George. *Phoenicia.* London: Longmans, Green, 1889.

58 Markoe, Glenn E. *Peoples of the Past: Phoenicians.* Los Angeles: University of California Press, 2000.

59 *Judges 5: 17.* In: Hartgdegen, Stephen J., Ceroke, Christian P., O'Boyle, Cardinal Patrick., Habig, Marion., O'Donnell, Cletus F. *The New American Bible.* Nashville – Camden – New York: Thomas Nelson, 1978.

60 Baucum, Walter. *Phoenicia.* www.uhcg.org/Lost-10-Tribes/walt3a-Phoenicia.html

61 Capt de La Falconnière, R. *Le Crepuscule de Babylone: Roman.* Paris; Eugène Figuière, 1936.

62 Goodchild, John A. *The Book of Tephi.* London: Kegan Paul, Trench, Trübner & Co, 1897.

63 Nolan, Daniel J. Ed: Goodchild, John A. *The Book of Tephi.* Bray, County Wicklow: Malbay, 2014.

64 www.stewartsynopsis.com/Israel.htm

65 Byron, Lord. *Don Juan.* In: McGann, Jerome J. Ed. *Lord Byron: The Major Works.* Oxford & New York: Oxford University Press, 1986.

66 http://en.wikipedia.org/wiki/River_Don,_South_Yorkshire

67 Massey, John Dunman. *Tamar Tephi: or, the Maid of Destiny. The Great Romance of the Royal House of Britain. 2nd Ed.* London: Covenant Publishing, 1924.

68 Charriere, Doris & Adams, Jack. *Tamar, the Tender Twig.* Colorado Springs: Chalet Publishing, 1997.

69 http://en.wikipedia.org/wiki/Tamar-class_lifeboat

70 http://en.wikipedia.org/wiki/Albion

71 http://en.wikipedia.org/wiki/River_Don,_Aberdeenshire

72 http://en.wikipedia.org/wiki/Rosemarkie_sculpture_fragments

73 www.ancientscripts.com/ogham.html

74 Sakwa, Richard. *Frontline Ukraine: Crisis in the Borderlands.* London: I B Tauris, 2015.

75 Vallancey, Charles. *Collectanea de Rebus Hibernicis.* Dublin: T Ewing, 1770–1804.

76 Murphy, Anthony. *Newgrange: Monument to Immortality.* Dublin: Liffey Press, 2012.

77 Ó Dónaill, Niall. *Foclóir Gaeilge Béarla.* Dublin: Oifig an Tsoláthair, 1977.

78 *Exodus 38: 22-23.* In: Hartgdegen, Stephen J., Ceroke, Christian P., O'Boyle, Cardinal Patrick., Habig, Marion., O'Donnell, Cletus F. *The New American Bible.* Nashville – Camden – New York: Thomas Nelson, 1978.

79 Childress, David Hatcher. *Introduction* In: O'Brien, Henry. *The Round Towers of Atlantis.* Longman: London, 1834.

80 Marlow, Christopher. *The Tragedie of Dido, Queene of Carthage.* In: Gill, Roma. Ed. *The Complete Works of Christopher Marlowe. Volume 1.* Oxford, Clarendon Press, 1987.

81 http://en.wikipedia.org/wiki/Carthage

82 Garland, Robert. *Hannibal.* London: Bristol Classical Press, 2010.

83 http://en.wikipedia.org/wiki/Ancient_Carthage

84 Charles-Picard, Gilbert & Colette. *Daily Life in Carthage at the Time of Hannibal.* (Translated from French by A E Foster) London: Allen & Unwin, 1961.

85 Lancel, Serge. *Carthage: A History.* (Translated by Antonia Nevill). Oxford: Blackwell, 1995.

86 Bagnell, Nigel. *The Punic Wars: Rome, Carthage and the Struggle for the Mediterranean.* London: Hutchinson, 1990.

87 Wormington, B H. *Carthage.* London: Robert Hale, 1960.

88 http://en.wikipedia.org/wiki/Cato_the_Elder

89 Miles, Richard. *Carthage must be Destroyed: The Rise and Fall of an Ancient Civilization.* London: Allen Lane, 2010.

90 jaysromanhistory.com/romeweb/engineer/art12.htm

91 Picard, Gilbert Charles & Picard, Colette. (Translated by Dominique Collon) *The Life and Death of Carthage: A Survey of Punic History and Culture from its Birth to the Final Tragedy.* London: Sidwick & Jackson, 1968.

92 Moore, Mabel. *Carthage of the Phoenicians: In the Light of Modern Excavations.* London: William Heinemann, 1905.

93 Groom, Nigel. *The Union Jack: The Story of the British Flag.* London: Atlantic Books, 2006.

94 jahtruth.net/liafail.htm

95 jahtruth.net/teltn.htm

96 *Genesis. 28: 10-12.* In: Hartgdegen, Stephen J., Ceroke, Christian P., O'Boyle, Cardinal Patrick., Habig, Marion., O'Donnell, Cletus F. *The New American Bible.* Nashville – Camden – New York: Thomas Nelson, 1978.

97 Cliff, Nigel. *The Last Crusade: The Epic Voyages of Vasco da Gama.* New York: HarperCollins, 2011; London: Atlantic Books, 2012.

98 http://en.wikipedia.org/wiki/Battle_of_Tara_(Ireland)

99 http://en.wikipedia.org/wiki/DonaldIII_of_Scotland

100 britam.org/namesakes.html

101 Larsson, Björn. *From Cape Wrath to Finisterre.* London: Haus Publishing, 2005.

102 jahtruth.net/tephisum.htm

103 *Genesis 30: 1-6.* In: Hartgdegen, Stephen J., Ceroke, Christian P., O'Boyle, Cardinal Patrick., Habig, Marion., O'Donnell, Cletus F. *The New American Bible.* Nashville – Camden – New York: Thomas Nelson, 1978.

104 *Genesis 49: 16.* In: Hartgdegen, Stephen J., Ceroke, Christian P., O'Boyle, Cardinal Patrick., Habig, Marion., O'Donnell, Cletus F. *The New American Bible.* Nashville – Camden – New York: Thomas Nelson, 1978.

105 *Joshua 18: 2-29* In: Hartgdegen, Stephen J., Ceroke, Christian P., O'Boyle, Cardinal Patrick., Habig, Marion., O'Donnell, Cletus F. *The New American Bible.* Nashville – Camden – New York: Thomas Nelson, 1978.

106 http://en.wikipedia.org/wiki/Tribe_of_Dan

107 http://en.wikipedia.org/wiki/bnei_brak

108 *Numbers. 2: 1-26.* In: Hartgdegen, Stephen J., Ceroke, Christian P., O'Boyle, Cardinal Patrick., Habig, Marion., O'Donnell, Cletus F. *The New American Bible.* Nashville – Camden – New York: Thomas Nelson, 1978.

109 jahtruth.net/bkofke.htm

110 Gawler, John Cox. *Dan – The Pioneer of Israel.* London: W M Guest, 1880.

111 Healy, John. *Ireland's Ancient Schools and Scholars. 6th Ed.* London: Burns & Oates, 1912.

112 Baldwin, Neil. *Henry Ford and the Jews: The Mass Production of Hate.* New York: Public Affairs, 2001.

113 www.ensignmessage.com/archives/tracingdan.html

114 www.israelite.ca/research/source/document/dan_in_ europe.html

115 O'Brien, Henry. *The Round Towers of Atlantis 1834.* Kempton, Illinois: Adventures Unlimited Press, 2002.

116 http://nolanfamilies.org/index.php?topic=roots

117 http://en.wikipedia.org/wiki/Tara_Brooch

118 Commons.wikimedia.org/wiki/File:Ardagh_chalice.jpg

119 http://en.wikipedia.org/wiki/Book_of_Kells

120 Ellis, Peter Beresford. *The Celtic Empire. The First Millenium of Celtic History* c. 1000 BC – 51 AD. London: 1990.

121 Morris, Marc. *The Norman Conquest.* London: Hutchinson, 2012.

122 Persephone. www.amazon.co.uk/Vikings-Neil-Oliver (book review)

123 Churchill, Winston. *A History of the English-Speaking Peoples. Vol 1. The Birth of Britain.* London: Cassell, 1956.

124 http://en.wikipedia.org/wiki/William_de_Burgh

125 http://en.wikipedia.org/wiki/Crusades

126 http://en.wikipedia.org/wiki/House_of_de_Burgh

127 D'Alton, E A. *History of Ireland: From the Earliest Times to the Present Day. Vol 4.* London: Gresham Publishing, 1912.

128 McCourt, Frank. *'Tis. A Memoir.* New York: HarperCollins, 1999.

129 Brogan, Hugh. *Longman History of the United States of America.* London & New York: Longman, 1985.

130 www.tullynallycastle.ie

131 wiki.bcw-project.org/commonwealth/horse-regiments/daniel-abbott

132 Lunacharsky, Anatoly Vasilievich. *Oliver Kromvil.* Moskva: Gos. izd-vo, 1920.

133 Rappaport, Helen. *The Last Days of the Romanovs.* London: Hutchinson, 2009.

134 Tzouliadis, Tim. *The Forsaken: From the Great Depression to the Gulags: Hope and Betrayal in Stalin's Russia.* London: Little, Brown, 2008.

135 Oxford English Dictionary Second edition on CD-ROM (v. 4.0)

136 Koenker, Diane P & Bachman, Ronald D. Eds. *Revelations from the Russian Archives. Documents in English Translations.* Wasshington DC: Library of Congress, 1997.

137 http://en.wikipedia.org/wiki/John_Bradshaw_(judge)

138 http://en.wikipedia.org/wiki/Codrington_Library

139 Carlyle, Thomas. *Oliver Cromwell's Letters and Speeches with Elucidations. Vol 1.* London: Chapman & Hall, 1846.

140 Pakenham, Eliza. *Soldier, Sailor: An Intimate Portrait of an Irish Family.* Weidenfeld & Nicolson, 2007.

141 Confucius. *The Sayings of Confucius: A New Translation of the Greater Part of the Confucian Analects with Introduction and Notes by Lionel Giles.* London: John Murray, 1907.

142 http://en.wikipedia.org/wiki/Reginald_Pole

143 Macauley, Thomas Babbington. *Essays Contributed to the Edinburgh Review: Machiavelli.* In: Trevelyan, G O. *Life and Letters of Lord Macauley. Vol 1.* 1876.

144 Solzhenitsyn, Aleksandr. *The Gulag Archopelago.* London: Harvill Press, 2003.

145 O'Casey, Sean. *Juno and the Paycock.* In: Atkinson, Brooks. *The Sean O'Casey Reader: Plays, Autobiographies, Opinions.* London: Macmillan & New York: St Martins Press, 1968.

146 Orwell, George. *Orwell Diaries 1938-1942.* https:orwelldiaries.wordpress.com/2012/03/14/14-3-42

147 http://en.wikipedia.org/wiki/Inclosure_Acts

148 Kligman, Gail & Verdery, Katherine. *Peasants Under Seige: The Collectivization of Rumanian Agriculture. 1949-1962.* Princeton & Oxford: Princeton University Press, 2011.

149 http://en.wikipedia.org/wiki/Agrarian_law

150 Thubron, Colin. *In Siberia.* London: Penguin, 2000.

151 Marlowe, Christopher. *The Jew of Malta.* In: Gill, Roma. Ed. *The Complete Works of Christopher Marlowe.* Oxford: Oxford University Press, 1995.

152 Duffy, Eamon. *The Stripping of the Altars: Traditional Religion in England 1400–1580.* New Haven & London: Yale University Press, 1992.

153 Machiavelli, Nicolò. *The Prince. Translated by Luigi Ricci.* London: Henry Frowde, 1906.

154 Strathern, Paul. *The Artist, the Philosopher and the Warrior: Leonardo, Machiavelli and Borgia: A Fateful Collusion.* London: Jonathan Cape, 2009.

155 Jenkins, Simon. *A Short History of England.* London: Profile Books, 2011.

156 Nolan, Albert. *Jesus before Christianity.* London: Darton, Longman and Todd, 1977.

157 Ridley, Jasper. *Henry VIII, King of England, 1491–1547.* London: Constable, 1984.

158 Knights, Charles. *Popular History of England: An Illustrated History of Society and Government from the Earliest Period to our Own Times. Vol 2. From Reign of Richard II to Edward VI.* London: Bradbury & Evans, 1856–1862.

159 D'Alton, E A. *History of Ireland: From the Earliest Times to the Present Day. Vol 3.* London: Gresham Publishing, 1912.

160 Vidal, Gore. *The United States of Amnesia.* www.gorevidaldocumentary.com, 2013.

161 O'Brien, Henry. *Translators Note.* In: Villanueva, Joaquin Lorenzo. *Phoenician Ireland.* (Translated by Henry O'Brien) London: W Thacker, 1837.

162 http://en.wikipedia.org/wiki/Geoffrey_Keating

163 D'Alton, E A. *History of Ireland: From the Earliest Times to the Present Day. Vol 6.* London: Gresham Publishing, 1912.

164 Robinson, Mary. *Everybody Matters: A Memoir.* London: Hodder & Stoughton, 2012.

165 Briscoe, Robert. (and Alden Hatch) *For the Life of Me.* London: Longmans, 1959.

166 http://en.wikipedia.org/wiki/Robert_Briscoe_(politician)

167 Staver, James. *Letter. Briscoe in Peoria.* Chicago Sunday Tribune. October 19, 1948.

168 http://en.wikipedia.org/wiki/List_of_Irgun_Attacks

169 Jeffery, Keith. *MI6: The History of the Secret Intelligence Service 1909–1949.* London: Bloomsbury, 2010.

170 http://en.wikipedia.org/wiki/Yitzhak_Shamir

171 Einstein, Albert. *Et al.* https://archive.org/details/AlbertEinsteinletter-TheNewYorkTimes.December41948 *Visit of Menachen Begin and Aims of Political Movement.*

172 http://en.wikipedia.org/wiki/Menachem_Begin

173 www.nobelprize.org/nobel_prizes/peace/laureates/1978/begin-facts.html

174 http://en.wikipedia.org/wiki/Nobel_Peace_Prize

175 http://en.wikipedia.org/wiki/Alfred_Nobel

176 Klug, Brian. *Being Jewish and Doing Justice: Bringing Agreement to Life.* London: Vallentine Mitchell, 2011.

177 http://en.wikipedia.org/wiki/Edwin_Samuel_Montague

178 www.jewishvirtuallibrary.org/source/history/montagumemo.html

179 http://jahtruth.net/britca.htm The Heraldic Symbolism of the Unicorn on the British Coat-of-arms

180 Orwell, George. *Why I Write.* London: Penguin, 2004.

181 http://en.wikipedia.org/wiki/North_West_Mounted_Police

182 Jordan, Neil. *Michael Collins* (The Movie). Geffin Pictures, 1996.

183 Béaslai, Piaras S. *Michael Collins and the Making of a New Ireland.* London: Harrap, 1926.

184 Leeson, David. *The Black and Tans: British Police in the First Irish War, 1920-21. DPhil Thesis.* Hamilton, Ontario: McMaster University, 2003.

185 Hattersley, Roy. *David Lloyd George: The Great Outsider.* London: Little, Brown, 2010.

186 Blake, Robert. *The Unknown Prime Minister: The Life and Times of Andrew Bonar Law 1858-1923.* London: Eyre & Spottiswoode 1955.

187 Holmes, Richard. *The Little Field Marshall: A Life of Sir John French.* London: Jonathan Cape, 1981.

188 Murphy, John A. *Bloody Fable of Kilmichael's Dead.* Irish Independent on Line. November 26, 2000.

189 Martin, Pierce. *Letter. Michael Collins is not my Hero.* Sunday Independent Oct 3, 2010.

190 MacKay, James. *Michael Collins: A Life.* Edinburgh: Mainstream, 1996.

191 Murphy, Brian P. *Charles William St John Burgess (Cathal Brugha).* Oxford Dictionary of National Biography. Oxford: Oxford University Press, 2004:8; 349--350.

192 Joyce, James. *Ulysses.* Oxford: Oxford University Press, 1993.

193 Maugham, W. S. *Of Human Bondage.* New York: George H Doran, 1915.

194 http://en.wikipedia.org/wiki/Yitzhak_HaLevi_Herzog

195 www.michaeljournal.org/piusXII.htm

196 http://en.wikipedia.org/wiki/Chaim_Herzog

197 http://en.wikipedia.org/wiki/Yaakov_Herzog

198 forward.com/articles/1688/the –shadow-that-never-went-away. Ben Beckerman. In: The Jewish Daily Forward.

199 http://en.wikipedia.org/wiki/Isaac_Herzog

200 Scammell, Michael. *Writers in a Cage.* Review of *Zhivago's Children: The Last Russian Intelligentsia.* New York Review of Books. 14 January 2010.

201 Foster, RF. Ed. *The Oxford History of Ireland.* Oxford: Oxford University Press, 1989.

202 Harries, Richard. *Thought for the Day.* BBC Radio 4. February 26, 2010.

203 Pearsall, Judy. *The New Oxford Dictionary of English.* Oxford: Oxford University Press, 1998.

204 Black, Edwin. *Nazi Nexus: America's Corporate Connections to Hitler's Holocaust.* Washington DC: Dialog Press, 2009.

205 Ford, Henry. *The International Jew: The World's Foremost Problem.* "Abridged from the original as published by the renowned industrial leader Henry Ford, Sr." "Appearing originally in the periodical published by the Ford Motor Co. "The Dearborn Independent." " Los Angeles, California: Gerald L K Smith, 192-.

206 Sinclair, Upton. *The Jungle.* London: William Heinemann, 1906.

207 Horwood, William & Rappaport, Helen. *Dark Hearts of Chicago.* London: Hutchinson, 2007.

208 Patterson, Charles. (Forward by Lucy Kaplan) *Our Treatment of Animals and the Holocaust.* Chapter 3 *From Slaughterhouse to Death Camp.* New York: Lantern Books, 2002.

209 Wasserstein, Bernard. *On the Eve: The Jews of Europe before the Second World War.* New York: Simon & Schuster, 2012.

210 Attributed to Voltaire.

211 Graham, Robert A, SJ. *The Vatican and the Holocaust: 860,000 Lives Saved –The Truth About Pius XII & the Jews.* www.jewishvirtuallibrary.org/jsource/anti-semitism/piusdef2.html

212 Lapide, Pinchas E. *The Last three Popes and the Jews.* Toronto: Souvenir Press, 1967.

213 Dalin, Rabbi David G. *The Myth of Hitler's Pope: How Pope Pius Rescued Jews from the Nazis.* Washington, DC: Regnery Publishing, 2005.

214 Novak, David. *Praise for the Myth of Hitler's Pope.* In: Dalin, Rabbi David G. *The Myth of Hitler's Pope: How Pope Pius Rescued Jews from the Nazis.* Washington, DC: Regnery Publishing, 2005.

215 Lapin, Rabbi Daniel. *Praise for the Myth of Hitler's Pope.* In: Dalin, Rabbi David G. *The Myth of Hitler's Pope: How Pope Pius Rescued Jews from the Nazis.* Washington, DC: Regnery Publishing, 2005.

216 George, Robert P. *Praise for the Myth of Hitler's Pope.* In: Dalin, Rabbi David G. *The Myth of Hitler's Pope: How Pope Pius Rescued Jews from the Nazis.* Washington, DC: Regnery Publishing, 2005.

217 Longerich, Peter. *Heinrich Himler.* Oxford & New York: Oxford University Press, 2012.

218 Chambers, Vanessa. *Republican Representative Randy Weber: Even Adolph Hitler thought it more Important than Obama to get to Paris. . .* MailOnline. January 13, 2015.

219 www.cato.org

220 Louie, Elaine. *Chronicle.* New York Times-on-line. August 25, 1995.

221 http://en.wikipedia.org/wiki/Carl_von_Clausewitz

222 http://www.quora.com/Why-did-Napoléon-feel-that-Machiavellis-The-Prince-belonged-to-him

223 Watson, Peter. *The German Genius: Europe's Third Renaissance, the Second Scientific Revolution and the Twentieth Century.* London: Simon & Schuster, 2010.

224 Woolf, Virginia. *Thoughts of Peace in an Air Raid*. In: *The Death of a Moth and Other Essays*. London: Hogarth Press, 1984.

225 Costello, John & Hughes, Terry. *The Battle of the Atlantic*. New York: Dial Press/J Wade, 1977.

226 Hamilton, Hugo. *The Speckled People*. London: Fourth Estate, 2003.

227 Black, Edwin. *IBM and the Holocaust: The Strategic Alliance Between Nazi Germany and America's Most Powerful Corporation*. New York: Random House, 2001.

228 Urwand, Ben. *The Collaboration: Hollywood's Pact with Hitler*. Cambridge Massachusetts & London: Harvard University Press, 2013.

229 http://en.wikipedia.org/wiki/John_Goodchild

230 Gregory, Augusta. *Gods and Fighting Men: The Story of the Tuaatha De Danaan and of the Fianna of Ireland Arranged and put into English by Lady Gregory. With a Preface by W B Yeats*. London: John Murray, 1904.

231 www.nli.ie?1916/pdf/3.4.3.pdf W.B. Yeates and the Irish Literary Revival.

232 Latham, Robert G. *Ethnology in Europe*. London: Jan Van Voorst, 1852.

233 www.britishempire.co.uk/biography/maugham.htm

234 http://en.wikipedia.org/wiki/list_of_works_by_W_ Somerset _Maugham.

235 Maugham, W Somerset. *The Summing Up*. London: Heine-mann, 1938.

236 http://en.wikipedia.org/wiki/Anton_Chekhov

237 Chekhov, Anton Pavlovich. (Translated by Michael Henry Heim) *To A S Suvorin August 29, 1888*. In: *Letters of Anton Chekhov*. London: Bodley Head, 1973.

238 Chekhov, Anton. *The Cherry Orchid*. In: *Two Plays by Chekhov – Translated with an Introduction and Notes, by George Calderon*. London: Grant Richards, 1912.

239 Chekhov, Anton Pavlovich. *The Island: A Journey to Sakhallin*. Translated by Luba and Michael Terpak). London: Century, 1987.

240 http://en.wikipedia.org/wiki/Charles_Vallancey

241 Dudley Edwards, Owen. *Sir Arthur Ignatious Conan Doyle (1859-1930)*. Oxford Dictionary of National Biography. Oxford: Oxford University Press, 2004:16;827-830.

242 Doyle, Arthur Conan. *Letter: Gelsemium as a Poison.* British Medical Journal. 20 September, 1879; 483.

243 Gilligan, James. *Violence: Our Deadly Epidemic and Its Causes.* New York: G P Putman's Son, 1966.

244 Steinbeck, John. *Cannery Row.* New York: Viking Press, 1945.

245 Murphy, Dervla. *Introduction.* In: Orwell, George. *Down and Out in Paris and London.* London: Penguin, 1989.

246 O'Brien, Edna. *Country Girl: A Memoir.* London: Faber & Faber, 2012.

247 Leeson, D M. *The Black and Tans: British Police and Auxiliaries in the Irish War of Independence, 1920-1921.* Oxford: Oxford University Press, 2011.

248 Dingley, James. *The IRA: The Irish Republican Army.* Santa Barbara, California: ABC-CLIO LLC, 2012.

249 Behan, Brendan. *The Hostage.* London: Methuen 1962.

250 http://en.wikipedia.org/wiki/John_de_Wogan_%28Justiciar_of_Ireland%29

251 Wheatley, Henry B. Ed. *The Diary of Samuel Pepys.* Cambridge: Deighton Bell, 1893.

252 http://en.wikipedia.org/wiki/Sack_of_Cashel

253 Abbott, Richard. *Police Casualties in Ireland 1919–1922.* Dublin & Cork: Mercier Press, 2000.

254 Nolan Daniel J. *Clippers: The Ships that Shaped the World.* Bray, County Wicklow: Malbay Publishing, 2011.

255 Gray, Chris. *Writers Riveting Memoir.* The Oxford Times: October 11, 2012.

256 Enright, Anne. *Country Girl by Edna O'Brien – Book Review.* The Guardian: 12 October 2012.

257 Bell, David A. *The Conductor – Book Review.* New Republic. 5 April 2012.

258 O'Casey, Sean. *Juno and the Paycock.* In: Atkinson, Brooks. *The Sean O'Casey Reader: Plays, Autobiographies, Opinions.* London: Macmillan & New York: St Martins Press, 1968.

259 Pakenham, Tom. *The Year of Liberty: The Bloody Story of the Great Irish Rebellion of 1798.* London: Hodder & Stoughton, 1969.

260 O'Ferrall, Fergus. *Daniel O'Connell.* Dublin: Gill & MacMillan, 1981.

261 Dunlop, Robert. *Daniel O'Connell and the Revival of National Life in Ireland.* London & New York: G P Putnam's & Sons, 1900.

262 Andrew Lowney Literary Agency. *Writers and Artists Yearbook 2015.* London: Bloomsbury, 2014.

263 Gallagher, Cian. *Review: Clippers: The Ships that Shaped the World.* Dublin: Inshore Ireland. February/March 2012;25.

264 Pappas, Theoni. *The Joy of Mathematics: Discovering Mathematics All Round You.* San Carlos, California: Wide World Publishing/Tetra, 1989.

265 X, Malcolm. *Black Revolution Speech New York 1964.* In: Jay, Anthony. Ed. *The Oxford Dictionary of Political Quotations.* Oxford & New York: Oxford University Press, 1996.

266 Young, Arthur. *A Tour of Ireland.* London, T Cadell, 1780.

267 D'Alton, E A. *History of Ireland: From the Earliest Times to the Present Day. Vol 5.* London: Gresham Publishing, 1912.

268 Hague, William. *William Pitt the Younger.* London: HarperCollins, 2004.

269 www.ewartbiggsprize.org.uk

270 Dudley Edwards, Ruth. *Patrick Pearse: The Triumph of Failure.* London: Victor Gollancz, 1977.

271 O'Brien, Conor Cruise. *My Life and Themes.* London: Profile, 1998.

272 Heeney, Seamus: *An Open Letter* (1983) en.wikipedia.org/wiki/The_Penguin_Book_of_Contempoary_British_Poetry

273 Kelly Richard J. *The Second Boer War/1898-1902: Context of Queen Victoria's Final Visit to Ireland in 1900.* www.vssj.jp/journal/10/kelly.pdf

274 Conrad, Joseph. *Some Reflections on the Loss of the Titanic – 1912.* In: *Notes on Life and Letters.* London: Dent, 1921.

275 Hurd, Douglas. *Robert Peel.* London: Weidenfeld & Nicolson, 2007.

276 http://en.wikipedia.org/wiki/Theobald_Mathew_%28temperance_reformer%29

277 http://en.wikipedia.org/wiki/Frederick_Douglass

278 http://en.wikipedia.org/wiki/Daniel_O%27Connell

279 Douglass, Frederick. *Part 1- Life as a Slave, Part II – Life as a Freeman.* In Stauffer, John. Ed. *My Bondage and my Feeedom.* New York: Random House, 2003.

280 Fenton, Laurence. *Frederick Douglass in Ireland – The "Black O'Connell."* Cork: The Collins Press, 2014.

281 http://en.wikipedia.org/wiki/Séan_MacBride

282 Churchill, Winston S. *(re: External Relations Act of 1936.) Foreign affairs Debate in the House of Commons.* In: *Winston S Churchill: His Complete Speeches. 1897–1963. Volume VII 1943-1949.* London: Chelsea House Publishers, 1974.

283 Paisley, Ian. *Oliver Cromwell: Address by Dr Ian Paisley, MP, MEP at the service of Thanksgiving for the life of Oliver Cromwell held in the Crypt of the House of Commons at Westminster on the 400th Anniversary of the Birth of Cromwell on Tuesday, April 15, 1999.* European Institute of Protestant Studies. Lessons from History. www.ianpaisley.org/articles. asp?ArtKey=cromwell

284 http://en.wikipedia.org/wiki/John_Reid_Baron_Reid_of_Cardowan

285 http://en.wikipedia.org/wiki/George_Galloway

286 http://irishconstabulary.com/topic/576/The-Macroom-Ambush-Graves-of-Auxiliary-Cadets#.VSqL3PmUddg

287 McKenna, Peter. *Little to Celebrate as UK Troops Withdraw from Afghanistan.* The Guardian: October 29, 2014.

288 Morris, Steven & Norton-Taylor, Richard. *Royal Marine must serve at least 10 Years in Jail for Taliban Murder.* The Guardian: December 8, 2013.

289 Chalmers, Robert. *Still standing: George Galloway reveals why his staunchly leftist outlook is still invariably right.* The Independent: June 17, 2014.

290 Ninh Bao. *The Sorrow of War.* Hanoi: Writers Association, 1991; London: Minerva, 1994.

291 http://www.intelligencesquared.com

292 http://en.wikipedia.org/wiki/Lewes_Bonfire

293 Shakespeare, William. *The Tragedy of Hamlet, Prince of Denmark.* In: Greenblatt, Stephen. Ed. *The Norton Shakespeare: Based on the Oxford Edition.* New York & London: W W Norton & Co, 1997.

294 https://www.gov.uk/government/news/80-million-start-up-loans-for-new-businesses

295 Howe, Irving. & Coser, Lewis. *The American Communist Party – A Critical History. 1919 – 1957.* Boston: Beacon Press, 1957.

296 Steinbeck, John. *The Grapes of Wrath.* London: Heinemann, 1939.

297 Hope, Christopher. *Budget 2012: £28 Billion of Royal Mail Pension Assets to pay down National Debt.* The Telegraph-on-line March 21, 2012.

298 Feierstein, Mitch. *Planet Ponzi. How Politicians and Bankers Stole your Future.*London: Transworld Publishers, 2012.

299 Peston, Robert. *Who Runs Britain: How the Super Rich are Changing our Lives.* London: Hodder, 2008.

300 Martin, Daniel. *Why Families will have to pay £656,000 in Tax: That's what the Average Household Forks out in a Lifetime.* Mail-Online January 30, 2012.

301 Kirkup, John. *Banks give us edge in global race, says PM.* The Daily Telegraph *November 13, 2012.*

302 Humphries, John. BBC *To-Day.* December 22, 2012.

303 Chekhov, Anton. *The Seagull.* In: *Two Plays by Tchekhof – Translated with an Introduction and Notes, by George Calderon.* London: Grant Richards, 1912.

304 https://www.ipsos-mori.com/researchpublications/researcharchive/2818/Doctors-are-most-trusted-profession-politicians-least-trusted.aspx

305 Evans, Harold. *How Thatcher and Murdoch made their Secret Deal .* The Guardian-on-Line April 28, 2015.

306 Douglas, Torin. *How Margaret Thatcher helped change Media Lanscape.* BBC-on-Line April 14, 3013.

307 www.levesoninquiry.org.uk/. . . /Transcript-of-the-morning-hearing-25-April-2012.pdf

308 www.levesoninquiry.org.uk/. . . /Transcript-of-the-afternoon-hearing-17-May-2012.txt

309 Wightman, Andy. *The Poor had No Lawyers: Who Owns Scotland (And How they Got It)* Edinburgh: Birlinn, 2010.

310 Beckett, Thomas. *Murphy.* New York: Grove Press, 1957.

311 Belloc, Hilaire. *On Sailing the Sea.* London: Mariners Library, 1951.

312 http://en.wikipedia.org/wiki/Lady_Justice

313 www.huffingtonpost.c.uk/ . . . *Courts Jail 107 People for not Paying BBC TV License Fines.* Huffington Post. October 10, 2013.

314 Wogan, Terry. *Mustn't Grumble. The Autobiography.* London: Orion books, 2006.

315 Jardine, Lisa. *Going Dutch: How England Plundered Holland's Glory.* London: HarperPress, 2008.

316 Holmes, Richard. *Marlborough: England's Fragile Genius.* London: Harper Press, 2008.

317 http://en.wikipedia.org/wiki/File:William_Hogarth_-_Gin_Lane.jpg

318 Bragg, Mervyn. *In Our Time.* http://www. bbc.co.uk/programmes/b03yqj31

319 Williams, Charles Richard. Ed. *Diary and Letters of Rutherford Birchard Hayes: Nineteenth President of the United States.* Columbus: Ohio State Archaeological and Historical Society, 1922.

320 Kincaid, Dennis. *British Social Life in India, 1608-1937.* London: Routledge & K Paul, 1973.

321 Bower, Tom. *Branson.* London: Fourth Estate, 2000.

322 Bruck, Connie. *The Billionaire's Playlist: How an Oligarch got into the American Music Business.* The New Yorker. January 20, 2014.

323 http://en.wikipedia.org/wiki/Peter_Sutherland

324 Blanding, Michael. *The Coke Machine: The Dirty Truth Behind the World's Favorite Soft Drink.* New York & London: Penguin, 2010.

325 http://www.bloomberg.com/news/articles/2013-06-07/vodafone-ceo-colao-s-pay-drops-30-to-17-1-million-on-bonus-cut

326 Grice, Andrew. *Vodafone £84bn tax Avoidance Bonanza: Nothing for Taxpayers in Verizon Deal while Bankers share £500m in fees.* The Independent-on-Line. September 2, 2013.

327 Galbraith, John Kenneth. *The Great Crash 1929.* New York & London: Penguin, 1954.

328 Newenham, Pamela. *Peter Sutherland to Retire as Goldman Sachs Chairman.* Irish Times-on-Line. May 20, 2015.

329 http:// en.wikipedia.org/wiki/David_J_O'Reilly

330 http://en.wikipedia.org/wiki/Condoleezza_Rice

331 http://en.wikipedia.org/wiki/Bill_Gates

332 Herrmann, Joshi. *University Challenge: A C Grayling's Project is halfway through Year One but Can the New College of Humanities, with its £18,000 Fees and American-style Courses, Silence Its Critics.* London: Evening Standard, 19 February 2013.

333 Paisley, Ian. www.publications.parliament.uk February 10, 2011.

334 Ngo, Jennifer. *Illegal Cigarette Booming despite Customs Bust.* South-China-Morning-Post-on-line. Hong Kong: January 4, 2014.

335 http://en.wikipedia.org/wiki/A_Counterblaste_to_Tobacco

336 https://fullfact.org/factchecks/does_smoking_cost_as_much_as_it_makes_for_the_treasury-29288

337 en.wikipedia.org/wiki/British_American_Tobacco

338 http://www.tobaccotactics.org/index.php/Kenneth_Clarke

339 Costello, Peter. *The Smoking Gun of the Iron Lady: Margaret Thatcher's Relationship with the Tobacco Industry.* Stanford-Medicine-on-Line. February 1, 2012.

340 Mychasuk, Emiliya & Terazono, Emiko. *Odgers Team still on Board.* Financial-Times-on-Line August 20, 2007.

341 http://en.wikipedia.org/wiki/Virginia_Bottomley

342 http://en.wikipedia.org/wiki/AkzoNobel

343 http://en.wikipedia.org/wiki/Smith_%26_Nephew

344 Waples, John and Lyons Tom. *British American Tobacco Recruits Bank Chief Richard Burrows as Chairman.* Clear the Air News Tobacco Blog. http://tobacco.cleartheair.org.hk/?p=1373

345 http://theconversation.com/call-time-on-soft-approach-to-big-alcohol-35769

346 Tran, Mark. *Alcohol Blamed for 40% rise in Liver Disease Deaths in 12 Years.* Guardian-on-line 20 October 2014.

347 Slack, James. *24-hour Drink Law Disaster.* Guardian-on-line 18 September 2013.

348 *Daniel 1: 12-14.* In: Hartgdegen, Stephen J., Ceroke, Christian P., O'Boyle, Cardinal Patrick., Habig, Marion., O'Donnell, Cletus F. *The New American Bible.* Nashville – Camden – New York: Thomas Nelson, 1978. 299.

349 O'Connell, Daniel P. *Richelieu.* London: Weidenfeld & Nicolson, 1968.

350 Conrad, Joseph. *Nostramo: A Tale of the Seaboard.* London & New York: Harper and Brothers, 1904.

351 Hastings, Max. *All Hell Let Loose: The World at War 1939-1945.* London: Harper Press, 2011.

352 http://en.wikiquote.org/wiki/Curtis_LeMay

353 http://en.wikipedia.org/wiki/ Curtis_LeMay

354 Lankov, Andrei. *The Real North Korea: Life and Politics in the Failed Stalinist Utopia.* Oxford: Oxford University Press, 2015.

355 Blake, George. *No Other Choice*. London: Cape, 1990.

356 Chomsky, Noam. *On Resistance*. New York Review of Books. December 7, 1967.

357 Rotblat, Joseph. *Leaving the Bomb Project*. http://www.reformation.org/joseph-rothblat.html

358 http://en.wikipedia.org/wiki/Joseph_Rotbalt

359 http://en.wikipedia.org/wiki/Russell-Einstein_Manifesto

360 http://en.wikipedia.org/wiki/Partial_Nuclear_Test_Ban_Treaty

361 Hughes-Wilson, Colonel John. *JFK: An American Coup D'Etat: The Truth Behind the Kennedy Assassination*. London: John Blake, 2014.

362 Petterson, Per. (Translated by Anne Born) *Out Stealing Horses*. London: Vintage, 2006.

363 King, Martin Luther. *Dictionary of Political Quotations*. Speech at New York Riverside Church April 4, 1967. Oxford: Oxford University Press, 1996.

364 https://en.wikipedia.org/wiki/Patrice_Lumumba

365 https://en.wikipedia.org/wiki/Patrice_Lumumba/ Mahony *JFK* (1983)

366 Kanza, Thomas. *The Rise and Fall of Patrice Lumumba: Conflict in the Congo*. London: Rex Collings, 1978.

367 www.historylearningsite.co.uk/final_speech_Charles.htm *Final Speech of Charles I*.

368 Curie, Eve. *Madame Curie*. London: William Heinemann, 1978.

369 Andreyev, Catherine. *A Moth on the Fence: Memoirs of Russia, Estonia, Czechoslovakia and Western Europe*. Kingston-Upon Thames: Hodgson Press, 2009.

370 Fox, Robert Lane *Alexander the Great Exhibition*. Ashmolean Museum Oxford, 2011.

371 Tolstoy, Lev Nikolajevic *On Patriotism*. www.panarchy.org/tolstoy/1894.eng.html

372 Shaw, George Bernard. *O'Flaherty VC*. In: *The Complete Plays of Bernard Shaw*. London: Constable, 1931.

373 Brink, Lindsey. *Human Capitalism: How Economic Growth has made Us Smarter and More Unequal*. Princeton & Oxford: Princeton University Press, 2013.

374 Chandler, Raymond. *The Long Goodbye*. London: Hamish Hamilton, 2009.

375 *Native American Proverb*. Engraved in Marble on the Seafront in Sliema, Malta.

376 Glick, Thomas F. *Islamic and Christian Spain in the Early Middle Ages*. Princeton, New Jersey: Princeton University Press, 1979.

377 Miller, Arthur. *A View from the Bridge*. In: Miller, Arthur. *Collected Plays*. London: Cresset Press, 1958.

378 Chadwick, Ray & Knights, Martin C. *The Story of Tunnels*. London: Andre Deutsch, 1988.

379 Depares, Ramona. *Hibs you're out of Line*. Times-of-Malta-on-line 3 January 2015. www.timesofmalta.com/articles/view/2015013/blogs/ hibs-youre-out-of-line.550448

380 Wolmar, Christian. *Blood, Iron and Gold: How the Railways Transformed the World*. London: Atlantic Books, 2009.

381 Allen, Geoffrey Freeman. *Railways in the Twentieth Century*. London: Brian Todd, 1990.

382 Jardine, Lisa. *Ingenious Pursuits: Building the Scientific Revolution*. London: Little, Brown, 1999.

383 Day, David. *Conquest: How Societies Overwhelm Others*. Oxford: Oxford University Press, 2008.

384 *Psalm 138:8* In: Hartgdegen, Stephen J., Ceroke, Christian P., O'Boyle, Cardinal Patrick., Habig, Marion., O'Donnell, Cletus F. *The New American Bible*. Nashville – Camden – New York: Thomas Nelson, 1978.

385 Sellink, J L. *Dutch Antique Domestic Clocks*. Leiden: H E Stenfert Kroese, 1973.

386 *Genesis. 35: 10–18*. In: Hartgdegen, Stephen J., Ceroke, Christian P., O'Boyle, Cardinal Patrick., Habig, Marion., O'Donnell, Cletus F. *The New American Bible*. Nashville – Camden – New York: Thomas Nelson, 1978.

387 *Exodus 35: 30-35*. In: Hartgdegen, Stephen J., Ceroke, Christian P., O'Boyle, Cardinal Patrick., Habig, Marion., O'Donnell, Cletus F. *The New American Bible*. Nashville – Camden – New York: Thomas Nelson, 1978.

388 Alvord, Katie. *Divorce your Car: Ending the Love Affair with the Automobile*. Toronto: New Society, 2000.

389 http://en.wikipedia.org/wiki/Rudof_Diesel

390 Bodley, R V C. *Admiral Togo: The Authorised Life of Admiral of the Fleet, Marquis Heihachiro Togo OM*. London: Jarrolds, 1935.

391 Eisenhower, David. *Forward.* In: Humes John C. *Churchill: The Prophetic Statesman.* Washington D C: Regenery History, 2012.

392 Blanke, David. *Hell on Wheels: The Promise and Peril of America's Car Culture, 1900-1940.* Lawrence, Kansas: University Press of Kansas, 2007.

393 www.who.int/gho/road_safety/mortality/en/

394 Boyd, William. *Not Yet, Jayette.* In: *On the Yankee Station.* London: Penguin, 1982.

395 Leon Krier. *The Architecture of Community.* Washington, DC: Island Press, 2011.

396 Mangan, James Clarence. *Ireland in the Seventh Century*: Prince Alfrid's Itenerary Through Ireland. In: Brown, M J. *Historical Ballad Poetry of Ireland.* Dublin & Belfast: The Educational Company of Ireland, 1912.

INDEX

ACKNOWLEDGEMENTS

I am particularly fortunate in having access to a number of great libraries and I would like to thank the staff of the following who have been most helpful: The Bodleian Library Oxford, The London Library, St James Square, London and the British Library, St Pancras, London. The Internet, and particularly Wikipedia, has proved invaluable. The caricature of the author was sketched by the late Emanoel Lee MCh FRCS and I am indebted to Janine Lee who gave it to me. And I wish to acknowledge the Irish National School teachers of the 1940s particularly the Christian Brothers who did so much for so many for so long.

While every effort has been made to trace the sources of material produced, the publisher will make proper acknowledgement in future editions in the event that any omission has occurred..